Jean Vigo

Manchester University Press

FRENCH FILM DIRECTORS

DIANA HOLMES and ROBERT INGRAM *series editors*
DUDLEY ANDREW *series consultant*

Jean-Jacques Beineix   PHIL POWRIE

Luc Besson   SUSAN HAYWARD

Bertrand Blier   SUE HARRIS

Robert Bresson   KEITH READER

Leos Carax   GARIN DOWD AND FERGUS DALEY

Claude Chabrol   GUY AUSTIN

Claire Denis   MARTINE BEUGNET

Marguerite Duras   RENATE GÜNTHER

Georges Franju   KATE INCE

Jean-Luc Godard   DOUGLAS MORREY

Diane Kurys   CARRIE TARR

Patrice Leconte   LISA DOWNING

Louis Malle   HUGO FREY

Georges Méliès   ELIZABETH EZRA

Jean Renoir   MARTIN O'SHAUGHNESSY

Coline Serreau   BRIGITTE ROLLET

François Truffaut   DIANA HOLMES AND ROBERT INGRAM

Agnès Varda   ALISON SMITH

FRENCH FILM DIRECTORS

Jean Vigo

MICHAEL TEMPLE

Manchester University Press

MANCHESTER AND NEW YORK

distributed exclusively in the USA by Palgrave

Published by Manchester University Press
Oxford Road, Manchester M13 9NR, UK
and Room 400, 175 Fifth Avenue, New York, NY 10010, USA
www.manchesteruniversitypress.co.uk

Distributed exclusively in the USA by
Palgrave, 175 Fifth Avenue, New York, NY 10010, USA

Distributed exclusively in Canada by
UBC Press, University of British Columbia, 2029 West Mall, Vancouver, BC, Canada v6T 1Z2

British Library Cataloguing-in-Publication Data
A catalogue record for this book is available from the British Library

Library of Congress Cataloging-in-Publication Data applied for

ISBN 0 7190 5632 2 *hardback*
EAN 978 0 7190 5632 1

First published 2005

14 13 12 11 10 09 08 07 06 05   10 9 8 7 6 5 4 3 2 1

Typeset in Scala with Meta display
by Koinonia, Manchester
Printed in Great Britain
by Bell & Bain Limited, Glasgow

Contents

List of plates

Series editors' foreword

To an anglophone audience, the combination of the words 'French' and 'cinema' evokes a particular kind of film: elegant and wordy, sexy but serious – an image as dependent on national stereotypes as is that of the crudely commercial Hollywood blockbuster, which is not to say that either image is without foundation. Over the past two decades, this generalised sense of a significant relationship between French identity and film has been explored in scholarly books and articles, and has entered the curriculum at university level and, in Britain, at A-level. The study of film as an art-form and (to a lesser extent) as industry, has become a popular and widespread element of French Studies, and French cinema has acquired an important place within Film Studies. Meanwhile, the growth in multi-screen and 'art-house' cinemas, together with the development of the video industry, has led to the greater availability of foreign-language films to an English-speaking audience. Responding to these developments, this series is designed for students and teachers seeking information and accessible but rigorous critical study of French cinema, and for the enthusiastic filmgoer who wants to know more.

The adoption of a director-based approach raises questions about *auteurism*. A series that categorises films not according to period or to genre (for example), but to the person who directed them, runs the risk of espousing a romantic view of film as the product of solitary inspiration. On this model, the critic's role might seem to be that of discovering continuities, revealing a necessarily coherent set of themes and motifs which correspond to the particular genius of the individual. This is not our aim: the *auteur* perspective on film, itself most clearly articulated in France in the early 1950s, will be interrogated in certain volumes of the series, and, throughout, the director will be treated as one highly significant element in a complex process of film production and reception which includes socio-economic and political determinants, the work of a large and highly skilled team of artists and technicians, the mechanisms of production and distribution, and the complex and multiply determined responses of spectators.

The work of some of the directors in the series is already known outside France, that of others is less so – the aim is both to provide informative and original English-language studies of established figures, and to extend the range of French directors known to anglophone students of cinema. We intend the series to contribute to the promotion of the informal and formal study of French films, and to the pleasure of those who watch them.

DIANA HOLMES
ROBERT INGRAM

Acknowledgements

I should like to thank the following people and organisations for their help and support with this project: the Arts and Humanities Research Board for the 'Research Leave' award that I received in 1999–2000; my employer Birkbeck College for its constant generosity, and my colleagues in the French Department for their understanding; the staff of the British Film Institute library in London and of the Bibliothèque du Film in Paris, especially Sophie Brégiroux and her colleagues at the Iconothèque. I am particularly grateful to Luce Vigo for her kindness in granting me access to her picture archives and for permission to reproduce the illustrations.

My heartfelt thanks also go to Rui Barbo, Nicole Brenez, Agnès Calatayud, Teresa Castro, Bernard Eisenschitz, Nick James, Peter Jennings, John Simmonds, Muriel Tinel, James Williams, and Michael Witt for their friendship and advice.

Finally, I dedicate this book to Isa Temple, whose love and encouragement have sustained me through the bad times, and brought me to the happier times ahead.

1

The cinema incarnate

Tous les cinéastes cherchent le Cinéma et le découvrent partiellement. Vigo est le Cinéma incarné dans un homme.[1] (Langlois 1986: 283)

This superlative assessment of the films and reputation of Jean Vigo was written in 1956 by no less a figure than Henri Langlois, the historic founder of the Cinémathèque française and one of the most influential personalities in twentieth-century film culture. It is possible that Langlois's words, composed for the celebration of the Cinémathèque's twentieth anniversary, may now sound somewhat extreme, excessive, even slightly absurd. For how can a single artist, man or woman, be said to embody in such a mysterious way the essence of an art form? Is it the legendary story of Vigo's tragic life that Langlois is evoking here? Or is it the exemplary nature of Vigo's work that Langlois seeks to identify with the very secret of cinema? Perhaps he means to suggest both these ideas, in other words, that through a mixture of the life and the art into a cultural emblem, such as 'Shakespeare' standing for Literature, 'Mozart' for Music, or 'Picasso' for Painting, the name of 'Jean Vigo' has come to evoke a certain idea of cinema, which Langlois has then projected onto a universal scale? Even if we allow for a degree of exaggeration, however, Langlois's identification of 'Vigo' and 'Cinema' must surely still seem paradoxical. After all, when this young French artist died in 1934 at the age of 29, he bequeathed just four films to his small group of admirers, and to a largely indifferent public. Two short documentaries – *À propos de Nice* (1930), *Taris ou la natation* (1931) –

---

[1] 'All filmmakers are searching for Cinema and discover it partially. Vigo is Cinema incarnate in one man.'

one short fiction – *Zéro de conduite* (1933) – and one full-length feature – *L'Atalante* (1934). The total running time of Vigo's slim filmography is less than three hours, and his complete works are reproduced in Gaumont's two-DVD box set, *L'Intégrale Jean Vigo* (2001), with plenty of room for extra features. And yet the most remarkable aspect of Langlois's paradox is that for several generations of film-lovers in the second half of the twentieth century, particularly in France but also more generally across the world, this bold claim that 'Vigo is Cinema incarnate' would have sounded neither shocking nor unreasonable. Indeed, it would more likely have been received as rather an elegant formulation of a commonly held belief.

Our aim in this book is to convey to the contemporary reader, especially the film student coming to Jean Vigo for the very first time, a sense of the awe and enthusiasm that those four films – *À propos de Nice, Taris ou la natation, Zéro de conduite,* and *L'Atalante* – have inspired among filmmakers, critics, historians, archivists and fans, ever since the tragic death of their creator in 1934. As a vital part of that story, we shall start in this first chapter by presenting the key biographical features of Vigo's early life, in particular the traumatic events of his childhood and the violent death of his father. In the following chapters, we shall focus on the quartet of films one by one. In Chapter 2, 'On the subject of documentary', we shall discuss how the two short documentaries, *À propos de Nice* and *Taris ou la natation,* were an experimental apprenticeship in the art of filmmaking. In Chapter 3, 'The personal and the political', we shall analyse his semi-autobiographical fiction *Zéro de conduite* as a fable of libertarian revolt. And in Chapter 4, entitled 'An unknown masterpiece', we shall examine how Vigo attempted the transition to mainstream cinema with *L'Atalante,* his only full-length feature film. For each work we shall relate the circumstances in which it was made, from conception through to exhibition, and discuss some of the most significant reactions that it provoked at the time and in later years. We shall also explore the structure, themes, technique and style of the work, drawing on Vigo's handful of theoretical writings, where these are appropriate (see the Select bibliography). The final chapter, 'Visions of Vigo', will situate in post-war French film culture the exceptional critical fortune of *À propos de Nice, Taris ou la natation, Zéro de conduite* and *L'Atalante,* which has transformed the slender corpus of a once almost unknown filmmaker into one of French cinema's greatest names.

So let us now begin with some basic biographical information about Vigo's extraordinary childhood, as well as some historical background to the key formative events of his early years.

A brief life

On écrit des articles, on parle de 'Jean Vigo', sans penser que c'est un pauvre petit bien malheureux.[2] (Salles Gomes 1988 [1957]: 37)

Jean Vigo was born 26 April 1905 at 25 rue Polonceau in the 18th arrondissement, not far from Montmartre in the North of Paris. He died on the other side of town, 5 October 1934, at 23 rue Gazan in the 14th arrondissement, opposite the Montsouris park. Expressed in such simple terms, just twenty-nine years between two dates and two places, this is indeed a brief life. Film history rightly remembers Vigo for his short and remarkable career as a filmmaker, from 1929 to 1934, and we celebrate the artistic legacy of his intriguingly unfinished work. But the story of his life before cinema, especially his family circumstances and childhood experiences, is no less extraordinary, and it throws an interesting light on the creative years that followed. His parents were Émily Cléro and Eugène Bonaventure de Vigo, although his father was more commonly known by his pseudonym of Miguel Almereyda. They had met as political activists, committed to the anarchist cause and the revolutionary overthrow of the French Third Republic at the turn of the twentieth century. This regime was an essentially conservative parliamentary democracy, built on the fragile social consensus that had come into being in 1870 after the loss of the Franco-Prussian War, the fall of Emperor Louis-Napoléon, and the bloody suppression of the Paris Commune. Although the final decade of the nineteenth century and the opening years of the twentieth tend to be remembered in popular culture as the 'Belle Époque', an age considered beautiful no doubt in contrast to the inconceivable horrors that were unleashed by the outbreak of the First World War in 1914, this period of French history was in fact marked by dramatic social conflict and considerable political

2 'People write articles and talk about "Jean Vigo" without realising that he's a poor unfortunate kid.' The phrase comes from a letter by Jean de Saint-Prix, October 1917.

uncertainty. After the sacrifices and losses of the Great War, it is understandable that the comforting images of peaceful stability and progressive reform evoked by the term 'Belle Époque' should be preferred retrospectively to the ugly memories of the era's 'Guerre Sociale' (as Miguel Almereyda had entitled the weekly newspaper that he founded in 1906). This social war was fought against a background of regular economic crises and political controversies; frequent strikes, street battles and police repression; the profoundly divisive Dreyfus affair and the separation of church and state; above all, the constant ideological pressure and revolutionary threats exerted on the Third Republic from the extreme right (nationalist, monarchist, catholic) and extreme left (socialist, syndicalist, anarchist). It was into this turbulent world of radical politics that Vigo was born in 1905, the year of the foundation of the French socialist party, or SFIO, by Jean Jaurès (whose assassination at the Café du Croissant in July 1914 Almereyda and son would later witness at close hand). There exist several contemporary accounts of the young 'Nono', as he was known as a child, being passed around anarchist meetings from comrade to friend, or left with neighbourly sympathisers while Jean's parents were otherwise politically engaged. The intense yet informal solidarity of these bohemian circles was later to be reproduced in the filmmaking community of faithful accomplices that formed around Vigo during his creative years.

The launching of *La Guerre sociale* in 1906 marks the start of the second phase of Miguel Almereyda's career, both ideologically and in terms of his integration into the political caste. Between 1906 and 1912, when he joins the Socialist Party, Almereyda's earlier revolutionary anarchism changes into a republican socialism, in other words, his political philosophy evolves from a belief in the destruction of the state as the means to transform society, towards a belief in the transformation of society by means of the state. This new ideological pragmatism is accompanied by Almereyda's entry into the corridors of power and the world of finance, a move that draws money, influence and protection towards the cause, but also confirms his changing social status from political outlaw to rising left-wing entrepreneur. Indeed, *La Guerre sociale* triples its circulation to some fifty thousand copies a week between 1908 and 1913, when Almereyda leaves to start a new venture, the satirical *Bonnet rouge*. By this time, however, Almereyda's financial affairs (*Le Bonnet rouge* is soon receiving support in cash from private businesses, government departments and possibly foreign sources) and personal life (several mistresses, houses, cars and increasingly ill health) have become so compromised and complicated that few of his erstwhile comrades-in-arms now recognise the young political prisoner of 1900, who had chosen his militant identity because it was an anagram of the anarchist slogan 'Y a la merde!' (literally, 'there's shit!'). But if many of his former friends consider Almereyda definitively lost to the revolutionary cause, it is unlikely that any of them could have imagined the dreadful circumstances of his impending political and personal downfall.

In August 1914, with the outbreak of the First World War, *Le Bonnet rouge*, and Almereyda in particular, soon became easy targets for the extreme right-wing press. For the next three years, Alphonse Daudet and *L'Action française* waged an unrelenting campaign against the supposedly 'defeatist' stance of Almereyda's pro-peace journal, constantly accusing 'Vigo the traitor' of unspecified, and therefore all the more terrible, crimes against France. Such persistent attacks eventually paid off, in July 1917, when the business administrator of *Le Bonnet rouge*, a certain Duval, was arrested coming back from one of his regular trips to Switzerland – with a cheque for 100,000 francs to be drawn on a German bank account! At this point, *Le Bonnet rouge* and Almereyda could no longer offer much resistance to the enraged criticism from the far right, nor to the more controlled assault from future national leader Georges Clemenceau. The latter, as part of his strategy to assume control of the flagging war effort, successfully exploited this murky affair, and launched a double attack on the two main political obstacles blocking his path to power: Louis Malvy, the Interior Minister, and Joseph Caillaux, the leader of the Radical party. Since both men had longstanding financial and political links with Almereyda, Clemenceau was able to accuse them of 'commerce with the enemy', by association with Duval and the 'affair of *Le Bonnet rouge*'. He thus succeeded in removing his opponents from the scene, at least until the end of the war. It is amidst this complex political manoeuvring that Vigo's father met his violent and mysterious end. Young Jean was in fact physically present when the police raided Almereyda's suburban villa at Saint-Cloud on 4 August 1917, then the offices of *Le Bonnet rouge*, where they found a number of compromising military documents in the safe. Almereyda was arrested, sent first to the Santé prison in the 14th arrondissement, then transferred for reasons of bad health to the Fresnes prison outside Paris. On the night of 13–14 August, Almereyda was strangled against the bars of his cell with his own shoelaces, and the following morning when the body was found a verdict of suicide was hastily agreed. He was 34 years old; his son Jean was 12.

My life as a kid

Who can imagine what effect such terrible events must have had on the young Jean Vigo? As we shall see later in this book, the figure of Miguel Almereyda returns to haunt Vigo's films in a variety of guises: it is the journalist's satirical venom that flows through *À propos de Nice*; his anarchist idealism that inspires *Zéro de conduite*; and his left-wing humanist values that inform the social realism of *L'Atalante*. Certainly Vigo was convinced all his life that Almereyda was innocent of 'commerce with the enemy', and that his father had been murdered in his prison cell as the victim of a political plot. It seems likely, however, that the son's sincere ambition to clear his father's name, through the legal process, was strongly discouraged by Almereyda's former anarchist comrades. They did not believe that their friend was guilty of treason, but rather they feared what else Jean might discover about Almereyda's private affairs and political entanglements, and that this information might tarnish the heroic image of his father that Jean had cherished throughout his adolescence.

Those teenage years were spent at a safe distance from Paris and the cruel spotlight of the 'Almereyda/*Bonnet rouge*' scandal. At first in semi-clandestinity, adopting the name 'Jean Salles' (after his paternal grandmother, Aimée Salles), Vigo pursued his secondary education from 1917 to 1925 at a number of locations across provincial France. He only returned to Paris occasionally in order to visit his mother, Émily Cléro. Immediately after Almereyda's death in 1917, Émily had decided to send her son away from Paris to Montpellier, where he was taken into the care of Almereyda's stepfather, Gabriel Aubès, whose family had already looked after Jean as a young child. We should note that it is Aubès, a professional photographer, who seems to have introduced Vigo to the art of images, teaching him the basic techniques of the craft, just as twenty years earlier he had trained the young Almereyda to be his photographic assistant. Together, Aubès and his wife Antoinette now took charge of Vigo's future, and in early 1918 a certain 'Jean Salles' was sent to school in nearby Nîmes, where the sympathetic headmaster turned a blind eye to the real identity of the infamous traitor's son. The following academic year, the young 'Salles' changed schools, from Nîmes to the college at Millau in the Midi-Pyrénées region. It was believed that the purer climate there would benefit Jean's already fragile health (like Almereyda and Eugène de Vigo, his paternal grandfather, the boy was considered 'tubercular', although in those days the term was probably employed to cover a whole range of ailments and conditions). For the next four years, until the age of 17, Vigo was an intern at Millau, after which he was transferred to another boarding school in Chartres, so that he could be nearer Émily Cléro in Paris. However, it would appear that during this period Jean became increasingly estranged from his mother, probably because of a disagreement about Almereyda's reputation. In July 1924, 'Jean Vigo', as he then called himself once more, finally completed his baccalaureate certificate, thus bringing to a close his strange journey through the French educational establishment.

What traces of this remarkable childhood do we find in Vigo's later works? We know from the evidence of a diary written by Jean in 1918–19, as well as from the testimony of many of his former schoolmates, that a number of incidents and aspects of this college life were later reproduced dramatically in *Zéro de conduite* (Vigo 1953: 77–95). These include the scene with the sleep-walking boy, the famous 'Can he go now, sir?' dialogue, the quasi-homosexual relationship between the young 'girl' and the older boy, even the names of several of the characters (Bruel, Caussat, Colin). At a more general level, Vigo's representation of the enclosed, heavily disciplined, semi-incarcerated existence of the children in *Zéro de conduite* retains such an odour of authenticity and anger about it that he must surely have been drawing on his personal recollections. The film captures perfectly the diffuse teen-spirit of boredom and rebelliousness that permeates such institutions (as Lindsay Anderson so compelling illustrated in *If ...*, his 1968 British remake of the film). We shall return to this topic in Chapter 3, 'The personal and the political', but let us note in passing how closely these biographical and historical aspects of our study of Vigo's work are interlinked with its aesthetic qualities, as well as its ideological dimension. As Vigo once stated to a journalist who asked him what *Zéro de conduite* was about: 'Ce film est tellement ma vie de gosse que j'ai hâte de faire autre chose'[3] (Chardère 1961: 68).

Love and cinema

Upon leaving the college at Chartres in the summer of 1925, Vigo moved temporarily to Paris, apparently already inspired with the idea of pursuing a career in cinema. It may well have been the photographer Gabriel Aubès who first suggested to him that one might seriously earn one's living in this manner, but in any case Vigo's utter lack of contacts and experience would mean that for the time being this project was little more than a young man's dream. In the autumn, like many a future artist uncertain of his way, he enrolled as a student at the Sorbonne, opting for courses in sociology and philosophy. Rather than cinema or higher education, however, it was Vigo's poor health that was to set the rhythm and direction of his life for the next few years. Having fallen seriously ill, early in 1926, Jean left his mother in Paris once more for the Aubès family in Montpellier, where medical examinations confirmed his lungs to be in such a delicate state that a period of convalescence in the mountains was strongly recommended. Thus in August 1926, at the age of 21, Jean was sent to the 'Espérance' clinic at Font-Romeu in the Pyrenees mountains of south-west France, not far from the Spanish border and the Andorra region where the Vigo family has its historic roots. There he would remain until the autumn of 1928, occasionally returning to Paris or Montpellier, but spending the majority of this time at the clinic, no doubt experiencing the fluctuations of depression and hope that necessarily accompany the evolution of such a chronic illness.

Looking at the course of Vigo's existence up to this point, marked as it is by poverty, illness, death, violence and exile, one could easily understand if the young man had simply given up on life altogether. Two crucial factors, however, seem to have carried him through this difficult and potentially fatal period. They are cinema and love. Firstly, his commitment to film, his passion to learn more about his chosen craft, were strengthened by reading some key texts in the early history

3 'This film is so much my life as a kid that I'm in a hurry to do something else.'

and theory of cinema. Léon Moussinac's *Naissance du cinéma*, published in 1925, was one of the first synthetic and intellectually ambitious accounts of cinema's origins, progression and contemporary artistic significance. As well as a film historian, Moussinac was a communist, which would certainly not have displeased Vigo at the time, and he was also one of the founders of the Amis de Spartacus, an important left-wing branch of the burgeoning 'ciné-club' movement that would later inspire the Amis du Cinéma set up and run by Vigo in Nice from 1930 to 1932. This combination of personal cinephilia and political action was a vital dimension of the new film culture that flourished across France in the 1920s, and the alternative distribution networks that grew out of the movement often succeeded in showing films that were banned for political or moral reasons – a fact of film life that Vigo would painfully encounter later in his career. We know that at Font-Romeu, Jean also read two other essential texts by key players in the French film renaissance of the period. One was *Photogénie* (1920) by Louis Delluc, probably the first serious professional film critic in French history, whose journalism had for a decade set the tone of informed debate and speculative thinking about cinema, until his early death in 1925. The other was *Le Cinématographe vu d'Etna* (1926), by Jean Epstein, whose stylish writing had taken film theory to poetic heights, and who like Delluc had also made the successful transition from cinephilia to criticism to personal filmmaking, notably with *La Belle Nivernaise* (1923) and *La Glace à trois faces* (1927). Seen from a clinic called 'Hope', on a mountain in southwest France, these three inspiring examples of a life in cinema – and, tangibly, of cinema as life – must have encouraged and revitalised Jean in his more desperate days.

The second major reason to live, even greater than cinema, was the love that Vigo encountered in the course of his stay at Font-Romeu. The young Elisabeth Lozinska, known as 'Lydu', was a fellow patient at the sanatorium, where she had arrived from Switzerland in 1926. The couple seem to have fallen in love at once and for life. In July 1928, they left the clinic together and moved into a chalet at nearby Super Bolquère, either because their health had miraculously improved, or more likely because they required some amorous privacy. By October they were engaged to be married and had decided to set up home in Nice, where the climate was considered better for their fragile constitutions. Newly invigorated, Jean intended to find employment at the Victorine Studios, which had opened in 1925 amid talk of a French 'Hollywood' on the Côte d'Azur. We get a sense of his deep commitment to cinema, and of his determination to succeed in his chosen field, from the optimistic tone of the following letter, written to Francis Jourdain shortly after the couple's arrival in Nice in December 1928. Significantly, Vigo was requesting help and contacts from Jourdain, a friend of Almereyda, who had worked as designer on Louis Delluc's *Fièvre* (1921) and *La Femme de nulle part* (1922):

> Alors je suis prêt à aller *n'importe où*, car matériellement cela s'impose tout de même et surtout je désire avec force apprendre le métier, et au plus vite. 'Une petite place d'assistant opérateur, s'il vous plaît.' Ah! quelle joie et soit dit sans ironie que d'astiquer un appareil, de le porter, etc. Mais je ramasserai le crottin des stars (de halage?) pour noter sur mon calepin une seule question de technique nouvelle pour moi.[4] (Lherminier 1984: 36)

Jean was soon to discover that breaking his way into the world of professional cinema would require all the help, contacts, optimism, patience, resilience and humour that this fragile and inexperienced young man was able to muster. However, Vigo's 'cinegraphic luck', as he once described it, was about to take a positive turn. When the young couple are married, on 24 January 1929, one of the most welcome and significant wedding guests was Lydu's father, Hirsch Lozinski. This Jewish industrialist, from Lodz in Poland, not only guaranteed his daughter a regular monthly allowance, he also promised his son-in-law a considerable sum of money, so that Vigo could finance his debut film independently. A few months later, Lozinski duly delivered his promise, and it was with this generous gift of 100,000 francs, an important sum at the time, that from the summer of 1929 Jean was able to start working seriously on his first film. He decided it would be an experimental documentary, 'on the subject of Nice'. After the tragic violence of his childhood, and the internal exile of his adolescence, Vigo's new life in cinema was about to begin.

---

4 'I'm therefore prepared to go *anywhere*, financially I have no choice and above all I have this powerful desire to learn the craft, as quickly as possible. "A little job as an assistant cameraman, please!" Oh! what joy, and I mean this without sarcasm, to polish a camera, to carry it, and so on. I'll even clear up the horse shit of stars if it means I can write down just one new technical point in my notebook.'

References

Chardère, B. (ed.) (1961), *Jean Vigo*, Lyons, Premier Plan.
Langlois, H. (1986), *Écrits*, Paris, Cahiers du cinéma/Cinémathèque française.
Lherminier, P. (1984), *Jean Vigo*, Paris, Pierre Lherminier/Filméditions.
Salles Gomes, P.E. (1988 [1957]), *Jean Vigo*, Paris, Seuil/Ramsay.
Vigo, J. (1953), 'Mon journal', *Positif*, 7, May 1953, 77–95.

2

On the subject of documentary

J'espère ma vie durant conserver l'état d'esprit du bonhomme qui réalise son premier film et qui n'est jamais très sûr de ce qu'on en pensera.[1] (Vigo 1966: 3)

In 1949, when the cameraman Boris Kaufman was asked to recall *À propos de Nice*, there came to his mind the following images and motifs from twenty years earlier:

Le point de vue documenté. Vieux Nice, les rues étroites, le linge suspendu entre les maisons, le cimetière baroque. Les plaisirs. Les régates. Les navires de guerre en rade. Les hôtels. L'arrivée de touristes qu'on tourna image par image avec poupées de quatre sous et chemin de fer d'enfants. Les usines. La vieille femme. La jeune femme changeant la robe (truquage) en pleine promenade et paraissant nue à la fin. L'enterrement, tourné image par image pour expédier cette cérémonie peu plaisante aux touristes. Les crocodiles. Le soleil. La femme autruche. Le Carnaval, la bataille des fleurs, les danses en ralenti. Les cheminées menaçantes au-dessus de cette gaieté absurde.[2] (Chardère 1961: 33)

1 'I hope my whole life to keep the state of mind of the fellow making his first film who is never very sure of what people are going to think about it.'

2 'The documented point of view. Old Nice, narrow streets, laundry suspended between the houses, the baroque cemetery. Pleasures. Yacht-races. Warships in the bay. Hotels. The arrival of the tourists that we filmed frame by frame with threepenny dolls and a child's train-set. Factories. The old woman. The young woman changing dresses (trick-shot) as she walks along and ending up naked. The burial, shot frame by frame to speed up a ceremony that's hardly suitable for tourists. Crocodiles. Sun-shine. The ostrich-woman. The Carnival, the battle of the flowers, the slow-motion dances. The industrial chimneys threatening above this absurd gaiety.'

These images of life as it was in the Mediterranean resort at the start of the 1930s (in fact just a few months after the massive Wall Street Crash of October 1929) have become so familiar to lovers of French cinema, and so famous as representations of the city of Nice, that it is hard to imagine how Jean Vigo, even as a young 'fellow making his first film', could ever have doubted 'what people are going to think about it'. Indeed, Vigo's independent entrance into cinema, À propos de Nice, is now considered nothing less than a documentary classic, a particularly fine example of the 'city-portrait' genre that flourished across the film-world in the late 1920s and early 1930s. It stands alongside such celebrated works as Charles Sheeler and Paul Strand's *Manhatta* (1921), Walter Ruttmann's *Berlin, a City Symphony* (1927) and Dziga Vertov's *The Man with a Movie Camera* (1929), those landmarks of a historical meeting between the documentary move-ment and the avant-garde, between experimental film and the cinema of experience. For some filmmakers of Vigo's generation, like Jean Lods (*Aujourd'hui/24 heures en 30 minutes*, 1928), Henri Storck (*Images d'Ostende*, 1929) and Joris Ivens (*The Bridge*, 1928), the urban landscape offered an exciting forum of political expression, as well as a laboratory of formal innovation. It is as if the new social order, to which they aspired, could already be foreseen through their artistic transformation of everyday urban reality. For other young hopefuls coming to cinema in the 1920s, it was the documentary format that provided an early working opportunity and an important learning experience in their practical education: thus Alberto Cavalcanti's *Rien que les heures* (1926), Marcel Carné's *Nogent, Eldorado du dimanche* (1929), Georges Lacombe's *La Zone* (1928), or indeed Robert Siodmak and Edgar Ulmer's *People on Sunday* (1929), all mark significant stepping-stones in long and distinguished careers in mainstream cinema. In the case of Jean Vigo, the experience of À propos de Nice fulfils the triple function of the documentary debut, since the film is at once a formal experiment, a social commitment and an apprentice-ship in filmmaking.

I'm planning to make a film about Nice

With the money received from his father-in-law, Jean made a trip to Paris in the summer of 1929 and bought himself a second-hand

Debrie Parvo, the lightweight 35mm camera appreciated by profes-
sionals for its sturdiness and reliability in action. He took his camera
to the park at Vincennes and shot some pictures at the zoo. Were
these then the first images that Vigo ever filmed? He clearly knew
how to work the Debrie Parvo, but it is worth noting that, at this point
in his career, his total film experience probably comprised no more
than a few weeks as volunteer assistant to the assistant of cameraman
Léonce-Henri Burel, on the set of Louis Mercanton's *Vénus* (1929) at
the Victorine studios. Back on the Côte d'Azur, he started researching
his topic. He read copiously about the cultural background and
history of Nice, keeping written notes of the visual ideas, motifs,
contrasts and images, which came to mind as he explored the city's
streets and examined its people. There is a tendency even among
Vigo's fans to denigrate the semi-poetic, descriptive text that he produced in this way, no doubt because we know that the filmmaker
himself ultimately rejected this approach as too schematic and
rhetorical a vision for his documentary essay:

> Dans toute la première partie, il est absolument important qu'en
> aucune manière la présence de l'homme et de son œuvre ne soit
> révélée. Le pays merveilleux était là, livré par la nature. Le pays est
> placé sous la tutelle du ciel et de l'influence de la mer. L'écran s'ouvre
> sur le ciel. Fuite des nuages, le ciel bleu est maître ici.[3] (Lherminier
> 1985: 69)

But the literary character of this draft scenario should hardly surprise
us, since Vigo had obviously read more books than he had seen films
at this point in his life, and had won prizes at school for written
composition – not for screenwriting! In fact what is more striking
about these remarkable notes is the highly visual quality of his
thinking, and his 'imagist' sense of the world's movement caught
between glimpses of a shifting reality:

> Les voyageurs sortent de la gare/le voyageur assis sur la valise/les
> commissionnaires/les employés d'hôtel/les taxis/les voitures/l'inter-
> prète/une porte d'hôtel qui s'ouvre/les grooms/un chasseur d'hôtel

3 'In all of the first part, it is absolutely important that in no way should the
presence of man or his work be revealed. The marvellous land was there, a gift
of nature. The land is placed beneath the protection of the sky and the influence
of the sea. The screen opens onto the sky. The clouds disappear, the blue sky is
the master here.'

court/on balaie une terrasse, une salle de restaurant/le maître d'hôtel arrange sa cravate/les hôtels vus de travers se redressent/un garçon arrange sa raie/l'arbre tordu se transforme en palmier/une palme/le balai du balayeur public/la vague qui apporte des saletés sur la plage/le balayeur, qui balaye/le casino de la jetée/les saletés petits tas/auprès du balayeur/en gros tas/auprès du balayeur/la mer/le balai/le balayeur s'en va/pousse sa voiture/vue de la promenade vide et sans arbres/les fauteuils sont préparés/la mer/les mouettes les arbres alignés/le ciel/le linge/les joueurs sortant du casino. Un joueur/le linge au vent/l'eau coule/les saletés dans l'eau/une femme passant ses bras au cou du joueur/la maison de la vieille ville avec la vigne grimpante/les sous roulent/le baptême dans la vieille ville/les gosses courant/les sous/la roulette/le jeu des doigts dans la ville/les fleurs avec un tuteur, le soin que l'on prend pour les fleurs/la culture des fleurs/la bataille des fleurs/coup de balai/les armes de NICE.[4] (Lherminier 1985: 70–1)

How does this poetic transcription of Jean's vision of Nice, however, become the purely filmic creation that is *À propos de Nice*? The turning point in this process is undoubtedly Vigo's encounter with Boris Kaufman, whom he met thanks to the documentary filmmaker Jean Lods, during a visit to Paris with Lydu in the autumn of 1929. Writing twenty years later, Kaufman vividly remembered this special moment in his life:

Jean Vigo est entré dans ma vie un jour d'automne 1929. Jamais il ne m'a quitté depuis, spirituellement. En ce moment, où l'audace fait

4 'The passengers leaving the station/the passenger sat on his case/the page boys/ the hotel employees/the taxis/the cars/the interpreter/a hotel door opening/the bell boys/a hotel messenger running/someone sweeping a terrace, a restaurant/the *maître d'hôtel* adjusting his tie/the hotels seen on their sides stand upright again/a waiter adjusting his parting/the twisted tree turns into a palm-tree/a palm/the broom of the garbage-man/the wave leaving rubbish on the beach/the garbage-man sweeping/the casino on the pier/the rubbish in little piles/near the garbage-man/in big piles/the sea/the broom/the garbage-man goes off/pushing his cart/view of the empty promenade no trees/the deck-chairs are ready/the sea/the gulls the trees lined up/the sky/the washing/the gamblers leaving the casino. A gambler/the washing in the wind/the running water/the rubbish in the water/a woman putting her arms round a gambler's neck/the house in the old town with the climbing vine/the rolling coins/the baptism in the old town/the kids running/the coins/the roulette wheel/the fingers game in the old town/the flowers with a support, the care taken with the flowers/the cultivation of flowers/the battle of the flowers/a sweeping movement/the arms of NICE.'

défaut dans l'entreprise cinématographique, je pense souvent à la manière dont Vigo s'est jeté dans la production.[5] (Chardère 1961: 28)

The two young men clearly hit it off from the start. While Boris was immediately touched by Vigo's humour, vivacity and desire for cinema, Jean could not fail to be impressed by Kaufman's practical experience and artistic credentials. Born in Bialystok, Poland, in 1902, Boris was the younger brother of cameraman Mikhail and filmmaker Denis Kaufman. The latter is better known to film history by the name of Dziga Vertov, the director of *Cinema-Truth* (1925), *The Man with a Movie Camera* (1929) and *Three Songs of Lenin* (1934), and probably the most influential figure to emerge from early Soviet cinema, along with Sergei Eisenstein. Just as significant to Vigo, no doubt, was the fact that his new friend had already made a film of his own, *Les Halles centrales* (1927), and had worked with Jean Lods (*Champs Élysées*, 1928) and Eugène Deslaw (*La Marche des machines*, 1928). Above all, Kaufman was open to immediate offers of employment:

Il m'avait demandé de lui présenter deux de mes films. Après la projection, il me déclara: 'J'ai l'intention de faire un film sur Nice, voulez-vous le faire avec moi?' C'était son premier film. Mais même pour les suivants, sa façon de choisir ses collaborateurs, la rapidité de son jugement, le courage de ses décisions, sont restés les mêmes. Comme je ne connaissais pas Nice, il m'invita à venir là-bas pour explorer et écrire le scénario avec lui. Il semblait aimer et détester cette ville où il avait été forcé de vivre les deux dernières années (avec sa femme) pour des raisons de santé. Nice se préparait au Carnaval. On peignait les palmiers sur la promenade, on bâtissait les énormes chars et les figures de plâtre. Le point focal qui s'imposait était la promenade des Anglais, le champ d'action (ou d'inaction) de la paresse internationale. La méthode consistait à surprendre les faits, actions, attitudes, expressions, et à cesser de tourner au moment même où le sujet devenait conscient d'être photographié. Le point de vue documenté.[6] (Chardère 1961: 28)

5 'Jean Vigo entered my life on an autumn's day in 1929. Never has he left me since, spiritually. At the present moment, with audacity absent from the cinematographic endeavour, I often think of the way that Vigo threw himself into production.'

6 'He had asked me to show him two of my films. After the screening, he declared: "I'm planning to make a film about Nice, do you want to do it with

Thus *À propos de Nice* is a genuine collaboration between two young filmmakers working as equal partners, although we can see from the handwritten contract, drawn up *post facto* by the two men on 7 March 1930, that a clear distinction is made between artistic and economic ownership of the work:

> 1. Il est fait un film sur Nice et ses environs – et cela en toute indépendance. 2. En collaboration totale. 3. Ce film sera la propriété artistique de chacun des deux réalisateurs. 4. Jean Vigo, qui apporte le capital, jouira seul de la propriété commerciale. 5. Jean Vigo s'engage à donner trois mille francs par mois à Boris Kaufman et à lui fournir gîte et table – cela jusqu'à ce que le film soit prêt à être présenté au public. 6. Ces conditions seront remplies à partir de 6 février 1930.[7] (Lherminier 1985: 62)

The fact that this document was signed one month after it was due to take effect indicates, however, that their agreement is based on mutual trust and practical complicity rather than on employment law. The contract is merely formalising a working relationship that had already been operative for some time, as the following letter from Vigo to Kaufman on 4 January 1930 makes quite clear:

> Il faudrait que je mette au point au plus vite notre scénario et que vous veniez en discuter sur place avec moi. Nous déciderons des appareils,

---

me?". It was his first film. But even for the later ones, the way he chose his collaborators, the speed of judgement, the courage of his decisions, all this remained the same. As I didn't know Nice, he invited me down there to explore the city and to write the scenario with him. He seemed to love and detest this city where for the last two years he (and his wife) had been forced to live for health reasons. Nice was preparing for the Carnival. The palm-trees along the promenade were being painted, the enormous floats and plaster figures were being constructed. The obvious focal point was the Promenade des Anglais, which is the centre of activity (or inactivity) for international sloth. Our method consisted of taking facts by surprise, actions, attitudes, expressions and of stopping the camera as soon as the subject became conscious of being photographed. The documented point of view.'

7 '1. A film made about Nice and its surroundings – in a spirit of complete independence. 2. And total collaboration. 3. The film will be the artistic property of each of the two filmmakers. 4. Jean Vigo, who supplies the capital, will hold exclusive rights to the commercial property. 5. Jean Vigo agrees to give Boris Kaufman three thousand francs per month and to provide him with board and lodging – this will continue until the film is presented to the public.' 6. These conditions will be fulfilled from 6 February 1930.'

objectifs, pellicules, qu'il convient de choisir – les lieux de nos futures prises de vues nous faisant la loi. Je vous demanderais ensuite de retourner pour deux ou trois jours à Paris afin de procéder aux achats et locations nécessaires.[8] (Lherminier 1985: 60)

We can also see from this letter how dependent Vigo was on Kaufman's practical know-how. This is hardly surprising, given the two men's relative film experience. However, what is really striking about Kaufman's later testimony is that, whatever else he may have learned or achieved in his subsequent career in Hollywood (notably working on Elia Kazan's *On the Waterfront*, 1954, and *Baby Doll*, 1956), the collaborative process of making *À propos de Nice* was as rewarding an adventure for him, as it was a precipitous initiation for Vigo. As he related the story to Édouard de Laurot and Jonas Mekas in 1955:

We developed a sketchy plan and from the outset I was fascinated with completely spontaneous shooting. To surprise people *in flagrante*, to do the shooting before they discovered they were being photographed. We wrote the final version of the script together and I went to Paris to get the equipment. This was Vigo's first experience in the movie field. Yet he was intuitively so well prepared for the cinema that his grasp of the medium seemed to me to be miraculous. His maturity of understanding, which confirmed itself a couple of years later in *Zéro de conduite*, made him capable of directing actors – both amateur and professional – without any sense of difficulty at all. He had a perfect ear, a perfect sense of the dramatic. In *À propos de Nice*, we split the physical area into several sections and it was quite carefully planned ahead of time. But some scope was left for spontaneity and improvisation. Otherwise, everything we shot had a pre-established place in the picture. We edited the film together without rejecting a single shot. We could not afford any waste and we tried to use cinematic language in an unorthodox way. For instance, when we went to the old Nice cemeteries, built in the Italian baroque style – mothers tearing their hair, desperate children, etc. – we shot it not to show the cemetery for itself but in such a way that the cemetery shots could be intercut with shots of the Promenade des Anglais and counterpoint them. (de Laurot and Mekas 1955: 4–6)

8 'I must get our scenario into shape as soon as possible so that you can come and discuss it with me down here. We'll decide on the cameras, lenses, and film-stocks that we need to choose – as dictated to us by the locations of our future shoot. I would then like you to return to Paris for two or three days so you can get on with the buying and hiring as necessary.'

Kaufman's admiration for Vigo is not unique. Most of Jean's collaborators speak of the young filmmaker, destined to die so young, with great sincerity and affection. What makes the cameraman's testimony so special, however, is that he focuses on their working relationship, on the qualities that Vigo revealed to him in action. For Boris, the experience of *À propos de Nice* would come to represent 'work in its ideal aspect', so it can be no surprise that he was delighted to renew their working relationship on *Zéro de conduite* and *L'Atalante*, making him by far the most significant collaborator in Vigo's short career:

> Tout ceci peut paraître naïf maintenant, mais nous étions sincères. Nous rejetions impitoyablement tout ce qui était pittoresque mais sans signification, contrastes faciles. L'histoire devait être comprise sans sous-titres ou commentaires. Nous tournions donc en comptant sur l'évocation d'idées par les associations visuelles seulement. C'est pour cela qu'au montage il nous a été facile de monter la promenade des Anglais avec le cimetière de Nice, où les personnages de marbre (style baroque) avaient les mêmes traits ridicules, mais pour l'éternité, que les humains de la promenade. Le travail avec Vigo, son goût sans erreurs, son intégrité, sa profondeur et sa légèreté, son non-conformisme, l'absence de routine de toute sorte, me prolongeaient dans un paradis cinématographique. C'était le travail dans son aspect idéal.[9] (Chardère 1961: 33)

The shooting was finished by the end of March 1930, the editing took place during April and May, and the film was ready by 28 May to be shown for the first time in public at the Théâtre du Vieux-Colombier in Paris. This was a prestigious avant-garde venue for two such young and unknown filmmakers. The joint press-release announced their debut work in these promising and intriguing terms:

9 'All this may seem naive now, but we were sincere. We rigorously rejected anything that was picturesque but meaningless, such as facile contrasts. The story was meant to be understood without intertitles or commentary. So when we were shooting we relied on the evocation of ideas purely through visual associations. That's why at the editing stage it was easy for us to cut between the Promenade des Anglais and the Nice cemetery, where the marble characters (baroque style) had the same ridiculous features, for all eternity, as the human characters on the Promenade. Working with Vigo, his faultless taste, his integrity, his depth and his lightness of touch, his non-conformism, the absence of any routine whatsoever, all of this maintained me in a filmmaking paradise. It was work in its ideal form.'

Jean Vigo et Boris Kaufman viennent de terminer leur film *À propos de Nice*. Ciel bleu, maisons blanches, mer éblouie, soleil, fleurs multicolores, cœur en liesse, telle apparaît d'abord l'ambiance niçoise. Mais ce n'est là que l'apparence éphémère, fugitive, et que la mort guette, d'une ville de plaisirs. Par delà cet aspect mortel, les jeunes cinéastes d'*À propos de Nice* ont voulu dégager le *devenir* d'une cité.[10]
(Salles Gomes 1988 [1957]: 70–1)

Let us now look more closely at the film that these two ambitious and gifted young men revealed to the world that night.

A city becoming cinema

The version of *À propos de Nice* that we see at the cinema and, perhaps more commonly, the one that we can watch on VHS or DVD, lasts approximately twenty-three minutes. In the critical discussion of Vigo's work, one sometimes finds mention of variously longer versions, occasionally stretching the film to forty minutes or more. These are presumed to have been truncated by external hands, or simply lost from sight. There is probably a degree of exaggeration in some of these accounts, which are no doubt influenced by the fact that Vigo's most famous film, *L'Atalante*, was mutilated beyond recognition for many years. What is certain is that the producers of *L'Intégrale Jean Vigo* (supervised by Bernard Eisenschitz with the cooperation of Luce Vigo) were able to locate one slightly longer version of the film, belonging to the filmmaker Jean Painlevé, which includes some extra shots and alternative sequences made available as bonuses on the DVD. According to Painlevé, it was Vigo himself who cut these images, which he considered superfluous. For the purposes of the following discussion, we shall refer to the version of the film available commercially in the Gaumont box set.

The story of *À propos de Nice*, as we saw from Kaufman's testimony, was meant to be understood without intertitles or commentary.

10 'Jean Vigo and Boris Kaufman have just finished their film *À propos de Nice*. Blue sky, white houses, bedazzled sea, sunshine, multicoloured flowers, hearts full of joy, such would appear at first the atmosphere of Nice. But this is only the ephemeral and transient appearance of a city of pleasures watched by death. Beyond this mortal aspect, the young filmmakers of *À propos de Nice* wanted to make visible the *becoming* of a city.'

Whether the film has a story is a debatable question, but in order to provide a commentary of the work's structure, themes, technique and style, we shall introduce a series of imaginary breaks, thus dividing it into four sections:

1   Welcome to Nice (0.30–3.30);
2   The idling rich (3.30–10.30);
3   Two worlds apart (10.30–17.40); and
4   The whole doomed to die (17.40–23.00).

Welcome to Nice (0.30–3.30)

A number of key themes and stylistic features are established in this introductory section. The film begins with an explosive image of a firework bursting open onto the night sky. There follows a series of three aerial shots, filmed from an aeroplane, which situate the city in relation to the coastline, the nearby port, the Mediterranean sea. This opening juxtaposition of the sky seen from below, and the world seen from above, introduces from the very start of Vigo's corpus one of the key figures of his film style, and À propos de Nice in particular. It is the stark contrast of high-angle overhead shots (plongée in French), in this case literally filmed from the sky, diametrically opposed to extreme low-angle shots (contre-plongée), here showing the heavens viewed from the city. Such a powerful, if potentially grandiloquent, figure is immediately undercut by the next sequence of images, shot frame by frame, so as to look like a cartoon or trick-film. A toy-train deposits two tourist dolls on a giant roulette table, presumably representing Nice's main casino, across which their innocent miniature bodies are swept by an unseen croupier's rake. The satirical theme of man's foolish pursuit of licensed pleasure is thus established, from the opening section of the film, in such a crude, almost childish, fashion that Vigo's social critique will never run the risk of becoming pompous denunciation. In fact we also know that one of the practical reasons why this sequence was shot in this way is that the filmmakers were not granted permission to record inside the casino, although to be fair to the city's authorities the couple were given more or less a free hand elsewhere.

The comical miniature scene of the tourists at the gaming table is followed by a series of expository images, which together set the tone and rhythm of much of what is to follow in À propos de Nice. Close-ups of the waves rolling onto the pebble beach, and more aerial shots from the plane, recall the broader social and natural context in which the petty human activities of the city will be represented. The palm-trees and the grand hotels lining the Promenade des Anglais are filmed from a variety of bewildering angles (above, below, even in rotation), disorienting our familiar sense of how this postcard-like scene would normally be perceived. Cleaners are shown sweeping the Promenade, waiters setting up the tables on the café terraces, both working to prepare the day's 'inactivities of the internationally lazy' (to paraphrase Kaufman). This contrast between the working and the leisure classes introduces another of the film's key themes: an unconscious society whose deep divisions cinema can explore. Finally, we see men painting the grotesque *papier-mâché* heads of the giant mannequins that will feature so strongly in Vigo's depiction of the Carnival procession, during the second half of the film. All of these images (waves, beach, aerial shots, palm-trees, hotels, workers, mannequins) are edited together at a pace gentle enough for each to be recognisable and meaningful, yet sufficiently lively to keep the rhythm of the film, and its representation of the world, always open and moving forward.

The idling rich (3.30–10.30)

The second section of *À propos de Nice* shows the idle rich indulging in a variety of pursuits and pastimes. It starts on the famous Promenade des Anglais, the camera performing a series of intricate movements through the crowds of tourists. Kaufman and Vigo probably rigged up some kind of 'dolly' to record these fluid images. Thus their camera appears to hover a few inches above the flowing pavement. It zigzags through the promenaders, who see it coming and dart out of its way. Or it follows the particular movements of curious individuals who catch its wandering eye. Among all the lazy tourists, the camera also captures the working gestures of people trying to make a living: road-cleaners sweeping the tourists' rubbish; hawkers displaying ties and sun-glasses for sale; photographers and cameramen recording the scene for posterity; a beggar showing her baby to an elegant young lady, who turns her head away from the request and from Kaufman's gaze. The camera then withdraws slightly from this shared promiscuity with the crowd, and the next shot shows the promenaders in medium long-shot, presumably filmed from a hotel window. It is from this same vantage point that the camera now raises its gaze, looking onto the beach, and then out towards the sea. Here the arrival of a hydroplane landing on the water introduces a new theme of sporting pastimes. Thus the gliding movement of the hydroplane is picked up in the images of the sails of racing yachts stirring in the wind. The sails in turn become the white clothes of tennis-players, whose exchanges of shots are alternated with images of spectators enjoying the energetic display of the sportsmen. The representation of each sporting activity is carefully edited so as slightly to overlap with the following one, thus creating a series of rhythmical echoes between the different gestures. In this way, the elegant tennis-players appear momentarily to exchange blows with the less sophisticated bowlers, right to left and back again, as if their sporting gestures were parallels of the class struggle. The intensely concentrated bowlers running towards the jack, left to right, lead into the rapid passing movements, right to left, of racing-cars filmed in the hills around Nice. From this competitive spectacle above the city we return to the sea, where the sweeping passages of the racing-cars are shadowed by the rapid movements of the yachts, now filmed flying through the water in full racing mode.

Slowing down these competitive rhythms, a change of pace occurs with a cut to the stately arrival of some dignitaries outside a grand hotel. We now return to the observation of café life on the Promenade. It looks like Kaufman and Vigo may well have used a hidden camera for some of these shots. They seem to be able to get so close, without disturbing the idling pursuits of their subjects. These pressing activities include: watching the world go by; trotting with a poodle, or strutting like an ostrich, along the Promenade; drinking, smoking, nibbling away one's boredom; gossiping and reading about the state of the world; sleeping in spite of the unsolicited entertainment of the street-musicians; preening and studying oneself just in case one is being observed. Vigo and Kaufman then strip this voyeurism down to its essence, with the famous sequence of the fashionable young lady, who appears repeatedly to change her dress by a series of super-impositions, until she is finally left stark naked in the same elegant pose. This reminder of the naked human form, equally desirable and fragile beneath all these layers of social nicety, leads to a series of representations of the body, which oscillate between vitality and decay. Thus we see bas-reliefs of semi-naked figures on elaborate facades; funerary statues in the cemetery to the east of the city; athletic swimmers and overdressed sunbathers on the beach; a comical sailor tanning himself in the sun until, through a trick of superimposition, his face becomes like the skin of a crocodile (which an inserted shot suddenly shows appearing so menacingly at the water's edge ...). This juxtaposition of grotesque humans and their animal counterparts (poodle, ostrich, crocodile) is comically in tune with the first ten minutes of the film. But there now occurs a clear change of tone and direction at this mid-point of *À propos de Nice*.

Two worlds apart (10.30–17.40)

The predominantly light-hearted satire of tourist pastimes in the first half of the film gives way to a more biting social critique, as we pass from the moneyed Promenade to the poor back-streets of the city. The transition is marked by a series of vertical shots, literally climbing up the facades of various buildings and reaching toward the sky. The camera appears to be searching for something beyond all this idle futility. By the fourth of these roving *contre-plongées*, we realise that the location has changed and that we are now exploring the steep and narrow streets of the old town. Here we have entered a different world, a parallel universe, which Vigo proceeds to fold into our consciousness of Nice. Thus the camera slowly descends to street level, revealing a group of working-class women cleaning clothes around a communal washtub. Here is a place where, compared to what we have seen of the city so far, people look, dress, act and interact differently. There is a busy energy in the gestures of the women, but also a collective spirit very different from the crowd of bourgeois individuals that we saw on the Promenade. These distinct forms of social behaviour are also recognisable in the children that Vigo and Kaufman film in the poorer parts of Nice. We see some boys carrying on their heads, like enormous hats, the vast *pissaladières* (a kind of pizza) that will be sold at the market. In contrast to the boredom and fatigue of the Promenade des Anglais, here we can feel the intense commitment of the group of children playing cards, or the popular street-game of *la mourre* (where you guess the number of fingers your opponent will draw from behind his or her back). This is far from a miserabilist vision of poverty, therefore. Indeed, one is reminded of Vigo's description of Carl Junghans's *Such Is Life* (1929):

Aussi ce jeune cinéaste n'exploite-t-il pas la grande pitié du pauvre bougre. S'il trimballe son appareil de prises de vue dans un quartier ouvrier, aux quatre coins d'un intérieur par trop modeste, à travers l'atmosphère lourde d'un bistrot et derrière un enterrement de troisième classe, c'est qu'en ce milieu sans doute, les êtres demeurent tout de même plus simples et qu'il lui parut plus facile de les décaper de leur rouille superficielle. Point de pittoresque: l'Homme.[11] (Lherminier 1985: 54)

This passage of *À propos de Nice*, however, does indicate the effects of poverty and its diseases: the fingers of the boys playing *la mourre* are contrasted with another boy's hands mutilated by a corrosive illness. And the smiling, vivacious faces of the children carrying the *pissaladières* to market are opposed to a disoriented young lad whose face is eaten up by a skin disease. Here the rubbish piling up in the gutter suggests a far less healthy environment than the spick-and-span surfaces of Nice's fashionable cafés and hotels. But none of this is presented with 'philanthropic myopia', to use Vigo's phrase. On the contrary, one of the striking features of this sequence in Old Nice is the way that the enquiring gaze of Kaufman's lens is constantly met head on, and returned, by its ethnographic subjects. Such a look of frank curiosity in the face of cinema's presence contrasts strongly with the avoidance of the camera, or the embarrassed sense of invaded privacy, which we see elsewhere in the film. This fact is confirmed at the end of this passage by one of the best looks-to-camera in French cinema: an alley-cat stares straight back at Kaufman from its gutter, as if to say 'So you think you're making a film about me, do you?', before darting out of shot, exit left.

This relationship of subject to camera changes, as soon as we return to bourgeois life in Nice. From the old town we switch to a hotel ballroom, where overdressed dancing couples hold each other and look at the camera with an awkwardly compromised air. Henceforth in *À propos de Nice* there will exist a structural tension between two political options: the bourgeois social order in crisis, and

11 'So this young filmmaker doesn't exploit the grand pathos of the poor hovel. If he carts his film-camera around a working-class area, to the four corners of a far too modest interior, through the heavy atmosphere of a cheap diner or following behind a third-class funeral, it's no doubt because in this milieu people remain simpler after all, and so to Junghans it seems easier to remove from them their superficial rust. Nothing picturesque: just Man.'

the popular world with its revolutionary potential. This second political possibility will be represented most evidently – but not unambiguously – by the Carnival parade, which dominates the rest of the film as a constant reference point in the rhythm of the editing. Thus the awkward jigging of the couples in the ballroom merges into the dancing figures of the parade, shot 'undercranked' so as to appear in accelerated motion. This transition from ballroom to Carnival is explicitly marked by a momentary, but very deliberate, loss of focus in the camera. What is the meaning of this striking optical effect of perceptual distortion and refocusing? Does it signal that the Carnival will offer a vision of an alternative world, a projection of a different social order? Or will it provide merely the exaggerated, grotesque continuation of the present unjust state of affairs? A number of delicately poised questions thus arise in this sequence, and they will remain to the end of the film. What is the sense of the camera's position, sometimes detached in the middle distance, sometimes caught up in the frenetic chaos of the Carnival crowd? How should we understand the staged violence of the 'battle of the flowers', which at times sees the dignified victims of the battle struggling to retain their social composure? Do these giant parading dolls represent the people as revolutionary excess, threatening to overcome the restrictions of bourgeois society? Or do they merely embody 'bread and circuses', the safely ritualised symbols of a politically controlled moment of licensed disorder? Finally, one might ask, how should we interpret the presence of Vigo himself in the image, disguised as a clown among a group of working-class women crazily dancing the cancan on a Carnival stand? Is this an expression of whose political side he is on? And in ethical terms, where does the filmmaker therefore stand in relation to this world that his film is representing? Is the artist an impartial observer of reality, or an active participant in its recreation?

All of these issues are raised by the filming of the Carnival, in particular by the way in which the procession is deployed as the central figure of the second half of the film. We can see, for example, how the Carnival scenes are alternated with a series of representations of the existing social order: a senior cavalry officer proudly prancing by; a military parade marking a more disciplined rhythm; warships sitting menacingly in the Bay of Nice; a Catholic cemetery awaiting the future arrival of all these dancing corpses; a priest wandering the streets mundanely distracted and alone; a funeral cortege speeded up like a chase scene in a burlesque comedy. Each time the editing poses the Carnival parade as an alternative political form of sociability. But is the spectacle itself a joyous anarchistic liberation from this strait-laced and oppressive world? Or is the show merely a nihilistic representation of this society's inevitable and ultimate self-destruction? Both interpretations seem viable, indeed it is perhaps this formal and political ambivalence that injects a certain frenetic energy, a pessimism of the intellect crossed with an optimism of the will, throughout the two final sections of the film.

The whole doomed to die (17.40–23.00)

In the concluding sequences of À propos de Nice, we can feel an intensification of this collective movement towards the death of a society whose days are numbered. While retaining the Carnival images as a constant reference point within the rhythm of the editing, the film reprises many of the key motifs depicted earlier in the work. Thus we see again the Promenade des Anglais, the café terraces, the uptight fatigue of the world-weary tourists; an invalid gentleman in an elaborate mechanical wheelchair; a close-up of trap-ponies reflecting on the folly of human existence; the narcissistic doorman of a grand hotel covered in military decorations; a shoe-shine boy frantically polishing a pair of elegant shoes until a trick-shot reveals the bare feet of the tourist beneath; a series of *contre-plongées* of passers-by (and their underwear) shot from inside a pothole in the Promenade; an athletic swimmer displaying some amusing tricks with his stomach muscles. However, edited into this rapid reprise of material familiar from the earlier sections of the work, there appears an insistent series of images filmed at the Nice cemetery, with its sombre tombstones, expressive statues, baroque angels, and hysterical symbols of grief and agony, all shot against the heavens above. These reminders of our common mortality are folded into the repeated slow-motion sequences of the increasingly sinister cancan dancers, as well as the return of the images of eternal nature with which the film began (the sea, the waves, the trees, the sky). For a few moments, we might think that the satirical and polemical tone of the second and third sections is about to turn metaphysical: 'Et le tout voué à la mort' ('And the whole is doomed to die'), as Vigo expressed it in one of his early literary sketches for À propos de Nice.

Doomed to die, certainly, but perhaps also destined for a revolutionary transcendence beyond that death? This appears not just a
legitimate question to pose at this point, but even the clear optimistic
message of the closing moments of the film. Thus the insistent
opposition of decadent Nice versus images of death, and images of the
Carnival, seems to give way to a more evidently political solution: the
death-throes of the bourgeoisie opposed to, and transcended by, the
revolutionary dynamism of the working class. The former is symbol-
ised by a rich old lady, who appears already to be wearing her cosmetic
death-mask and her funereal finery. She is shown repeatedly looking
up at the sky, towards what we imagine is the genteel last resort of her
celestial retirement (a Nice among the clouds). But the reverse shot is
edited so that her polite gaze in fact meets a series of oppositional and
shocking images. Firstly, she appears to be looking up the skirts of the
dancing women, then her look encounters the giant phallic symbols
of smoking industrial chimneys. She laughs nervously, and we see an
image of a Carnival doll's head, uncannily resembling her own and
symbolically turned upside down. Is this the sign of her social class's
impending downfall? If so, then the rugged smiling faces of her class
enemy, the fraternal factory workers, appear to be laughing in solidarity at her impending fate. Finally, the bourgeoisie meets its destiny
in the revolutionary fire itself, represented by the images of smoke
and red-hot coals flowing through the foundry. These are the metaphorical flames in which the ruling order will be destroyed, and out of
whose ashes a new and better world will be born. If this rhetorical
imagery seems inflammatory and excessive, we should not forget that
this is 1930, just a few months after the spectacular financial crash of
October 1929. Such a candidly utopian view of revolutionary upheaval
is part of a common political discourse, employed by the extreme
right as well as the extreme left. It is a vision that Vigo and Kaufman
would have absorbed from the left-wing political culture of the times,
and that Jean in particular had no doubt inherited from his father's
youthful anarchistic ideology of purifying destruction and redemptive
violence. One could even suggest that there is an element of personal
revenge in Vigo's depiction of an unjust society turned upside down –
and going up in flames.

Towards a social cinema

It was certainly this political dimension of *À propos de Nice* that Vigo chose to emphasise when he introduced the second screening of the film at the Théâtre du Vieux-Colombier on 14 June 1930:

> Dans ce film, on assiste à un procès d'un certain monde [...] Le film tend à la généralisation de grossières réjouissances placées sous le signe du grotesque, de la chair et de la mort, et qui sont les derniers soubresauts d'une société qui s'oublie jusqu'à vous donner la nausée et vous faire le complice d'une solution révolutionnaire.[12] (Lherminier 1985: 67)

Likewise, the handful of reviewers who first saw the film (it would be commercially distributed for a while by Pathé-Nathan in 1931, before joining the film club and art house circuit in later years) also tended to stress its explicit political ambitions. These were both praised and criticised by Jean-George Auriol, for example, in his severe but very interesting review of the film published in *La Revue du cinéma*, December 1930:

> Vigo a eu une idée derrière la tête: comme peu de metteurs en scène possèdent de telles idées, il convient de le féliciter. Presque tous les documentaires relèvent du Haut Commissariat au Tourisme ou de recherches esthétiques périmées. La place est libre pour des pamphlets cinégraphiques auxquels la sordidité où nous vivons fournira une matière et une espérance inépuisables. Les rues de Nice, les monuments hôteliers, les faces de chair des hivernants et les têtes de carton du carnaval mourant, les malheureuses tentations sexuelles offertes aux vieux bourgeois, les poules, les vieilles dames également attirées par les petits chiens et les jeunes amants, ces éléments traditionnels de la poésie distinguée peuvent alimenter un réquisitoire dirigé contre cet Eldorado dangereux [...] Malheureusement l'intention a dépassé l'exécution: au lieu du film tranchant que lui permettaient les photographies souvent excellentes de son opérateur, Vigo a bâti un film nuageux où le pamphlet est noyé dans des contrastes usés depuis les Romantiques. On voit des gros vieillards ramollis: le comique; puis des ouvriers brûlent les mannequins du Carnaval: le tragique. Une

---

12 'In this film, we are attending the trial of a certain world [...] The film tends towards the generalisation of vulgar pleasures placed beneath the sign of the grotesque, of flesh and death, and these are the final spasms of a society which has let itself go to the point of making you sick and inspiring you to become part of a revolutionary solution.'

vieille dame fait la jolie et jette sur les passants des boules de coton: le plaisir; un cimetière apparaît alors: c'est la mort; tous les spectateurs méditent la vanité de la vie. Vigo ne nous entraîne pas hors des chemins usés et la bourgeoisie ne s'en porte pas plus mal. Il est d'autre part naïf de prouver que les bourgeois sont haïssables parce qu'ils sont laids et ronflent en dormant; tous les prolétaires n'ont pas la figure d'un dieu et ce n'est pas la Révolution qui guérira tout le monde des polypes et des végétations. Il y a des contrastes, des images plus efficaces contre la bourgeoisie. Jugeons Vigo seulement sur ses bonnes intentions.[13] (Chardère 1961: 5–6)

The tone of Auriol's article may sound a little harsh, since *À propos de Nice* is unquestionably considered a classic of the experimental documentary tradition. While offering a useful counterpoint to this consensual view, Auriol's contemporary reaction also provides a viewpoint that must necessarily escape any critic or historian writing about the film since Vigo's premature death in 1934. For it reflects a true sense of *À propos de Nice* as the debut work of a young filmmaker, with his whole life before him. To some extent, Vigo himself seems to have shared this provisional view of his first film. His own

13 'Vigo had an idea at the back of his head. He should be congratulated, as few directors have such ideas. Almost all documentaries derive from the Tourist Board or from outworn aesthetic experiments. There's room for cinegraphic pamphlets for which the sordid nature of our lives will provide inexhaustible materials and cause for hope. The streets of Nice, the monumental hotels, the fleshy faces of the winter-tourists, the cardboard heads of the dying Carnival, the unhappy sexual temptations proposed to the old bourgeois gentlemen, the prostitutes, the old ladies equally attracted by little dogs and young lovers, all these traditional elements of distinguished poetry can support the prosecutor's attack against this dangerous Eldorado [...] Unfortunately, the intention was greater than the execution. Instead of the sharp-edged film that his camera-man's often excellent images enabled him to make, Vigo has constructed a clouded film in which the pamphlet is obscured by contrasts outmoded ever since the Romantics. One sees comfortable, fat old men, i.e. the comic; then workers burning the Carnival mannequins, i.e. the tragic. An old lady thinks she's pretty and throws cotton-balls at the passers-by, i.e. pleasure; then a cemetery appears, i.e. death, so all the spectators think about the vanity of life. Vigo doesn't take us beyond the usual approaches, and the bourgeoisie comes out of it unscathed. In any case it's naïve to prove that the bourgeois are despicable because they're ugly and snore when they're asleep. Not all proletarians have god-like features, nor will the Revolution cure the world of polyps and adenoids. There exist contrasts and images that are more effective against the bourgeoisie. Let us judge Vigo only on his good intentions.'

presentation of *À propos de Nice* demonstrates a degree of reserve and humility that we can easily forget in the context of Vigo's posthumous greatness:

> Il ne s'agit pas aujourd'hui de révéler le cinéma social, pas plus que de l'étouffer en une formule, mais de s'efforcer d'éveiller en vous le besoin latent de voir plus souvent de bons films [...] traitant de la société et de ses rapports avec les individus et les choses. Car voyez-vous, le cinéma souffre davantage d'un vice de pensée que d'une absence totale de pensée [...] Un appareil de prise de vues n'est tout de même pas une machine pneumatique à faire le vide. Se diriger vers le cinéma social, ce serait consentir à exploiter une mine de sujets que l'actualité viendrait sans cesse renouveler. Ce serait se libérer de deux paires de lèvres qui mettent 3000 mètres à s'unir et presque autant à se décoller. Ce serait éviter la subtilité trop artiste d'un cinéma pur et la supervision d'un super-nombril vu sous un angle, encore un autre angle, toujours un autre angle, un super-angle; la technique pour la technique.[14] (Lherminier 1985: 65)

What is striking about this presentation, apart from the wit and lightness of Vigo's prose, is the lucidity with which this 25-year-old debutant positions his work, in relation to what he perceives as the state of French cinema in 1930: the limited ambitions of commercially successful formulas; the purist impasse of the experimental avant-garde; and the demands of a political cinema that wishes to go beyond mere good intentions (*pace* Auriol) and ideologically correct messages. In search of a fraternal reference point on the contemporary filmmaking scene, Vigo turns to no less a figure than the then relatively unknown Luis Buñuel, whose *Un chien andalou* (1929) the

---

14 'It is not my aim today to reveal to you social cinema, nor is it to strangle it with a formula, but rather to try and awake in you the latent desire to see good films more often [...] i.e. films that deal with society and with its relationship to individuals and things. For I can assure you that cinema suffers more from an abuse of thought than from a total absence of thought [...] A film-camera is not after all a pneumatic machine for creating a void. To move towards social cinema would mean agreeing to exploit a source of subjects that would be endlessly renewed by current events. It would mean freeing ourselves from the sight of two pairs of lips that take 3,000 metres of film to come together and almost as long to come apart. It would mean renouncing the over-artistic subtlety of pure cinema and the super-view of a super-navel gazed at from this angle, then another angle, always another angle, a super-angle; technique for technique's sake.'

previous year had provoked a response more violent and dramatic than even the most committed surrealist rebel could have desired:

> *Un chien andalou* est une œuvre capitale à tous les points de vue: sûreté de la mise en scène, habileté des éclairages, science parfaite des associations visuelles et idéologiques, logique solide du rêve, admirable confrontation du subconscient et du rationnel.[15] (Lherminier 1985: 66)

While sympathetic to the 'savage poetry' of Buñuel's 'precise and courageous' social critique, Vigo remains nonetheless confident of his own distinct path:

> Se diriger vers un cinéma social, c'est donc assurer le cinéma tout court d'un sujet qui provoque l'intérêt; d'un sujet qui mange de la viande. Mais je désirerais vous entretenir d'un cinéma social plus défini, et dont je suis plus près: du documentaire social ou plus exactement du point de vue documenté. Dans ce domaine à prospecter, j'affirme que l'appareil de prise de vues est roi, ou tout au moins président de la République. Je ne sais si le résultat sera une œuvre d'art, mais ce dont je suis sûr, c'est qu'il sera du cinéma. Du cinéma, en ce sens qu'aucun art, aucune science ne peut remplir son office. Le Monsieur qui fait du documentaire social est ce type assez mince pour se glisser dans le trou d'une serrure roumaine, et capable de tourner au saut du lit le prince Carol en liquette, en admettant que ce soit spectacle digne d'intérêt. Le Monsieur qui fait du documentaire social est ce bonhomme suffisamment petit pour se poster sous la chaise du croupier, grand dieu du Casino de Monte-Carlo, ce qui, vous pouvez me croire, n'est pas chose facile. Ce documentaire social se distingue du documentaire tout court et des actualités de la semaine par le point de vue qu'y défend nettement l'auteur. Ce documentaire exige que l'on prenne position, car il met les points sur les i. S'il n'engage pas un artiste, il engage du moins un homme. Ceci vaut bien cela. L'appareil de prise de vues sera braqué sur ce qui doit être considéré comme un document, et qui sera interprété, au montage, en tant que document. Bien entendu, le jeu conscient ne peut être toléré. Le personnage aura été surpris par l'appareil, sinon l'on doit renoncer à la valeur 'document' d'un tel cinéma. Et le but sera atteint si l'on parvient à révéler la raison cachée d'un geste, à

---

15 '*Un chien andalou* is a capital work in every regard: the confidence of the mise en scène, the cleverness of the lighting, the perfect knowledge of visual and ideological associations, the solid dream-logic, the admirable contrast of the subconscious and the rational.'

extraire d'une personne banale et de hasard sa beauté intérieure ou sa caricature, si l'on parvient à révéler l'esprit d'une collectivité d'après une de ses manifestations purement physiques. Et cela, avec une force telle, que désormais le monde qu'autrefois nous côtoyions avec indifférence, s'offre à nous malgré lui au-delà de ses apparences. Ce documentaire social devra nous dessiller les yeux. À *propos de Nice* n'est qu'un modeste brouillon pour un tel cinéma.[16] (Lherminier 1985: 67)

Such modesty certainly becomes Vigo's first film, which we may no longer be able to think of as a mere 'sketch', but whose achievement is perhaps more justly appreciated for its unfinished, essayistic, playful and prospective qualities, rather than for the immaculate perfection that its classical status can misleadingly suggest. Like all good

16 'Working towards a social cinema means therefore providing cinema in general with a subject that provokes interest; a subject that shows its teeth. But I should like to talk to you about a kind of social cinema which is more clearly defined and to which I feel closer: it is social documentary, or more exactly the documented point of view. In this unexplored territory, I declare that the camera is king, or at the very least president of the Republic. I don't know if the result will be a work of art, but I do know that no art nor science can fulfil its function. The gentleman who makes social documentaries is a guy who's thin enough to slide into a Romanian key-hole, and able at the crack of dawn to film prince Carol in his night-shirt, if such a spectacle is indeed worthy of our interest. The gentleman who makes social documentaries is a fellow who's sufficiently small to position himself beneath the chair of the croupier, that great god of the Monte-Carlo casino, an exploit that is far from easy, you can believe me. The social documentary may be distinguished from the pure documentary and from the weekly newsreels because of the point of view adopted openly by its author. This type of documentary requires you to take sides, because it underlines its commitment. This may not be the mark of an artist, but at least it's the mark of a man. Which is certainly just as valuable. The film-camera will train its sights on material to be considered as documents, and at the editing-stage those documents will be interpreted as such. Conscious play-acting cannot be tolerated, of course. The characters must be surprised by the camera, otherwise one would have to abandon the 'document' value of such a cinema. And the target will have been reached if we succeed in revealing the motivation hidden behind a gesture, or if from an everyday person encountered by chance we obtain a sense of inner beauty or even a caricature. Or if we succeed in revealing the spirit of a social group from one of its purely physical manifestations. This will be so powerful that henceforth the world we frequented with indifference will in spite of itself be revealed to us beyond its appearances. The social documentary will have to open our eyes. À *propos de Nice* is merely a modest sketch of such a cinema.'

documentaries, it is best understood dynamically as an experiment and an experience in the truth of cinema, openly imperfect because formally open onto the world that it encounters in a ludic and lucid exchange. It is this filmic intelligence and sense of fun, discovered in the making of *À propos de Nice*, which Vigo now reinvested into his following project, the short documentary study of the champion swimmer, Jean Taris.

In at the deep end

In terms of Vigo's career, no doubt the most meaningful feature of *À propos de Nice* was neither its formal qualities nor its ethical dimension – but the simple fact that he had actually made a film. He was no longer just an enthusiastic young man with an ambition and a desire for cinema, he now had something to show that could prove his worth and help him find a way into the industry. As a project, Vigo's second film could hardly be more different from *À propos de Nice*, since *Taris ou la natation* (also known as *La Natation par Jean Taris, champion de France* and *Taris, roi de l'eau*) is a semi-journalistic piece about a famous and popular sports star, Jean Taris. It was commissioned for the sports section of *Le Journal vivant*, a news-cum-documentary unit managed by Constantin Morskoï for the recently formed GFFA (Gaumont, Franco-Film and Aubert). The commission had come Vigo's way because of a personal recommendation from the pre-eminent woman of 1920s French cinema, Germaine Dulac. This influential critic and filmmaker (*La Souriante Madame Beudet*, 1922, *La Coquille et le clergyman*, 1928) had recently been appointed with Guy Ferrand as head of production at GFFA, and she would later become head of production at the newsreel service, *Gaumont-Actualités*. Although *Taris ou la natation*, as we shall see, is a very interesting piece in its own right, notably for its witty handling of an imposed subject, the film is equally significant as a case-study of Vigo's attempted integration into mainstream French film culture during the early 1930s. Indeed it is often forgotten that the years 1929 to 1934, coinciding with Vigo's brief career, also correspond on a broader scale to the French industry's delayed and slightly panicked transition to the production and exhibition of synchronised sound films. As is always the case during such periods of change, there was considerable uncertainty and confusion across the whole film world, but also many opportunities appeared for those who were quick and keen enough to move with the times. The story of *Taris ou la natation* illustrates this point very well, since Vigo's lucky break at GFFA arose partly from the ambitious fusion of three companies, Gaumont, Franco-Film and Aubert, into a new French 'major', and partly from the urgent need to produce sound films (in this case documentary shorts) as quickly and cheaply as possible.

In this context, the independently financed *À propos de Nice* became a professional capital of experience that Vigo could bring to the shifting French labour market of 1930. Although its experimental documentary format had necessarily limited its potential distribution on the commercial network, we should not underestimate the strategic importance of the film's screenings at the Théâtre du Vieux-Colombier in May and June 1930, and its longer run at the Studio des Ursulines in October and November of that year. These were discrete but fashionable venues for the exhibition of the latest avant-garde tendencies and of new talent in general, so among the few spectators who saw *À propos de Nice* were people of considerable influence: writers, critics, actors, filmmakers, producers. Thanks to these screenings, for example, Vigo met his distant cousin Albert Riéra, who would later collaborate with him on the scenarios for *Zéro de conduite* and *L'Atalante*; Jean Dasté, who performed in both those films; and the actor René Lefèvre, whose social relations at the race-track (as we shall see) would lead to Vigo's crucial meeting with the producer Jacques Louis-Nounez in 1932. It is therefore no surprise that, as a result of the exposure that he had received at these Paris venues, the relatively unknown Jean Vigo should be invited to take his debut film to the second Congress of Independent Cinema held in Brussels from 27 November to 1 December 1930. Apart from showing *À propos de Nice* to a sympathetic international public of avant-garde filmmakers (perhaps with the hope of a wider European distribution through the film club and art house circuit), Vigo was able to establish some useful contacts for his future career, and also for the Amis du Cinéma association that he had set up in Nice that September.

Among the numerous encounters and discussions at the congress, Jean notably met the Dutch documentary filmmaker Joris Ivens, and became firm friends with the Belgian filmmaker Henri Storck, who would later work on *Zéro de conduite*. Apparently, Storck's *Images d'Ostende* (1929) received a less than positive response from Vigo, who loudly criticised the film during its screening, but the two young filmmakers' relationship was born from their heated exchanges after the projection. According to Storck's recollections in 1964, the congress also led directly to the commissioning of Vigo's second film, *Taris ou la natation*:

> J'avais fait la connaissance de Jean Vigo au Congrès du cinéma indépendant qui se tint à Bruxelles vers la fin de 1930, et où, comme tous les spectateurs, j'avais été frappé par l'originalité de style et de pensée, la nouveauté et la liberté de ton d'*À propos de Nice*. Germaine Dulac qui venait d'être appelée aux importantes fonctions de directrice de la production à Gaumont-Franco-Film, la plus puissante société de l'époque avec Pathé-Nathan, avait assisté aux projections de ce Congrès dans l'espoir de découvrir de jeunes cinéastes auxquels elle pourrait confier la réalisation de courts métrages [...] Germaine Dulac nous fit des promesses à nous deux et les tint. Elle engagea Vigo pour tourner le film sur Taris.[17] (Lherminier 1984: 114)

In fact this was not the first time that Dulac had taken a practical interest in Vigo's film activities, since she had come to Nice to celebrate the inaugural programme of the Amis du Cinéma in September 1930. Given that this energetic young man already had at that time an artistically original and technically competent debut film to his credit, it may well be the case that Dulac arranged the *Taris ou la natation* commission for Vigo before they renewed their acquaintance in Brussels. This sequence of events is confirmed by the fact that in November 1930 Vigo was already writing notes about Jean Taris's career:

> Jean Taris est né à Versailles le 6 juillet 1909. Son père lui apprend à nager dès l'âge de huit ans. C'est en 1924, quand il a quinze ans, qu'il assiste aux exploits d'Américains venus pour les Jeux Olympiques [...]

17 'I had first met Vigo at the Congress of Independent Cinema that was held in Brussels towards the end of 1930, and where I had been struck, like all the spectators, by the originality of style and thought, the novelty and freedom of tone of *À propos de Nice*. Germaine Dulac, who had just been given important production responsibilities at Gaumont-Franco-Film, the biggest company at the time along with Pathé-Nathan, had been present during the screenings at the Congress hoping to discover young filmmakers to whom she could entrust the realisation of some short films [...] She made promises to both of us and she kept them. She hired Vigo to make the film about Taris.'

notamment les exploits de Johnny Weissmuller le passionnent.[18]
(Lherminier 1985: 103)

The text then lists some of Taris's sporting records and achievements, describes his training regime as well as certain technical aspects of competitive swimming, and even sketches out some ideas for specific shots and sequences. As these notes indicate, the brief for *Taris ou la natation* was pretty straightforward, a reportage whose tone and content set it a world apart from the complete artistic freedom and financial independence of *À propos de Nice*. This commission seems much closer in format to the kind of five-minute item that today we might see in a television sports programme: some biographical and statistical information about a star and his exploits, plus some technical tips and encouragement for aspiring swimmers in the audience. In the early 1930s, the social contract between sports and the media was well established, so a figure such as Jean Taris was not just an outstanding sportsman, whose exploits regularly featured in the print and film journalism of the day. He was also a modest prototype of the modern 'sports personality', who is willing to communicate to his fans, via the popular media, something of his exemplary passion and athletic know-how. Taris certainly seems to have been an extremely cooperative subject for this brief film portrait, granting Vigo more than one personal interview (from which we can imagine the preparatory notes to derive), and showing considerable patience in the face of the technical rigours of filmmaking, as well as the artistic demands of the young filmmaker. The main shoot took place in January 1931 at the swimming pool of the Racing-Club de France, rue de l'Élysée, Paris. It seems likely that Vigo had chosen this location because its underwater portholes offered the exciting possibility of filming Taris's familiarly heroic body in various unconventional poses, and from a series of surprising angles. In addition to these swimming pool sequences, which already suggest a film that is stretching the formal restrictions of the brief, Taris's presence was required for some studio-based special effects, which Vigo wanted to mix into the straight-and-narrow format of the journalistic reportage.

18 'Jean Taris was born in Versailles on 6 July 1909. His father teaches him to swim at the age of 8. In 1924, aged 15, he witnesses the exploits of American swimmers competing at the Olympic Games [...] and he is particularly inspired by the exploits of Johnny Weissmuller.'

Finally, of course, there was the new technical question of recording and editing sound (including Taris's spoken commentary). This was still a relatively undeveloped process, which the young filmmaker was encountering for the first time, and without the reassuring presence of Boris Kaufman (this is the only occasion that he was absent from the crew). It was lucky for Vigo that Taris was used to the discipline of training!

Given all these contextual factors – the transitional technology, the journalistic brief, the sporting topic, Vigo's professional inexperience and demanding artistic vision – let us now take a closer look at *Taris ou la natation* as a work in its own right. In terms of content, the film has two basic ambitions. It is a portrait of Jean Taris, and a swimming master-class by a famous champion. A short introductory section of approximately two minutes sets the mood and scene of the film. Over the credits we hear children singing the following jaunty tune: 'Maman, les petits bateaux qui vont sur l'eau ont-ils des jambes? Mais oui, mon gros nigaud, s'ils n'en avaient pas ils marcheraient pas!'[19] (Lherminier 1985: 107). The mixed tone of the piece is established from the start. The film will be instructive but comical, and the sporting pedagogy will be communicated with an ironic smile. We are then introduced to the main location of *Taris ou la natation* with a shot of the entrance to the swimming pool at the Racing-Club de France, whose cooperation in the making of the film is duly recognised by a superimposed intertitle. Then we hear the recorded sound of a cheering crowd, as the image cuts to a close-up of a megaphone almost filling the screen. Behind the megaphone, we can just about see the face of a race official (possibly played by Vigo himself?), who presents the true star of the show: 'Jean Taris, détenteur de 23 records de France, toute distance de 100 à 1500 mètres; champion d'Angleterre des 500 et 880 yards; recordman du monde des 800 mètres'[20] (Lherminier 1985: 107). Here Taris himself appears for the first time. We see him poised for action, in a series of slightly static and self-conscious poses, on the starting blocks of the pool. These three angles show us the champion's body, which will become the principal motif

19 'Mummy, do the little boats that go on the water have legs? Of course they do, little fool, if they didn't they wouldn't be able to walk!'
20 'Jean Taris, holder of twenty-three French records, all distances from 100 to 1,500 metres; champion of England at 500 and 880 yards, world record holder at 800 metres.'

of the whole work. He is shot from above (high-angle overhead), from below (water level), and head-on, now looking into the camera for the explosive moment when the starter fires his pistol: 'Attention. Ready? BANG!'. As Taris dives headlong into the water, Vigo cuts to what is probably stock newsreel footage of a real swimming race, since it is clearly shot at another location, an open-air pool rather than the Racing-Club de France. The editing now alternates quickly between these 'live' images of a genuine contest, and staged shots of Taris swimming in the water at the indoor pool. We can easily tell that the two sets of images are from different sources, because the winner in the real race is wearing a black full-length bathing costume, whereas Taris (whom we assume to be the winner of his imaginary competition) is only wearing white trunks. Along the poolside in the newsreel pictures, we can see several press photographers running up and down, in search of spectacular images of the sporting battle. This sense of a dramatic climax sets up the final shots of the introductory racing sequence, whose purpose is to show us Taris in his natural element of water, and in his cultural position of budding media star. Thus Vigo cuts from the authentic footage of the end of the real swimming race, to a close-up of Taris's fingers touching home. This is followed by an overhead shot of the champion looking up from the water at a movie-camera, which is supposedly recording his moment of victory. At this point in the surviving version of *Taris ou la natation*, there seem to be some missing frames, since certain written accounts (Pierre Lherminier's, for example) describe the transition from the introductory section of the film to the main pedagogical section, in terms of a *mise en abyme* of the sports/media relationship. According to Lherminier, a reporter from Gaumont's very own *Journal vivant* approaches Taris after his victory and asks for an interview, to which the star responds as follows: 'Je suis né à Versailles le 6 juillet 1909; dès l'âge de 8 ans mon père m'apprend à nager. La natation s'impose et se réalise plus facilement que la marche'[21] (Lherminier 1985: 109). Henceforth it is the voice of Taris that picks up the task of the commentary, which for the next five minutes (the central and dominant section of the film) describes the different styles and techniques of swimming. Thus the crawl, the breast-stroke, the back-

---

21 'I was born in Versailles 6 July 1909; my father taught me to swim from the age of 8. Swimming is necessary and can be learned more easily than walking.'

stroke, even the 'sturgeon' and the 'over-arm stroke', are all explained and demonstrated by the champion: 'Tout homme flotte. L'eau est son domaine comme celui du poisson. Sans doute quelques mouve-ments à connaître: mais il suffit de se mettre à l'eau. On n'apprend pas à nager en chambre'²² (Lherminier 1985: 109). This mixture of reassuring encouragement and practical advice is amply and diversely illustrated by a rigorous visual study of the master swimmer in action, showing us how it should be done.

This pedagogical section of *Taris ou la natation* is probably the aspect of the commission that Vigo found the least inspiring on paper, given his profound aversion to authority in general, and to the educational system in particular. It is important to signal therefore that he does his best to keep the task as interesting for his film audience, and for himself, as it is instructive for the sporting public. Thus he brings comic touches to the representation of the young woman practising the breast-stroke 'in her bedroom' (balanced in mid-air on a stool wearing full bathing costume and a bonnet), as well as to the shots of the champion diving into the water and then (by reverse-motion) flying back out again. These gags provide some visual light relief from the didactic and demonstrative use of the sound track. This cuts between Taris's voice imparting rather dull instruc-tions, and the studio-produced sound effects of churning water. In terms of Vigo's corpus as a whole, what is most significant about *Taris ou la natation* is the evident pleasure that he derives from the filming of the human form. In the course of these five minutes, we get to know the champion's customised body at least as intimately as we will later discover the adolescent boys of *Zéro de conduite*, the passionate young lovers of *L'Atalante*, and of course the tattooed splendour of Michel Simon's decorated torso in the same film. Here we are treated to Taris in slow-motion, reverse-motion, and filmed underwater. We see his whole body in full flow, as well as selected features of the hero's arms, legs, back, chest and stomach. All of this is elegantly shot and cut, with a wide variety of camera-angles and movements. The relative crudity of the unmixed soundtrack (which can only incorporate either the voiceover or the water-effects, but not both at

22 'Man floats. The water is his domain as it is that of the fish. Yes, there are some movements to be learned: but you just have to get your feet wet. You can't learn to swim in your bedroom.'

the same time) even lends a certain rhythmical force and momentum to what might otherwise seem rather dryly demonstrational passages.

The final two minutes of *Taris ou la natation* return us to the playful and reflective tone of the opening section. Here we can recognise some of the most celebrated images of this generally neglected work. As has often been pointed out by commentators, the sequence showing Taris swimming about underwater foreshadows the marvellous moment in *L'Atalante*, when another Jean (Dasté) plunges desperately into the river, in order to look for his lost lover, Juliette. In *Taris ou la natation*, the signal for the closing change of tone comes, appropriately enough, at the point where the instructional commentary reaches the technical question of 'the tumble-turn' ('le virage'). Now Vigo twists the swimming-lesson into a pure celebration of the playful body, a motif of freedom and pleasure that we also find in the Carnival sequences of *À propos de Nice* and throughout *Zéro de conduite*. The soundtrack cuts to silence, as we see Taris abandoning his sporting status in favour of the ludic dimension of swimming as bodily liberation and improvisation, rather than physical discipline and competitive efficiency. The champion shows us a couple of properly executed tumble-turns, but then just starts showing off and generally messing about. He crawls on the floor of the pool, he twists and rolls around, he pretends to take an under-water nap, he blows bubbles and pulls funny faces at the camera, which is recording all this silliness from behind the portholes of the Racing-Club de France. As a final flourish, Vigo magically pulls Taris out of the water, with an impressive reverse-motion dive. Then he employs a trick-shot to switch the semi-naked sporting hero back into his civil attire of three-piece suit, sombre overcoat and bowler-hat. The fully dressed champion takes one final look at the camera overhead, raises his bowler to the audience, and walks off into the distance. But here Vigo decides to superimpose this studio-shot of Taris fully dressed over a watery image of the swimming-pool, so that what the viewer appears to see is the great sportsman walking on water. The semi-divine status of the champion in his media incarnation could hardly be more neatly expressed or more wittily satirised, depending on the audience's point of view. As the film ends, we hear once again the opening musical ditty, returning to remind us of the work's profound philosophical message: 'Of course little boats have legs, otherwise they couldn't walk!'.

It would seem that Vigo's slightly irreverent handling of the commission for GFFA was not especially appreciated by his employers. Indeed, according to Constantin Morskoï's testimony, recorded by Pierre Lherminier some forty years later, the first edited version of *Taris ou la natation* that Vigo produced was only 80 metres long, rather than the expected 300. As a result, Morskoï decided to bring in the more experienced Jean Arroy, in order to help the young man rework the materials into something worth showing as part of *Le Journal vivant*. Perhaps this editorial intervention can in part explain why Vigo later claimed to Henri Storck that he disliked the film, 'à l'exception de peu de vues sous l'eau' ('apart from a few of the underwater shots') (Lherminier 1985: 99–101). Hearing such a complaint from Vigo himself, one might wish to exclude *Taris ou la natation* from the artist's already brief corpus, or at least to relegate it to the status of footnote or curiosity. A more constructive approach, however, would be to situate Morskoï's anecdote in the context of the time (how could he have known that he was dealing with a future genius?), and to interpret Vigo's frustration as a stage in his development as an artist. He may well have resented the managerial interference of Morskoï and the professional assistance of Arroy. It is clear, however, from the evidence of the surviving version of *Taris ou la natation*, that Vigo fully seized the opportunity offered by this reportage. Not only did he enjoy himself and entertain his audience, he also learned more about film technique (especially sound) and the medium's full expressive range. Although it represents a very different form of learning experience from the case of *À propos de Nice* – the imposed exercise of an industrial commission rather than an independently financed adventure – *Taris ou la natation* tends to confirm our hypothesis that the documentary tradition has functioned historically as a kind of informal film school for the young and curious. Like many a filmmaker before and since, Vigo in 1931 was still an enthusiastic debutant, acquiring from the documentary format a fresh technical know-how, a hands-on experience of working in the industry, and above all an imaginative knowledge of the world in which cinema seeks a role and sometimes finds its place.

References

Chardère, B. (ed.) (1961), *Jean Vigo*, Lyons, Premier Plan.

de Laurot, É. and Mekas, J. (1955), 'An Interview with Boris Kaufman', *Film Culture*, summer, 4–6.

Lherminier, P. (1984), *Jean Vigo*, Paris, Pierre Lherminier/Filméditions.

Lherminier, P. (1985), *Jean Vigo: œuvre de cinéma*, Paris, Cinémathèque française/Pierre Lherminier.

Salles Gomes, P.E. (1988 [1957]), *Jean Vigo*, Paris, Seuil/Ramsay.

Vigo, J. (1966), 'Lettre à Léon Moussinac', *Jeune cinéma*, 15, May, 3.

3

The personal and the political

Frapper la balle, n'importe où, n'importe comment, n'importe quand![1] (Salles Gomes 1988 [1957]: 98)

Having completed *Taris ou la natation* in January 1931, the 25-year-old Jean Vigo now had two short films to his credit. One was an amateur experimental documentary with a small but significant critical reputation, the other a journalistic commission, which had introduced him to the world of professional filmmaking, and in particular to one of the major French production companies of the early 1930s, GFFA. As a double-sided calling-card, independent artist and director-for-hire, this was no mean achievement for a young man with few social connections, whose entrance into adult life has been seriously delayed by a tragic childhood, a fragmented education and persistently poor health. The next eighteen months, however, were to prove a most frustrating period for Vigo. All the numerous leads and projects that he pursued during this time would fail, one after the other, to capitalise on this promising start to his career. In the spring of 1931, Jean was back in Nice, trying to find work in the studios of the Côte d'Azur. The ever benevolent Germaine Dulac set up a potential job for him as script assistant on Jean Grémillon's *Daïnah la métisse* (1931). But this almost caused a rift between Vigo and his young friend Henri Storck, when the Belgian 'foreigner' was offered the post instead of the 'local boy' desperately looking for meaningful employment. The latter's angry reaction (soon appeased when Storck gallantly withdrew from the production) may seem less unreasonable

1 'Strike the ball, no matter where, no matter how, no matter when!' Vigo's notes for *Cochet ou le tennis*.

if we consider Vigo's personal circumstances at this point in his life. His young wife, Lydu, was experiencing a difficult pregnancy, with a baby due in June 1931. The couple's financial situation, despite the regular allowance from Hirsch Lozinski, and the modest income from the Amis du Cinéma film club, suddenly appeared quite alarming from the perspective of these new responsibilities. As a result, Jean was even obliged to sell the Debrie Parvo, with which he and Kaufman had shot *À propos de Nice*. In June, with the birth of daughter Luce imminent, Vigo decided to turn down the chance to cover the Tour de France that summer, as part of a sports newsreel team. In the autumn, he accepted an offer to work for GFFA and their German partner UFA, directing the French-language sequences of a multiple-language-version film, adapted from Louis Verneuil's stageplay *Pile ou face* (1924). But even this fairly uninspiring prospect came to nought, when in November the production encountered serious delays and Vigo was eventually released from the team. Finally, in the winter of 1931–32, he was invited to make a sports documentary about the tennis star Henri Cochet, one of the famous 'four musketeers' of French tennis, who dominated the sport at that time.

We can see from the surviving evidence related to *Cochet ou le tennis*, on which Jean collaborated with his friend, the journalist Charles Goldblatt, that this project was quite similar to *Taris ou la natation*. Like its predecessor, it would have trodden a fine line between respecting the journalistic tenor of the brief, and exploiting the didactic commission as a pretext for filmic fun, and for the development of personal themes and passions. Comparing the notes for *Cochet ou le tennis* published by Pierre Lherminier, and Salles Gomes's description of another outline for the film, we remark Vigo's familiar interest in the study of human forms, especially the elegant economy of the sportsman (Lherminier 1985: 355–63; Salles Gomes 1988 [1957]: 97–9). We also recognise the idea of expressing a sporting lesson through example and enthusiasm rather than dry pedagogical instruction; the importance that Vigo accords to freedom and play in the education of children; and his gentle satire of those 'accessible gods' that sports stars had already become in popular culture. In a final apotheosis, for example, reminiscent of Jean Taris's 'walking on water', Henri Cochet was to appear on a cloud, disguised as an angel, with tennis rackets for wings! We can also see from this material for *Cochet ou le tennis* that certain of these motifs would soon find a more fully poetic and more explicitly political expression in *Zéro de conduite*. In the latter, Vigo was to develop his heart-felt denuncia-tion of the oppressive educational system, as well as his lyrical celebration of adolescent fun and games. As for *Cochet ou le tennis*, at first the outline was approved by the production team at GFFA, and Vigo was even encouraged to expand his scenario and assemble a crew, with a view to start filming Cochet in Monte Carlo. By February 1932, however, the momentum for the project had broken down. This was partly because the potential distributors of the film had expressed doubts about its commercial acceptability, and partly because Vigo refused to respond constructively to their demands for changes (Vigo 2002: 43). On this evidence, it seems that by mid-1932 Jean's sense of his artistic independence (perhaps inspired by the exceptional circumstances of *À propos de Nice*) might soon have become incom-patible with a long-term career in the cinema. What he needed to find, by some miracle, was a film producer who, like his father-in-law, would pay for the kind of personal films that Vigo wanted to make, without any serious concern for financial viability, let alone a return on his investment.

The miracle happened

Je ne sais pas si c'était son charme ou son enthousiasme contagieux qui a permis à Vigo de trouver un commanditaire pour *Zéro de conduite*. En tout cas, le miracle s'est accompli, et nous voilà sur le plateau des studios Gaumont.[2] (Chardère 1961: 33–4)

Throughout its long evolution, alongside the dominant presence of major studios and integrated corporations, the ecology of the French film business has always featured a strange breed of rogue producers, whose independent frame of mind and love of cinema leads them to support the most unlikely filmmakers and the least acceptable films. Among them, we can include Pierre Braunberger, Anatole Dauman, Mag Bodard; the role-call is long and illustrious. It was just such a figure that Vigo was to encounter in July 1932, a year and a half after

2 'I don't know if it was his charm or his contagious enthusiasm that helped Vigo to find a backer for *Zéro de conduite*. In any case, the miracle took place, and there we were on the set of the Gaumont studios.' The speaker is Boris Kaufman.

making *Taris ou la natation*. At the time, he must have considered
giving up the fight to be a filmmaker, despite his brave words to Henri
Storck:

> Je n'ai peut-être pas beaucoup de chance cinégraphique; mais en vérité
> c'est tout de même le moindre de mes soucis. J'ai deux mains, et je
> finirai bien par agripper quelque chose ou quelqu'un. Quand on sait ce
> que l'on veut, on est patient et tenace.[3] (Lherminier 1984: 164)

Fortune may well favour the brave, but what is certain is that the
filmmaker's luck miraculously changed the day that Jacques Louis-
Nounez entered his life. The circumstances of their meeting were
related by the actor René Lefèvre, many years later, in Jacques
Rozier's film about Vigo for French television:

> Je revenais en voiture des courses d'Auteuil. Et dans la voiture, il y
> avait un petit propriétaire de chevaux de courses que je connaissais
> vaguement, qui s'appelait Nounez, et qui a profité de la circonstance
> pour me demander pourquoi le cinéma français était tellement
> statique, tellement bloqué sur des histoires de fesses qui commençaient
> à manquer d'un petit peu d'intérêt, et s'il y avait parmi les nouveaux
> venus des gens susceptibles de faire un peu mieux. Je lui ai dit: 'Si, j'en
> connais un, mais il n'a pas de capitaux, et les producteurs ne sont pas
> tellement d'accord avec lui. C'est un type qui s'appelle Jean Vigo. Il a
> fait un documentaire, à mon sens absolument sensationnel: *À propos
> de Nice*. Il a des idées originales et une conception du cinéma qui
> pourrait vous plaire, à condition que vous vouliez devenir command-
> itaire de films.' 'Mais pourquoi pas?' m'a dit Nounez. 'Donnez-moi
> l'adresse de votre ami.'[4] (Lherminier 1985: 115)

When they met at Louis-Nounez's office on 23 July 1932, in spite of
Vigo's growing scepticism about the workings of the film business,

3 'Perhaps I don't have much luck in cinema; but in truth it's the least of my
  worries. I've two hands, and I'll end up grabbing hold of something or someone.
  When you know what you want, you're patient and tenacious.'
4 'I was driving back from Auteuil and in the car was a minor racehorse owner I
  vaguely knew called Nounez. He took the opportunity to ask me why French
  cinema was so static, so fixated on sex stories that were beginning to lose any
  interest, and whether amongst the newcomers there was anyone likely to do a
  bit better. I said: "Yes, I know one, but he hasn't any capital and the producers
  don't like him. He's a guy called Jean Vigo. He's made a documentary that I
  think is absolutely brilliant, *À propos de Nice*. He has original ideas and a
  conception of cinema that you might enjoy, if you want to become a financial
  backer." "Well why not?" said Nounez. "Give me your friend's address."'

the son of Almereyda and the enlightened entrepreneur soon established a personal understanding and a working relationship. According to Henri Storck's testimony, Vigo was pleasantly surprised to find a producer who actually liked cinema and who was generally 'sympathetic'. As for Louis-Nounez, he would later recall how he had been immediately struck by the young man's blend of melancholy and good humour (Salles Gomes 1988 [1957]: 106). Interviewed for Rozier's film in 1964, he described Vigo as idealistic and sensitive, but also as a refined and exceptional person, capable of inspiring great loyalty and affection (Lherminier 1984: 108). It appears that from this initial encounter there emerged three possible ideas for films, two of which remained live projects in Vigo's mind during the next few months. The first, a fiction film about Vigo's schooldays, was clearly the project that was to become *Zéro de conduite*, although its original title was *Les Cancres* ('The Dunces'). As for the other two, one was a semi-documentary film about breeding race-horses in the Camargue region of France's south-east, an idea that for many years was wrongly believed to be Louis-Nounez's pet-project rather than Vigo's (because the producer was mistaken for a horse-breeder hailing from that region). The other was a dramatised account of the life of Eugène Dieudonné, an anarchist of Almereyda's generation and acquaintance, who had been sentenced to death, and then to hard labour at the penal colony in French Guyana, but who was eventually pardoned and released, after several escapes and a media campaign led by the journalist Albert Londres (Lherminier 1985: 413). On the evidence of these three projects, it is worth noting that Vigo's imagination had been far from idle during the year and a half of unemployment that he had experienced since *Taris ou la natation*. Two of the three outlines that he and Louis-Nounez began to discuss were clearly very personal stories, undeniably linked to Vigo's early life experience, and to the political culture of rebellion that the militant Almereyda had communicated to the future filmmaker. In the autumn of 1932, however, a decision had to be made about which of the three projects to pursue in the short term, and it was agreed to postpone the development of the film about Dieudonné, which had provisionally been entitled *Évadé du bagne* ('Fugitive from the penal colony'). In view of the subsequent fate of *Zéro de conduite*, it is highly ironic that the producer and the filmmaker should decide to defer the most politically sensitive of the three films, because they were concerned about incurring the wrath of the censors. By contrast, 'La Camargue' was developed and researched by Vigo, right up to October 1932, as his correspondence with Henri Storck confirms, but ultimately this more expensive project, which would have involved higher production costs, including travel allowances and location shooting, was abandoned in favour of *Les Cancres*, or *Zéro de conduite* as it was henceforth to be known (Lherminier 1984: 167).

In early December 1932, Vigo presented a script to Louis-Nounez, and an agreement was struck between artist and producer. The sense of their agreement needs to be understood in the wider context of the deal that Louis-Nounez had been negotiating with GFFA that autumn, while Vigo had been writing, researching and moving his young family to Paris (23 rue Gazan, in the 14th arrondissement, near the Montsouris park). The commitment by GFFA was to provide approximately 100,000 francs worth of hardware, i.e. studio-time, sets and props, cameras and lighting, sound-recording equipment, a stills-photographer, a projection-room, and facilities for mixing and editing. In return for all this, Louis-Nounez agreed to deliver artistic and technical services of an equivalent financial value, i.e. script, director, actors, crew, a musical score, as well as film stock, laboratory expenses and transport. This division of risks and responsibilities indicates not only that Louis-Nounez was unambiguously playing on the same side as Vigo, and that artist and manager form a team who were soon having to deal with the heavyweight structures of the Gaumont studios. It also shows that the novice producer was risking his own capital, and strategically setting up as positive an environment as possible for Vigo's personal vision to express itself.

From the start, however, two major logistical restrictions were placed on the making of *Zéro de conduite* by the management at GFFA. In terms of studio-time, the company was only offering eight working days, plus five days allowed for location shooting. Similarly, the length of the final work was strictly defined at 1,200 metres, since the film is intended as a short feature ('moyen métrage') of approximately forty-five minutes, to be shown in the first part of the show ('en première partie'), before the main feature film. Such contractual details may seem trivial, in relation to the grander stakes of artistic self-expression. But they go a long way towards explaining the elliptical structure and rough edges of *Zéro de conduite*, which many of its earliest spectators found either amateurish or confusing, while later generations have on the contrary been seduced by the film's charming qualities of formal liberty and magical improvisation. If we look at the timetable for the filming of *Zéro de conduite*, we will understand more clearly the restrictive circumstances in which the film was to be made: for the studio work, 24 December, 27–31 December, 3–4 January; for the exteriors, 5–7 and 8–9 January. Only thirteen days to produce a miniature masterpiece, a forbidding task compared to the total liberty that Kaufman and Vigo had enjoyed for the making of *À propos de Nice*. The studio filming was set to take place at the Gaumont premises near the Buttes-Chaumont, in the 19th arrondissement. Then the exteriors were to be shot at the college of Saint-Cloud, and in the streets of that chic Parisian suburb. Here, let us not forget, Vigo had spent some of his early childhood with his father Almereyda, to whose memory *Zéro de conduite* was a personal and political homage. From 12 to 24 December, Jean hastily assembled a gang of faithful friends, whom film history has come to call 'la bande à Vigo': cameraman Boris Kaufman (assisted by Louis Berger), assistant directors Albert Riéra and Pierre Merle, assistant producer Henri Storck, songwriter Charles Goldblatt, composer Maurice Jaubert. Out of necessity, most of the crew also appeared in the cast, along with acquaintances such as the actor Jean Dasté (the sympathetic teacher), Robert le Flon (the teacher known as 'Pète-Sec'), writer Louis de Gonzague-Frick (the Prefect), artist Raphaël Diligent (a fireman). Even Vigo's concierge was roped into the production, playing the teacher 'Bec-de-Gaz'! In the role of the little school principal, the professional actor known as 'Dauphin the dwarf' was engaged. But otherwise the majority of the performers in *Zéro de conduite* were non-professional actors, especially the children, whom Vigo chose mainly from the popular Parisian neighbourhood of the 19th arrondissement, near the Gaumont studios. Two important exceptions were Gérard de Bédarieux, the son of a poet, interpreting the key role of the 'girl' Tabard, and Louis Lefebvre, in the role of Caussat, a local tearaway whom Vigo had met in the Montsouris park near his home.

The first week of filming at the Gaumont studios started on time. But it soon became evident that the shooting schedule was going to be almost impossible to respect. This did not escape the attention of the studio managers, who had been instructed to keep an eye on the film's efficient progress. More alarming for all concerned was the state of Vigo's health. The filmmaker virtually collapsed under the combined pressure of the impossible timetable and the psychological stress of keeping the project artistically viable. Vigo was rapidly coming to terms with the mounting problems of the shoot. He knew already that some of his ideas would certainly have to be cut from the scenario, that the sound scenes were proving technically unsatisfactory, that most scenes would have to be shot in one take, and that certain members of the crew and cast were finding the delicate art of chaos a little more difficult to compose than they had perhaps imagined before Christmas eve 1932. By 31 January, Vigo was too sick to carry on, and even after the enforced break over the New Year, he was not yet in a fit state to return to work. Fortunately, Riéra and Merle managed to persuade Gaumont to grant a deferral for the final two days of studio filming until 6–7 January. Somehow, at midnight on the last day of shooting, this first stage of the production came to a feverish and frazzled conclusion.

We can get a sense of the chaotically creative atmosphere during the making of *Zéro de conduite*, from the following lively description, published by the journalist André Négis (another friend of Vigo's) in *Cinémonde*, 2 February 1933:

Les trois murs d'un dortoir percés de fenêtres qui ne donnent sur rien. Des lits saccagés, des oreillers éventrés, des plumes partout. Par terre, entre les lits, une douzaine de gosses en chemise, en pyjama, sont vautrés sur des matelas entassés. Dans une alcôve faite de trois rideaux, un homme en chemise est ligoté sur son lit verticalament dressé. On dirait d'un Christ, et c'en est bien un: le Pion crucifié des élèves infernaux. Nous sommes aux studios Gaumont et Jean Vigo tourne les intérieurs de son film *Zéro de conduite*, qu'on verra prochainement. Autour de lui, une jeune équipe s'agite, ardente, zélée: Boris Kaufman (frère du grand metteur en scène russe Dziga Vertoff) plus qu'un opérateur, un collaborateur, et son second, Berger; Riéra, le peintre, qui s'est fait assistant par affection pour son cousin Vigo; Henri Storck et Pierre Merle. Ce n'est pas rien, je vous jure, que de conduire, discipliner, que de tirer quelque chose de ces vingt gosses recrutés un peu partout, arrachés à l'arrière-boutique, à l'école, à la mansarde, au trottoir. Vigo les a longuement triés sur le volet de Paris. Il lui est arrivé d'en suivre dans la rue, au risque de passer pour un individu de mœurs douteuses. Mais ce que ce petit bonhomme veut, il le veut bien. Ainsi, à cette minute, avec ses yeux caves, ses joues creusées, sa toux de grippé, ses trente-neuf de fièvre, c'est dans son lit qu'il aurait dû rester. Mais on tourne, les frais courent et il est là aphone, agacé, pestant, jurant. Comme il n'a plus un son de voix, Riéra lui prête la sienne qui est magnifique: un vrai haut-parleur électro-dynamique [...] Jean Vigo, une bonne lame dans un mince fourreau. Le symbole de la volonté tenace. Ce jour, il l'a tant désiré! Tourner un scénario de lui![5] (Chardère 1961: 66–7)

The report closes with the image of Vigo dangerously poised 'sur le toit d'une maison de Saint-Cloud, par un temps de chien' ('on the roof of a house in Saint-Cloud, in dreadful weather'). He is about to confide to Négis the secret of his future projects: 'mais la toux lui coupe la parole' ('but his coughing cuts off his words') (Chardère 1961: 68). Reading this dramatic and vivid account, one can almost imagine an invisible second unit, recording the 'making of' *Zéro de conduite* for the future biopic of Jean Vigo, the patron saint and martyr of French cinema! Of course, Négis could have had no idea of the terrible fate awaiting the film at the hands of the censors, nor of the premature death of its director. It is worth observing, however, that even in 1932 certain elements of the 'myth of Vigo' (see Chapter 5) are already informing the narrative account of *Zéro de conduite*'s production. We can see the continuation of this tradition, some twenty-

5 'A dormitory with only three walls and windows looking out onto nothing. Ransacked beds, disembowelled pillows and feathers everywhere. On the floor, between the beds, a dozen kids in nightshirts or pyjamas are stretched out on piles of mattresses. In an alcove made of three curtains, a man is tied up on a bed that's standing vertically. He looks like Christ, and that's what he is: it's the warden crucified by infernal schoolkids. We are at the Gaumont studios and Jean Vigo is shooting the interiors for his film *Zéro de conduite*, shortly to be released. Around him a young team is busy at work, enthusiastic and zealous: Boris Kaufman (brother of the great Russian director Dziga Vertov) is more of a co-director than a cameraman, assisted by Berger; Riéra, the painter, is acting as assistant-director out of affection for his cousin, Vigo; and there's Henri Storck and Pierre Merle. It's quite a feat, I can assure you, to direct, discipline, and get results from these twenty kids recruited from shop-works, from school, from attic-rooms, from the streets. Vigo spent a long time sifting through Paris to find them. Occasionally he followed some of them in the street, at the risk of passing for a fellow of dubious morals. But what this little fellow wants he wants badly. Thus it is that at present, with his sunken eyes, his hollow cheeks, his raking cough, his thirty-nine degree fever, he should really have stayed in bed. But the camera's turning, the bills are mounting, and there he is voiceless, irritated, cursing, swearing. As his voice has gone, Riéra lends him his own magnificent voice, a real electro-dynamic loudspeaker [...] Jean Vigo, a trusty blade in a narrow sheath. The symbol of tenacious will power. He has longed for this day for so long! To film his own scenario!'

five years later, when the biographer Salles Gomes minutely recounts the surveillance and repression of Vigo's creativity by the clock-watching Gaumont functionaries. Thus, as midnight approaches on 7 January 1933, there only remain ten minutes of the allocated studio-time – and there's still one sequence to shoot! Somehow the miracle happens (although in fact this is one of the many scenes that will later be left on the cutting-room floor), and Vigo duly turns to the Gaumont employee, pausing only to adjust his hat: 'Monsieur, j'ai terminé, bonne nuit!' ('Sir, I have finished, good night!') (Salles Gomes 1988 [1957]: 117–23). If the invisible second unit really had been filming the biopic, no doubt Vigo, in that impossible version, would have said to the studio manager: 'Monsieur, je vous dis merde!' ('Sir, to you I say: shit!'), thus echoing the most famous line of *Zéro de conduite*, when René Tabard makes his revolutionary declaration of independence.

The same dynamic of creative disorder can be found in Kaufman's account of the film's production, but for him the relationship between art and chaos is perceived more clearly in terms of aesthetic invention. The impossible restrictions of the shoot, combined with Vigo's energy and desire for cinema, produce a rare fusion of the forces of contingency and improvisation:

> Quoique ce soit son premier film avec des acteurs professionnels, son oreille sûre aux dialogues et aux intonations, son horreur du cabotinage, lui permirent de triompher de son manque d'expérience, et même de le tourner à son avantage. Sa science de la mise en scène avait presque atteint sa maturité, totalement dépourvue de routine. On nous trouvait extravagants, parce que nous tournions au dortoir dans une obscurité presque totale (et ceci avec pellicule peu sensible); parce que nous tournions au ralenti (240 images par secondes) la scène de révolte au dortoir. À Saint-Cloud, nous avons scandalisé la population avec la procession des enfants menés par Jean Dasté, poursuivant une jeune femme. Vigo employait toute méthode nouvelle qui lui semblait justifiée pour exprimer l'idée initiale. Par exemple, Dasté marchant à la Charlot (Vigo cite Chaplin et sa philosophie, comme on cite un classique dans la littérature) ou le ralenti dans la procession d'enfants qui est une chorégraphie poétique de l'impossible accompli, dont Vigo a dû rêver dans son enfance.[6] (Chardère 1961: 33–4)

6 'Although it was his first film with professional actors, he was able to overcome this lack of experience, and even turn it to his advantage, thanks to his fine ear for dialogue and intonation, and his horror of overacting. His skills as a director

Starting on 10 January, the location filming, as Négis and Kaufman suggest, was conducted at the same slightly crazy (and, for Vigo, rather dangerous) rhythm as the work accomplished at the Gaumont studios. Over the next twelve days, the exteriors were shot at the Belleville-La Villette train station (the opening sequence of the film), in the playground of the college, and in the streets of Saint-Cloud. Once more, Vigo and friends were obliged to drop a number of planned scenes from the scenario, and they shot virtually all the other scenes in one take. In addition to the time-pressure and the budgetary restrictions imposed by GFFA, now there was bad weather to contend with, as well as the imminent departure of Kaufman for Switzerland, where he was committed to working on another film. By 22 January the filming was finished, for better or for worse. Then Vigo spent the next six weeks putting together an initial edit of the film, which was shown to the crew and other friends on 4 March. It would appear that Vigo and his relatively inexperienced collaborators were surprised, and slightly disappointed, by what they saw (Salles Gomes 1988 [1957]: 124–5). There was a significant gap between the film that they had imagined they were making, during those frenetic four weeks, and the rough-edged, elliptical, and at times barely audible version of *Zéro de conduite* which they discovered on the screen that day. The truth is that as Vigo was editing the material, which they had shot in such a hasty fashion, he was obliged to make further cuts from the scenario, in order to meet the target of 1,200 metres agreed between Louis-Nounez and GFFA. As for the question of sound, this was the dimension of the film where the team's relative lack of technical know-how was most noticeable, especially the recording of the dialogue, which at certain points was unintelligible, or at least difficult for the spectator to match to the relevant source. However, this was also the aspect of

had almost reached maturity, and were totally devoid of routine. People found us extravagant, because we filmed the dormitory scenes in almost total obscurity (and without a particularly sensitive film-stock); because we filmed in slow motion (240 frames per second) the rebellion-scene in the dormitory. At Saint-Cloud, we shocked the residents with the procession of children led by Jean Dasté who is following a young woman. Vigo used any new method that seemed to him justified in order to express his initial idea. For example, Dasté walking in the manner of Chaplin (Vigo cites Chaplin and his philosophy, as one cites a classic in literature) or the slow-motion of the children in revolt, a poetic choreography of the impossible and something that Vigo must have dreamed about during his childhood.'

the film which, thanks to the brilliant musical contribution of Maurice Jaubert, would change the most significantly, between the 'technical' preview of the film on 4 March and its 'corporative' presentation to critics, distributors and other invited personalities, on 7 April 1933 at the Cinéma Artistic, rue de Douai, in the 9th arrondissement.

Given Jaubert's creative role in *Zéro de conduite*, and later in *L'Atalante*, it is important to situate his working relationship with Vigo. At the time of the Amis du Cinéma in Nice, Vigo had made the acquaintance of this young composer, who had come to the film club one evening to accompany Alberto Cavalcanti's *Le Petit Chaperon Rouge* (1929), only to discover that the print of the film had not arrived in time from Paris (Vigo 2002: 45). This curious personal contact, between an atheistic radical filmmaker and a politically committed Catholic composer, soon developed into an important friendship for both men, and Jaubert would go on to write the music for *L'Atalante*, as well as *Zéro de conduite*. Born in 1900 in Nice, the son of a distinguished barrister, Jaubert was a highly gifted pianist and classically trained composer, who was looking to break out of the ideological impasse of 1920s modernism, in music and the other 'high' arts (Porcile 1971). He saw in cinema a possible way of making contemporary music more socially engaged, and relevant to a broader popular audience. Before the coming of 'talkies', Jaubert had already worked on the musical accompaniment for Jean Renoir's *Nana* (1926) and Hanns Schwartz's *The Wonderful Lies of Nina Petrovna* (1928). But it was in the 1930s that he flourished, notably working as musical director at Pathé-Natan from 1932–35, and writing scores for many classics of the early sound period: for Vigo, of course, but also for René Clair (*Quatorze juillet*, 1932, *Le Dernier milliardaire*, 1934), Julien Duvivier (*Un carnet de bal*, 1937, *La Fin du jour*, 1939), the Prévert brothers (*L'Affaire est dans le sac*, 1932) and Marcel Carné (*Drôle de drame*, 1937, *Quai des brumes*, 1938, *Hôtel du Nord*, 1938, *Le Jour se lève*, 1939). In addition to this work in the commercial mainstream, Jaubert's collaboration with filmmakers such as Jean Lods, Henri Storck, and Jean Painlevé shows his affinity with the socially committed tendency of experimental cinema. Like Vigo, he seems to have had little time for the purist avant-garde of the late 1920s. In the case of *Zéro de conduite*, although Jaubert had to work quickly, he studied very closely Vigo's initial edit a number of times, and together the couple managed to produce in the short time available a sound composition that goes well beyond the received idea of musical accompaniment. Indeed their work stands out, in 1933, as a serious attempt to take cinema into the field of a truly audiovisual art. The most celebrated instance of the couple's experimental collaboration on *Zéro de conduite* is no doubt the 'reverse' sound track for the slow-motion sequence of the children's carnivalesque rebellion in the school dormitory. For this scene of primitive liberation, Vigo asked his friend to compose a suitably joyous and yet disturbing piece of music. In response, Jaubert came up with the idea of writing the score 'backwards', and then instructed the musicians to play it 'straight'. This meant that when the recording was played in reverse, during the final sound mix, a recognisable melody, albeit strange and disorienting, would emerge from the sonic distortion. If anarchist regimes have national anthems, this is probably what they sound like.

Happily it isn't perfect

When *Zéro de conduite* was shown in public for the first time, at the trade screening in April, the audience's reactions were violently split, mainly along lines of personal loyalty on the one hand, and ideological prejudice on the other. Thus the children appearing in the film, and their parents, were pretty delighted to see themselves portrayed on the screen. Likewise Vigo's extended family of artistic friends and political sympathisers were full of enthusiasm and vociferous approval. The more significant reaction, however, came from the professional critics and potential distributors, who in the main found the film artistically amateurish and morally offensive. In their eyes, *Zéro de conduite* was either a loosely assembled string of badly filmed childish gags, or an attempt at avant-garde scandal and political provocation, in the manner of Luis Buñuel's *Un chien andalou* (1929) and *L'Âge d'or* (1930). It is likely that Vigo and friends left the screening somewhat discouraged, perhaps already fearing the worst for the film's chances of getting a fair hearing from the press, and a proper distribution on the commercial circuit. The most touching document relating to the trade screening is a short note to Vigo written on 16 April 1933 by Louis-Nounez, who clearly must have seen the need to console his protégé and encourage him to turn his mind already towards future projects and rewards:

Cher Vigo. J'ai été heureux de vous entendre hier au soir et d'avoir de vos nouvelles. Je regrettais beaucoup de vous quitter, j'aurais aimé que vous ayez de votre première représentation de *Zéro de conduite* un souvenir encore meilleur. Je pense que vous connaissez les hommes puisque vous avez beaucoup souffert. Gardez votre confiance entière, votre film est très bien; il n'est pas parfait heureusement. Mais vous le savez, c'est ce qui fait votre force et c'est ce qui affirmera votre valeur et contribuera à votre réussite. Mon souvenir à tous ceux que j'ai senti vos amis, ma pensée respectueuse à votre femme, à vous mon affection et mon amitié.[7] (Lherminier 1984: 108)

Over the next few weeks, a number of critical articles appeared in the press. Most of these either adopted an overtly hostile attitude to *Zéro de conduite*, or focused exclusively on the film's controversial qualities. Thus Pierre Ogouz in *Marianne*, 19 April 1933, was one of the more positive reviewers:

Une œuvre exceptionnelle, que l'on va siffler et discuter. Un film dont on ne comprend pas qu'un grand circuit se soit assuré la distribution. Haineux, violent, destructeur, rancunier, il semble gonflé de toute l'amertume que son auteur doit garder d'un misérable passé de pensionnaire. Infecté de grossièretés, nocif et âpre, il stigmatise les pédagogues vicieux et bornés et chante avec désespoir un hymne à la liberté. Photographie confuse et mauvaise, qui ajoute à l'angoisse de l'histoire. Œuvre ardente et hardie. M. Jean Vigo en est l'auteur: un Céline du cinema.[8] (Salles Gomes 1988 [1957]: 148)

---

7 'Dear Vigo. It was good to hear you last night and to get your news. I was very sorry to leave you, I'd have liked you to have had an even better memory of your first showing of *Zéro de conduite*. I believe that you know mankind, because you have known great suffering. Keep your confidence intact, your film is very good, happily it isn't perfect. But you know, it's what makes you so strong, and it's what will confirm your value and contribute to your success. My regards to all those friends I felt were with you, and my respects to your wife; to you goes my affection and my friendship.'

8 'An exceptional work that will be booed and disputed. A film whose distribution by a big commercial circuit is difficult to understand. Hateful, violent, destructive, vengeful, it seems to be infused with all the bitterness that its author has kept from an unhappy past in a boarding school. Infected with crude language, poisonous and sharp, it attacks the vice-ridden and narrow-minded pedagogues, and desperately sings a hymn of liberty. Confused and bad photography, which adds to the anguish of the story. An ardent and bold work. M. Jean Vigo is the author: a Céline of cinema.'

Even more troubling for Vigo and Louis-Nounez was the fact that several reviews carried rumours of complaints about the film, from Catholic and other right-wing organisations. Some even predicted forthcoming difficulties with the Board of Film Control. The film's planned commercial release (with Jean Benoît-Levy's *La Maternelle*, 1933) was ominously deferred. Although it was now clear to all concerned that the censors were going to demand at least the removal of certain morally or politically shocking scenes or phrases, nobody was expecting the exceptionally harsh verdict announced by the Board of Film Control. Citing the film's supposed 'dénigrement de l'instruction publique' ['defamation of state education'], they decided unequivocally to refuse *Zéro de conduite* a 'visa of exhibition'. This effectively meant an outright ban of the film, with no room for compromise or accommodation.

There has been considerable debate as to why *Zéro de conduite* was banned in such a brutal manner. Some observers insist on the political opposition of the censors to a film signed by 'the son of Almereyda', at a time when France was experiencing a serious economic and social crisis. In his presentation of the film in Brussels, in October 1933, Vigo himself claimed that the order to ban the film came directly from the Ministry of the Interior. We cannot know whether this was an explicit reason for the interdiction, but certainly the political climate of France in the early 1930s had returned to the violent and hateful atmosphere of the 1900s and 1910s, the period of Almereyda's militant heyday and tragic death. The emergence of Fascism, at home and abroad, had introduced a newly divisive element into traditional political debate, creating a radical split in the democratic centre of the Third Republic, and forcing the parties into bitterly opposed extremes. It is hard to appreciate in hindsight the sheer violence of the daily political confrontations in Parliament, in the press, and in the street-battles of Paris. We should recall, however, that in February 1934, less than a year after the banning of *Zéro de conduite*, not only did Édouard Daladier's government collapse under pressure from extreme right-wing demonstrations, but the Republic itself almost fell victim to a quasi-Fascist *coup d'état*. Seen in this broader historical perspective, the fate of a single film, even a masterpiece by Jean Vigo, is a relatively minor concern. We should not exaggerate therefore the political significance of the ban, which means so much more to film-history and cinephiles than it ever did to chairman Edmond Sée, and his sensitive colleagues on the Board of Film Control. The latter had probably forgotten the title of *Zéro de conduite* and the names of Vigo–Almereyda as soon as their decision had been ratified. The film was eventually granted an exhibition visa in 1945, after the Liberation of France. It was shown commercially for the first time at Pierre Braunberger's Panthéon cinema in November that year, appropriately on a double-bill with André Malraux's *Espoir* (1939), which had also been banned for political reasons in the complex aftermath of the Spanish Civil War. Within a decade, *Zéro de conduite* had become a film-club favourite and was soon considered a classic of left-wing political filmmaking. Along with *L'Atalante*, it forms one of the immovable foundation stones of Vigo's critical reputation and cultural legend. So let us now take a detailed look at *Zéro de conduite*, especially in terms of its narrative structure and major thematic concerns.

The children's plot

'Ce film est tellement ma vie de gosse que j'ai hâte de faire autre chose' (Chardère 1961: 68).[9] It is fair to say that Vigo's striking and candid remark to a friendly journalist, André Négis of *Cinémonde*, during the making of *Zéro de conduite*, has tended to set the tone of much critical discussion of the film. When an artist makes an explicit claim (repeated in the presentation to the film club in Brussels, 17 October 1933) that his work is autobiographical in nature, it is hardly unreasonable for critics, and *a fortiori* biographers, to pursue this line of enquiry seriously and to establish the degree of correspondence between the real life and its creative transposition. What Salles Gomes in particular has demonstrated is that the parallels are often exact yet overdetermined, so the film's representation of college life, for example, is in fact an amalgam of Vigo's diverse memories (some happy, some sad) of his schooldays at Millau and Chartres. Together they recreate the institutional atmosphere and repressive culture that we see in *Zéro de conduite*, the perverse behaviour of the teachers and their pupils, even particular dramatic incidents, such as the sleep-walking boy in the dormitory, or the 'haricot beans' protest (Salles

9 'This film is so much my life as a kid that I'm in a hurry to do something else.'

Gomes 1988 [1957]: 111–14). In his writing of the scenario, Vigo clearly draws on multiple sources and real emotions, blending these different elements into a composite picture whose authenticity has struck so many critics and spectators over the years, both on a personal level and on a wider political scale. This technique of transposing fragments of lived experience into an emotionally enhanced fiction is evident in Vigo's composition of the main children's characters, mixing and matching aspects of a number of his former schoolmates. Thus Bruel, Caussat, Colin, Tabard, all of these kids really existed, but in the bodies of many different children that Vigo had known or, in certain cases, that Vigo himself had been in an earlier life. For example, the answer to the most obvious question about *Zéro de conduite*'s autobiographical status – 'Who is Jean Vigo in the film?' – seems to be that young 'Jean Salles' is to be found a little in Tabard (the sensitive loner who turns into the rebel leader), a little in Bruel (the older boy whose intimacy with the 'girl' Tabard raises such suspicion), a little in Caussat (the tough kid boasting of his erotic Sunday exploits with his correspondent), and even a little in Colin (whose shame about his family origins reflects the young Vigo's enforced clandestinity). Finally, regarding the true basis of the events in *Zéro de conduite*, we should not forget the memory of Miguel Almereyda, who is clearly a personal reference point for the film's political narrative. Indeed Jean had even read his father's account of his own terrible experiences in the children's prison known as the 'Petite Roquette' (Salles Gomes 1988 [1957]: 111). Yet Almereyda's ghostly presence in the story can only be materialised through the kind of imaginative transposition of precise memories into symbolic fiction that constitutes Vigo's self-taught screenwriting method.

It is with a sense of the film's construction in mind that we shall now analyse the narrative structure and thematic development of *Zéro de conduite*, focusing therefore less on the biographical facts of Vigo's young life (for which, see Chapter 1) than on the manner of their transposition into screen fiction. This experience was, let us not forget, Vigo's first attempt at film narrative, since the structure of his two documentaries, *À propos de Nice* and *Taris ou la natation*, is in both cases more of an argument (association of ideas and images; construction by themes and subjects) than a dramatic story (plot, action, characters; linear time and the rhythm of scenes). Whereas

L'Atalante, his second and final chance at fiction, is in fact an adaptation of a scenario written by someone else (see Chapter 4), *Zéro de conduite* is his very own tale, not just in the autobiographical sense, but also because Louis-Nounez's generosity as a producer had enabled him to follow his personal inspiration and to pursue freely the themes of liberty and justice that were so close to his heart. In order to present our discussion of *Zéro de conduite* as clearly as possible, we shall divide the film's forty two minutes into eight sections, as presented in the following table.

Section	Timing	Duration
1 Back to school	1.10–6.10	5 minutes
2 In the dormitory	6.10–12.10	6 min
3 Play and study	12.10–18.40	6 min 30 sec
4 Promenade in town	18.40–25.30	6 min 50 sec
5 Sunday life	25.30–28.00	2 min 30 sec
6 Protest begins	28.00–33.10	5 min 10 sec
7 Open rebellion	33.10–38.15	5 min 5 sec
8 Revolution's here!	38.15–41.35	3 min 20 sec

Although these section divisions are ours and not Vigo's, we shall aim to demonstrate not only that they respect the organic development of the film, its characters and principal themes, but also that each section can in turn be subdivided into two reflecting parts (A and B), within a complex pattern of narrative correspondences and thematic echoes. In fact, for a screenwriting debutant, Vigo succeeded in building an extremely simple and elegant scenario. This challenges the commonly held idea that *Zéro de conduite* should be considered a triumph over its structural infelicities and the difficult circumstances of its production. The following table presents a more detailed breakdown of that basic pattern.

Section	Description	*Intertitles*	Timing
0	Titles (song)	*Zéro de conduite.* *Young devils at college.*	0–1.05
	Intertitle #1	*The vacation is finished.* *The return to school.*	1.08
1A	Train		1.10–4.30
1B	Station		4.30– 6.10
2A	Dormitory: night		6.10–10.00
2B	Dormitory: morning		10.00–12.10
	Intertitle #2	*The children's plot.*	12.13
3A	Playground		12.15–15.20
3B	Classroom		15.20–18.40
4 (A/B)	Promenade (4A)/ principal's office (4B)		18.40–25.25
	Intertitle #3	*Sunday. Caussat at his correspondent's house.*	25.28
5A	Sunday: Caussat		25.30–26.00
	Intertitle #4	*And Colin with Mother Beans, his Mum.*	26.03
5B	Sunday: Colin		26.05–28.00
6A	Refectory: protest (beans)		28.00–29.30
6B	Classroom: protest (*merde!*)		29.30–33.10
7A	Dormitory: rebellion (night)		33.10–36.25
	Intertitle #5	*The next morning, fatigue is the four rebels' accomplice.*	36.28
7B	Dormitory: rebellion (morning)		36.30–38.15
8 (A/B)	Fête: revolution (8A/playground) (8B/rooftop)		38.15–41.35
End	FIN (song)		41.40

1. Back to school

1A: The train

In narrative and thematic terms, the opening intertitle of *Zéro de conduite* – 'Vacation is over. Back to school' – could hardly be more succinct. Thus the first section introduces the dominant dramatic opposition of the film, between the free-flowing energy and conviviality of the schoolboys and the repressive culture of the educational regime into which they must enter in order to become socially trained citizens. As the film opens, we are following two boys returning to school by train: first Caussat (gloomily contemplating alone his impending doom) and then Bruel, whose final moments of freedom we witness, before they are both delivered like prisoners to the awaiting guard. This is Parrain, the teacher known as 'Pète-Sec', who has come to escort them back to the confines of the institution. As is Vigo's manner, however, the boys act out this difficult drama in a simple and comical sequence, whose gags and good humour sweeten the rather bitter political message that it conveys. Notably, Caussat and Bruel perform for each other a series of increasingly obscene tricks and visual gags, which celebrate the playful sexuality and crude pleasures of adolescence. Thus, since Caussat has a toy trumpet, he will necessarily stick it up his nose, or some other available orifice. Since Bruel has a couple of balloons, he will of course turn them into a pair of breasts, in order to fondle them *ad libendum*. And since Caussat has a bunch of feathers, there is only one part of his anatomy where they demand to be displayed to his friend. However, the sense that the children's moral licence is about to expire is signalled by the train's arrival at the station. A sudden jolt brings crashing to the floor the anonymous sleeping body, which we have seen once or twice sitting crumpled in the corner of the compartment. 'Il est mort!' ('He's dead!'), the boys exclaim, interrupting their manly enjoyment of a couple of fine cigars.

1B: The station

From their smoke-infested 'non-smoking' compartment, they emerge reluctantly onto the station platform. They know that, in spite of their extemporising distractions, this time the holidays really are finished. 'On ne va pas beaucoup rigoler encore cette année' ('We're not going to laugh much this year, again'), they observe as they realise that it is 'Pète-Sec', who has come to take them back to school for the new term. The sinister figure of the teacher is also awaiting two other characters of strategic importance in the film's narrative, whom this introductory section neatly folds into its dramatic exposition. One is the supposed 'dead man' from the train, who turns out to be the new teacher, Huguet, played by Jean Dasté. 'Il a l'aspect ahuri de quelqu'un qui se réveille. Il paraît à la fois confus et ravi', as Vigo describes him in his notes (Lherminier 1985: 141).[10] Indeed, this character will occupy a significantly ambivalent position in the film's *dramatis personae*, switching allegiance between the school authorities to whom he belongs, and the oppressed children with whom he sympathises. The other important figure to appear on the foggy station platform is René Tabard, the hyper-sensitive, long-haired boy, accompanied by his mother. She has come to ask Parrain for permission to keep her troubled son at her side, just one more night. Tabard is the innocent and troubled child through whom scandal, and ultimately rebellion, will arrive at the college and turn the world upside down. Thus, in this introductory section, Vigo has presented to the audience the three future rebels of his story (Caussat, Bruel, Tabard), one of the children's major oppressors (Parrain), and the unstable dramatic element of Huguet, the dreamer who is divided between order and liberty. On a thematic level, Vigo has established the key motifs of pleasure and freedom, both of which are seen as precious but fragile qualities, always in danger of repression from the school institution. Finally, the two scenes in the train and the station have neatly transported us to the college, which will provide the main dramatic setting of the story. As Parrain leads the boys back to school, we follow them as if they were returning to prison.

2. In the dormitory

In this second section, divided into 'night' and 'morning', Vigo slows down the narrative process, in favour of thematic development. What counts in these eerily intense passages is the oppressive atmosphere and sombre mood of the miniature prison where the children are enclosed. It is from this collective incarceration that the boys will later free themselves in section 7, the reverse-image of section 2.

10 'With the astonished look of someone who has just woken up, he appears both confused and delighted.'

2A: Night

Having said goodbye to the outside world and its minimal margins of liberty, the boys are now to be found in the school dormitory, at night. Here we discover the very heart of Vigo's story: the systematic repression of the children's natural freedom. This vision, however, is conveyed neither through philosophical dialogue nor through melodramatic incident. What we see, as the darkness of the railway station gives way to the semi-obscurity of the dormitory, is a regimented space, two columns of children's beds with docile little bodies lying in them like so many adolescent corpses. Kaufman's camera set-up cuts a deep diagonal line through this space. It runs from the left-hand side of the frame, where the General Supervisor (or 'Bec-de-Gaz', as he is known) has come to make his final check-up of the night, to the locked doors at the far end of the dormitory, where a seemingly blind supervisor in dark glasses keeps watch like a weird sentinel. A silence reigns over this whole scene, only broken by the occasional order barked in the dark by 'Pète-Sec', who responds to the stirrings and chattering of the children with immediate punishment ('Au pied de mon lit jusqu'à onze heures!' ['Stand by my bed until eleven o'clock']) or threats of deprivation ('Consigné dimanche!' ['Consigned to school on Sunday!']). In visual terms, we find here one of Kaufman and Vigo's signature shots, the high-angle overhead. In the context of *Zéro de conduite*, this is an especially appropriate figure, since it represents a spatial universe where the children are under surveillance at every moment, regulated, disciplined, controlled in their every movement throughout the night and day. Even their sleeping bodies are supervised and punished. Even the right to piss and shit freely is subject to permission:

> 'Monsieur, il peut y aller?'
> 'Monsieur, j'ai mal au ventre!'
> 'Monsieur, il peut y aller, quoi? Il a mal au ventre!'[11]
> (Lherminier 1985: 145)

In the end, of course, the boy 'goes', realising that in any case 'the old fool' is already asleep. This minor incident is significant from a thematic point of view, on two counts. Firstly, it shows how Vigo will invariably use comical touches of quite basic humour to attenuate the

---

11 '"Can he go, sir?"/"Sir, I've got stomach ache!"/"Can he go, sir, he's got stomach-ache!"'

harshness of his political message. Beyond that, however, we should note that this ideological content is never overly deterministic. It is always open to the initiative, ingenuity and invention of the free individual. Thus, however powerful Vigo's depiction of the school as prison may be, there is never any sense in *Zéro de conduite* that its prison-like regime is the reflection of an infallible social order. Vigo's ideology is often harsh, but never pessimistic. Thus the college is always also just a bunch of imbeciles and obsessives, whom the children will eventually outwit, and who sooner or later will become the sacrificial victims of the revolution. At this point in the narrative, however, the future rebellion is a long way off. And so, for now, all that violence and upheaval will remain pent up and constrained by the orderly rows and institutional discipline of the dormitory. Instead, what we see is an eloquent symptom of such repression. This is the disturbing sequence with the sleep-walking child, who uncannily retraces in reverse the sinister steps of the General Supervisor's final round. The other boys watch the sleepwalker in fascination and fear, mesmerised by this psychosomatic embodiment of their anger and anxiety, terrified that if they should wake him their comrade will 'die' from the shock.

2B: Morning

When morning comes, the children are roughly awoken by the supervisors, even though they have not slept enough during the night. Then they are hurriedly assembled for the day's regulated activities of eating, learning, exercising and sleeping again. It is the individual child's body, and the regimented body of the children as a group, that provide Vigo and Kaufman with the simple focus of their silent eloquence. The bed covers are rudely pulled back by the supervisors, to reveal the dozy bodies of adolescents – not soldiers or prisoners – who would like to rest their barely formed limbs a few minutes longer. No chance of such understanding from their teachers, however, and soon the kids are dressed in their school clothes, lined up like borstal boys and marched off for feeding time at the refectory. This is the first day of the new school year, and so it will set the rhythm for the weeks and months to come. As the boys march out of the dormitory, we know as well as they do what boredom lies before them. Thus Vigo, in these two highly atmospheric dormitory scenes, succeeds in evoking the college's whole monotonous daily routine of moral surveillance and corporal discipline. This impressive effect is achieved, we should note, with virtually no dialogue, and with a minimum of dramatic incident. The essence of the institutional spirit is captured in the filmic expression of its restrictive spaces and oppressive silence.

3. Play and study

This third section, in narrative and thematic terms, develops the representation of the school's regime, especially the strict regulation of the children's natural energies into fixed periods of study, interspersed with brief breaks of carefully supervised 'play'. At the same time, Vigo gradually sows the seeds of future rebellion throughout these two scenes, which were shot respectively in the real playground at Saint-Cloud, and in the artificial classroom that his team reconstituted at the Gaumont studios.

3A: Play

'The Children's Plot', thus one of the film's rare intertitles informs us that there is potential trouble ahead. We discover Caussat, Bruel and Colin in the playground, discussing their revolutionary plans and preparations (from which Tabard is at this stage significantly excluded). The playground is represented as a relatively free space, compared to the dormitory, classroom or refectory. Here we witness the children running around as individuals, or forming little groups of two or three. We see them playing games, like the street kids in *À propos de Nice*. They manage to find little pockets of resistance, here and there, discussing secrets behind a wall or a tree, smoking an illicit cigarette in the toilets, creating a margin of liberty beyond the gaze of the teachers and supervisors. At this point in the story, the strategic role of Huguet in the film's development is confirmed and elaborated. The new teacher is clearly struggling to retain the proper dignity and discipline of his supervisory functions. He is constantly drawn, by curiosity or sheer desire, towards the children's games. We sense that he would rather join in the fun rather than interfere and control the boys' activities. Significantly, Huguet himself is supervised by 'Bec-de-Gaz', the creepiest of the school staff, for whom surveillance is more of a perverse hobby than a professional necessity. Whenever Huguet is tempted by the children's games, grabbing hold of their football and charging around the playground with the kids in pursuit, or entertaining them with a decent imitation of Chaplin's policeman in *Easy Street* (1917), the General Supervisor is never far from the action. He is always watching at the window, or lurking in the background, ready to call the kids and their unwilling keeper back into line, back to the reality of institutionalised boredom.

3B: Study

This pattern of relationships is developed in the brief classroom scene, which in structural terms will later be reprised, and dramatically inverted, in section 6. Here, not only does Huguet again show himself totally incapable of imposing discipline on the children's study-time, he even encourages and adds to the disorder. Just as bored as the children, he decides to demonstrate to the boys his impressive hand-standing talents, and his curiously filmic ability to make an ink-drawing, which he sketches balanced on one hand, transform itself into an animated cartoon of Napoleon. (This is just one of the surviving special effects sequences that Vigo would have liked to include in the film in greater number, if time and money had allowed.) Even more striking, from a narrative point of view, is the manner in which Huguet covers up the children's future rebellion, whose existence he has somehow detected. Just as, earlier in the playground, he blocked the General Supervisor's view at a key moment, so here in the classroom he pretends to confiscate and rip up the kids' plans, rather than see the plot fall into hands of the authorities. The narrative signal is clear. The sympathetic Huguet has gone over to the other side, even though we do not yet know where that switch of allegiance will ultimately lead. Finally, in respect of the third section as a whole, it is worth noting that this is a section of Vigo's scenario where several passages were reduced or cut entirely (Lherminier 1985: 148–55). Notably, there was going to be an elaborate slapstick and effects sequence involving Caussat, a football and several broken windows. Vigo also wrote a fascinating montage scene in the playground, where the rhythm of social discipline subjugating the children's every movement was to be conveyed by a staccato passage of freeze-frames, whistles and handclaps, reminiscent of passages in Dziga Vertov's *The Man with a Movie Camera* (1929).

4. Promenade in town

In this fourth section, Vigo takes the story out of the confines of the college, and into the streets of Saint-Cloud. In fact, this section of *Zéro de conduite* is structured in parallel sequences, the promenade in Saint-Cloud (4A) alternating with the scenes in the school Principal's office (4B). While the boys are meant to be enjoying a healthy march through the bourgeois suburb, the little Principal and 'Bec-de-Gaz' discuss the scandalous question of Bruel and Tabard's intimate relationship. They are troubled by the rumours of homosexuality which, apart from its intrinsic moral evil, may unfortunately bring shame on the college, at the important annual celebration of the school fête. One could argue that questions of sex and sexuality, whether desired, imagined, pursued or repressed, dominate the central fourth and fifth sections of *Zéro de conduite*'s narrative and thematic structure. Sections 1 to 3, we could say, prepare the dramatic ground of the story, by introducing the context, the atmosphere, the characters, and the key motifs. At the end of the film, sections 6 to 8 will explode the essential problematic of the drama, by progressively unleashing the rebellion that leads to the film's revolutionary climax. These key middle sections, 4 and 5, both of which remove the action in part to the outside world, may therefore be seen as that crucial period of any good story, where a certain confusion and complexity reign, thus allowing the big themes of the narrative to mature, and to find their full dramatic expression. The promenade itself (although originally much more complex in Vigo's scenario) is a beautifully executed sequence, worthy of a silent chase comedy. It begins in relatively correct order, as the boys are lined up for inspection by the pompous Principal. But it then descends step by step into chaos. Firstly, the inattentive Huguet forgets that he is responsible for thirty young children, and wanders off on his own. Then the boys run wild all over town for a while, only rejoining Huguet at the moment he decides to pursue an attractive young bourgeois lady (who is quickly scared off by the sight of a teenage horde arriving hot on the chase). Just as the situation is getting completely out of hand, the rain comes pouring down, dampening everyone's ardour no doubt, but also sending the whole disorderly crew back to the school for cover. Last to arrive at the college are Tabard and Bruel, sharing an overcoat for protection. This flagrant sign of their 'excessive friendship' is the last straw for the morally panicked Principal. He calls Tabard into his office, in order to have a fatherly word with the troublesome (and soon very troubled) young boy. Unable to speak openly about homosexuality, the Principal mumbles and stutters a few moral and psychological clichés, until his anxiety can be contained no more. We see him in an illuminated *contre-plongée*, his hair standing on end, and his horrified expression conveying the institutional fear of sexual diversity. This shot provides a grotesque climax to the discussion between the Principal and 'Bec de Gaz', which we have seen developing throughout this section, as Vigo cuts back and forth between the promenade in Saint-Cloud and the college. Their words provide a moralising commentary on the state of events in the school: the approaching school fête, the need to maintain appearances for the special day, the group of Caussat, Bruel and Colin as potential trouble-makers, the rumours about Tabard and Bruel. It is this fear of a sexual scandal that proves too much for the Principal's sense of the school's civic image. But when faced with the innocent Tabard, the Principal cannot express his anxieties in a comprehensible manner. This linguistic repression, which is also sexual and political, will not just backfire in the short term (the boy has no idea what the Principal is talking about), it will ultimately explode into rebellion and revolution, violently and spectacularly, come the big day of the school fête. When Tabard returns to the classroom after his interview with the Principal, we can already see that a real crisis is brewing. Ashamed, he refuses to sit next to Bruel, such is the poor kid's confusion and anger. Indeed, for a film that generally maintains a light heart and a sense of humour, despite its extreme political message, this is one of the most poignant moments in *Zéro de conduite*. It introduces a dimension of emotional pain, which will powerfully re-emerge in Tabard's defiant protest against the school's hypocritical prurience.

5. Sunday life

Given the dramatic events to come, we could argue that this fifth section serves to defer the onset of the film's explosive dénouement in sections 6 (protest), 7 (rebellion) and 8 (revolution). Equally, it helps to deepen our understanding of the characters of Caussat and Colin, the two other rebel children, who will combine with Bruel and Tabard, at the end of the film, to turn the world on its head. What we see in

this section is Caussat and Colin's contrasting experiences of Sunday
life (that is, when they are not 'confined to premises' on the day of
rest). Colin (5B) is obliged to stay at home with his mother, known as
'Mère Haricot' ('Mother Beans'), who works in the school kitchen as
the eternal purveyor of haricot beans, while Caussat (5A) gets to spend
some time with his 'chick', in other words his bow-ribboned and
bespectacled correspondent of the opposite sex. In this double
dominical portrait, we first see Caussat enjoying the young girl's
playful charms. These seem to involve her blindfolding him, then
standing on a chair, so that he cannot look up her skirt, while she
hangs a goldfish bowl from a lamp by the window. In Vigo's scenario,
this was originally to be followed by another scene, in which Caussat
was going to boast about his correspondent's erotic charms, and his
imaginary sexual conquests. By contrast, Colin's Sunday is spent
either sulking or irritating his mother in the school kitchen. Here, his
only distraction is to pinch some chocolate and take it to Bruel and
Tabard, who are waiting for him outside. In narrative terms, this
scene is important because it shows Colin's acceptance of Tabard as
one of the key conspirators of the forthcoming rebellion. When Colin
returns to the kitchen, Vigo produces another of those felicitous
slapstick sequences, which are an intrinsic dimension of the film's
ideology, as well as offering moments of light relief. For Vigo, comedy
is political, a sign of freedom and a promise of happier times. Here, in
the school kitchen, Colin accidentally drops his rubber ball into his
mother's cooking pot, and, fearing her angry reaction, disappears out
the door. Like a skilled sportswoman, 'Mother Beans' picks the ball
from the pot, and in one flowing movement hurls it angrily towards
the doorway. With perfect timing, Colin reappears, offers the
audience a cheeky smile, catches the ball on the bounce, and vanishes
up the stairs again, exit stage right. Do we really need to interpret the
explicit political message of this sequence? Probably its secret would
have been revealed in the laughter of the children (and the adults)
who were prevented from seeing *Zéro de conduite* in 1933. If Vigo had
possessed the means to make the film as his heart desired, he would
no doubt have added more of these comical scenes, and extended
them. It is this intrinsically subversive quality of his comedy, and the
kind of liberating laughter that it incites, which the Board of Film
Control condemned as 'defamation'. Their repression of laughter
thus reproduces the dismal moralising of the college Principal in the

film. Like Colin's bouncing ball, however, there is an irrepressible joy in Vigo's work that will always return to inspire us.

6. Protest begins

The final third of *Zéro de conduite*, i.e. sections 6 (protest), 7 (rebellion) and 8 (revolution), together form a unified crescendo. This rising and expanding movement of revolt starts with Tabard's confused and embarrassed pout in the Principal's office, and finishes with one of the most memorable images of the revolutionary sublime in cinema history: the four rebels free and joyful, shot in *contre-plongée* on the rooftops of the college, heralding the coming of a happier world.

6A: Refectory
At first, the children's protests take shape modestly enough in the school refectory, with a noisy and spontaneous demonstration against the monotonous menu of beans, beans and more beans. This is a development that logically follows on from the exchanges between Colin and 'Mother Beans', in the preceding section. The refectory is shot in the high-angle overhead manner, which we recognise from a number of scenes in *Zéro de conduite*, especially the dormitory and classroom sequences. The effect is different, however, since now we are positioned as witnesses of unexpected events, which surprise us and evolve before our eyes. It is almost as if Kaufman were a lucky cameraman, who just happened to be in the right place at the right time, in order to record these remarkable acts of rebellion as they unfold. As the anti-beans protest begins to grow in fervour and strength, Vigo shows us young Colin in close-up (a rare occurrence in this film, whose focus is predominantly held on the collective adolescent body rather than its individual faces). Thus we see Colin's painful realisation that the target of his comrades' demonstration and rebellious chant is, after all, his own mother: 'Down with Mother Beans! Down with Mother Beans!'. It is important to signal that Bruel and Caussat, rather than the school supervisors, call the protest to a halt, when they see that Colin is embarrassed and upset. In narrative terms, their kind initiative clearly signals to the audience that henceforth it is the boys who will dictate the course of events in the dénouement of the film's dramatic climax.

6B: The classroom

The anger and frustration that have been released in the refectory are just the beginning of the real trouble to follow. The next scene in the classroom picks up the rhythm of rebellion where the beans-protest left off. Now the spontaneity of the latter has been folded into the purposeful plotting of the four conspirators, Caussat, Bruel and Colin, plus their fiery new recruit, Tabard. Only the rough-edged Caussat is still reluctant to admit him into their gang: 'C'est une fille, je te dis! Qu'est-ce qu'il sait faire?' ('He's a girl, I tell you! What can he do to help us?'). A drum-roll on the soundtrack (previously used in the film as a sign of school discipline, now a signal of revolutionary struggle) tells us that the answer to Caussat's question is on the way. Sure enough, it is the rebel Tabard whom we now see enter the classroom, where the vile and sweaty chemistry teacher is about to receive an unexpected lesson in the dangers of handling explosive adolescents. When the teacher starts fondling Tabard's hands ('Oh, mon petit, on ne prend pas de notes, aujourd'hui?' ['Oh, my little one, are we not taking notes this morning?']), his opportunistic expression of avuncular concern provokes a violent reaction from the troubled boy. Suddenly Tabard withdraws his hand from the teacher's ambiguous gesture, and when the latter tries to justify his action ('Je ne te dis que ça ...' ['I was only saying ...']), the rebel cuts him short, and utters for the first time his celebrated cry of freedom: 'Et moi je vous dis Merde!' ('And I say to you: Shit!'). We should note perhaps that when Vigo wrote this line for Tabard, he may well have had in mind a very similar phrase ('Et je vous dis Merde!') which Almereyda's anarchist newspaper, *La Guerre sociale*, had once employed as a banner headline addressed to the French government (Salles Gomes 1988 [1957]: 144). Thus the deep link between *Zéro de conduite*, Vigo's childhood, and the memory of Almereyda, is poetically forged by Tabard's magical exclamation. From this point in the film, the revolutionary touch-paper has been lit. Henceforth, the dramatic tension and narrative rhythm will rise from scene to scene. Thus, when the Principal himself comes to the classroom, magnanimously declaring that the school disciplinary committee can only 'forgive' Tabard, in exchange for a full public apology, the rebel responds by doubling his offence, and hurling his revolt all the louder: 'Monsieur, je vous dis Merde!' ('To you, sir, I say: Shit!').

7. Open rebellion

7A: The dormitory, night

On that scandalous note, significantly struck by Tabard the 'useless girl', we see the children's general discontent, and occasional acts of protest, merge and mutate into a fully-blown riot in the dormitory. The scene is one of the best known and most frequently commented of Vigo's work. As such, it is often analysed as an isolated sequence, apart from the rest of the film. We can usefully remark therefore that this second dormitory sequence in the film is in fact the reverse-image of the dormitory sequence in section 2. In the same way, section 6's refectory and classroom scenes are a narrative inversion of the playground and study sequences of section 3. We could even argue that the sublime finale of section 8 is the thematic counterpoint of the return to school in section 1. Thus the figure of inversion, the political reversibility of the current social order, is inscribed in the formal structure of Vigo's story. Here, in section 7A, the strictly regimented space of the dormitory, with its military rows of tidy beds, bursts into a riotous mess. The previously dormant and docile adolescent bodies now burst into 'effervescence' (to use Vigo's expression). They dance for joy, turn the beds upside down, thump each other and assault the supervisors with their pillows. This stirs up a storm of white feathers, which symbolically purify the site of their collective subjugation. Promoted to revolutionary leader, it is Tabard who in the middle of the riot climbs onto the roof of the college to plant the rebel flag. Again it is René who reads the kids' revolutionary statement:

> 'La guerre est déclarée! À bas les pions! À bas les punitions! Vive la révolte! La liberté ou la mort! Plantons notre drapeau sur le toit du collège! Demain, tous, debout avec nous!'[12] (Lherminier 1985 : 181)

7B: The dormitory, morning

In contrast to section 2, the coming of the new day in the dormitory marks the determined continuation of the rebellion, rather than a return to order. Indeed, if the fantastically carnivalesque parade of the previous night is probably the formal high-point of *Zéro de conduite* (this is where we hear Jaubert's famously inverted hymn of freedom),

12 '"War is declared! Down with supervisors! Down with punishments! Long live the rebellion! Liberty or death! We plant our flag on the college roof! Tomorrow, everyone, rise up with us!"'

it is the crucifixion of 'Pète-Sec' the following morning that was no doubt one of the most morally offensive sequences for chairman Edmond Sée and the Board of Film Control, back in 1933. Having sacrificed their supervisor in this suitably blasphemous manner, the four main conspirators head off to their hideout, in the school attic, ready for the next phase of rebellious action. This will be a paramilitary attack, directed against the decorous ceremonies of the college's annual day of celebration.

8. Revolution's here!

8A: The playground

'Caussat, Colin, Bruel, Tabard se sont enfermés dans le grenier. C'est étonnant, on n'a jamais vu ça!', declares a worried teacher to the Principal (Lherminier 1985: 187).[13] But everything is ready for the school fête. The local government Prefect has arrived, and it is too late now to change the arrangements, or even to deal with the coming crisis. Thus handshakes and bows are duly exchanged, hats removed, flowers and prizes distributed. Even the fairground dolls, whom Vigo has chosen to represent the various community dignitaries, seem very happy with the ceremonial procedures. The town firemen attending the show perform some appropriately safe yet impressive acrobatic manoeuvres, while 'Bec-de-Gaz' keeps a nervous watch for potential trouble in the attic. Suddenly the attack comes from the roof of the college instead, and the four rebels pelt the party of distinguished guests, with an artillery of offensive materials: old school books, empty tin cans, smelly boots, muddy footballs and broken tennis-rackets. While the other children (and Huguet) respond joyfully to the outbreak of hostilities, the dignitaries run for cover. The firemen, followed by the school staff, rush to the attic in order to deal with the rebels and extinguish their revolutionary flame. But the boys can no longer be caught. At this point in the film, the revolt has gone too far for the gang of four to be merely disciplined and punished, 'confined on Sunday for bad behaviour'. In the final images of *Zéro de conduite*, Vigo's story has thematically switched to another plane altogether. It abandons the relatively realistic narrative of the children's rebellion in

13 'Caussat, Colin, Bruel, Tabard have locked themselves in the attic. It's astonishing, we've never seen anything like it!'

a boarding school, and attains a higher realm of extreme utopian ideals. Having climbed from the attic onto the roof, the boys appear untouchable and heroic. They have become iconic symbols of the revolutionary struggle, rather than just a bunch of 'young devils at college'. Shot in *contre-plongée* against the sky, they are free from human injustice. They have transcended the perverse and repressive regime of the school, and now they are about to ascend into an anarchistic paradise. Thus they wave their arms victoriously, as they march up the slanting roof towards the horizon. But their triumphal gestures are no longer even directed to their comrades below. Henceforth they form the symbolic vanguard of a future grand rebellion, the legendary 'grand soir' of the French revolutionary tradition. At this climactic moment of the film, the opening theme song returns. The voices are still childish, and the sentiments puerile, but the song has now acquired the deeper resonance of a joyous hymn to freedom:

> 'Leur beau drapeau dans la bataille / A volé aux quatre vents / Ils ont reçu de la mitraille / Des petits pois des éléphants / Des petits pois des éléphants / Ce sont les gars de notre école / Qui ont gagné la partie / Et les voilà repartis / Hardi les gars chacun son rôle!'[14] (Lherminier 1985: 190)

As a final note on this stunning conclusion to the film, it is worth looking at the first ending that Vigo wrote for *Zéro de conduite* in his scenario. This originally involved the boys' disappearance from the attic raising momentarily the tragic question of a collective suicide ('Se sont-ils suicidés?' ['Have they committed suicide?']). But the worried audience would soon have realised that in fact the kids had simply escaped from the college premises, in the midst of all the confusion. And the last shot would have shown the four boys walking off arm in arm into the distance, like the vagabond characters of René Clair's *À nous la liberté* (1932) and Charlie Chaplin's *Modern Times* (1936). Why did Vigo decide to change the ending? The suggestion of suicide would have been an unhappy, and dramatically inappropriate, reminder of Almereyda. Likewise, the switch to the revolutionary sublime provides a more inspiring send-off for the truly anarchistic

---

14 '"Their fine flag in the battle / Has been ripped to shreds / They got a good pelting / With dried peas and elephants / With dried peas and elephants / It's our schoolmates / Who won the day / And off they go again / Courage, boys, each to his role!"'

message of *Zéro de conduite*. Despite the many qualities that he shares with Clair and Chaplin, Vigo's ideology goes deeper than their gently humanistic optimism. For Clair and Chaplin, freedom is a couple of pals on the open road, rather than a political ideal that must be fought for, if necessary through a bloody and collective struggle. In the words of the heroic René Tabard, the choice of direction is stark, and the road ahead more dangerous: 'La liberté ou la mort! En avant! En avant!' ('Liberty or death! Forward! Forward!').

The responsibility of the artist

For Vigo, at the age of 28, after the banning of *Zéro de conduite*, there was only one way forward, and that was to keep going forward. Death may well already have had an invisible eye on his fragile body, as we now know. But Jean would take full advantage of the remaining eighteen months of liberty before him, notably the opportunity to make a mainstream feature film, *L'Atalante*, which somehow Louis-Nounez persuaded Gaumont to entrust to the controversial young director of *Zéro de conduite*. Given Louis-Nounez's renewal of faith in Vigo, and the news during the summer of the deal with Gaumont, it is perhaps unsurprising that he should seem in remarkably upbeat mood about his life as a filmmaker, when he was invited to Brussels to present his banned film at the Club de l'Écran, 17 October 1933:

> Je m'étonne un peu de me trouver sur cette estrade tout seul. J'aurais préféré, étant donné l'esprit dans lequel a été réalisé *Zéro de conduite*, vous offrir à la manière des girls anonymes, comme préface fugitive à la projection du film, un salut chorégraphique en compagnie de tous mes collaborateurs. Une ronde aurait, je crois, avantageusement remplacé tous mots bafouillés. Je songeais aussi à vous amener quelques membres de la Censure française, qui finissent le plus souvent par devenir, à coups de ciseaux, les véritables auteurs d'un film. Mais j'ai craint qu'ils ne s'abîment dans le voyage.[15] (Lherminier 1985: 123)

15 'I'm a little surprised to find myself on this stage all alone. Given the spirit in which *Zéro de conduite* was made, I would have preferred, in the manner of anonymous dancing girls, to have performed a choreographic salutation accompanied by all my collaborators, as a fugitive preface to the film's projection. A rondo, I believe, would have favourably replaced any mumbled

Rather than play the role of sacrificial victim and martyred artist, Vigo modestly emphasises the collective nature of film work and responds with humour to the grievous assault of the censors. Their violence, he maintains, is a misunderstood form of love, a 'charming' expression of their desire for amorous 'exclusivity'. The censors must in fact be the film's greatest admirers, since they could not stand the idea of anyone else's gaze spoiling it: 'il ne faut qu'aucun autre regard que nos beaux yeux ne le souille' ('it must not be that any gaze other than our beautiful eyes should sully this film'). And yet, despite the jokes about collective authorship and jealous censors, Vigo also reveals a sharp sense of personal responsibility for the fate of *Zéro de conduite*. He goes on to develop this theme in political, moral and aesthetic terms. Firstly, on a political level, he makes the anecdotal claim that the censors had already been instructed by the Minister of the Interior to ban the film, even before they had had the chance to see it. In Vigo's eyes, this can only be an act of political persecution, aimed directly at the 'son of Almereyda'. It is therefore addressed indirectly at his father, Miguel. In this sense, he is more than willing to take the ban personally, since it is purely a political act of vengeance rather than a moral criticism or aesthetic critique of the work.

Then, as if to underline more explicitly the ethical link between the personal and the political aspects of his responsibility as an artist, Vigo insists upon the genuinely autobiographical status of *Zéro de conduite*. This is a striking exaggeration on his part, since most of the biographical evidence seems to suggest that the film's authenticity is poetic rather than literal, an imaginative enhancement and intensification of Vigo's childhood memories. But the tone that the filmmaker adopts in his presentation is unambiguously direct: 'je ne me suis permis dans ce film aucune littérature, nulle invention, n'ayant eu qu'à me pencher à peine pour retrouver des souvenirs'.[16] The film, Vigo proceeds to claim, far from being a vague evocation of past experience, is in fact an attempted reconstitution of real events from his childhood. In the following passage, therefore, it is almost as if he were prepared to countersign the film's authenticity, scene by scene,

---

words. I also thought of bringing along some members of the French board of censorship, who very often, by dint of scissor-work, end up becoming the true authors of the film. But I was afraid they might get damaged in transit.'

16 'In this film I did not allow myself any literature, no invention whatsoever, I barely needed even to bend down in order to retrieve my memories.'

not only as a faithful transcription of his own intense feelings of grief, loss, loneliness, and abandonment, but also as a sincere homage to the comradeship and rebelliousness that he shared with his fellow inmates:

L'enfance. Des gosses que l'on abandonne un soir de rentrée d'octobre dans une cour d'honneur quelque part en Province sous quelque drapeau que ce soit, mais toujours loin de la Maison, où l'on espère l'affection d'une mère, la camaraderie d'un père, s'il n'est déjà mort. Et alors, je me sens pris d'angoisse. Vous allez voir *Zéro de conduite*, je vais le revoir avec vous [...] Sans doute, je retrouve dans le comparti-ment qui sème les vacances les deux amis de la rentrée d'octobre. Bien sûr il se dresse là, avec ses 30 lits identiques, le dortoir de mes huit années d'Internat, et je vois aussi Huguet que nous aimions tant et son collègue le pion Pète-Sec, et ce surveillant général muet aux semelles crêpe de fantôme. À la lumière du bec de gaz demeuré en veilleuse, le petit somnambule hantera-t-il encore mon rêve cette nuit? Et peut-être le reverrai-je au pied de mon lit comme il s'y dressait la veille de ce jour où la grippe espagnole l'emportait en 1919. Oui, je sais, les copains Caussat, Bruel, Colin, le fils de la cuisinière, et Tabard, que nous appelions la fille, et que l'administration espionnait, torturait, alors qu'il eût besoin d'un grand frère, puisque Maman ne l'aimait pas [...] Tout est représenté, le réfectoire aux haricots, la classe et l'étude où l'un de nous dit un jour tout haut et deux fois ce que nous pensions tous. J'assisterai donc encore à la représentation du complot qui nous donna tant de mal, la nuit au grenier, au chahut qu'il fut, à la crucifixion de Pète-Sec telle qu'elle fut, à la fête des officiels que nous avons troublée en ce jour bien nommé de la Sainte Barbe. Partirai-je encore du grenier, notre unique domaine, par les toits vers un ciel meilleur?[17] (Lherminier 1985: 124)

17 'Childhood. An October night at the start of term, kids abandoned in the courtyard of a school somewhere in the provinces, beneath some flag or other, but always far from home and the desired affection of a mother, the camaraderie of a father, unless he's already dead. Now I feel myself consumed with anxiety. You're going to see *Zéro de conduite*, I'm going to see it again with you [...] No doubt I shall rediscover in the train compartment those two friends returning from vacation for the start of term. Of course there will appear, with its thirty identical beds, the dormitory of my eight years at boarding school. And I shall also see Huguet, whom we loved so much, and his colleague the warden Pète-Sec, and the silent chief supervisor with his ghostly crepe soles. In the light of the gas-lamp left on low, will the little sleepwalker haunt my dreams again tonight? And perhaps I shall see him again at the foot of my bed, as he appeared to me the night before he was swept away by the Spanish flu in 1919? [...] Yes, I

Finally, on the question of artistic responsibility, having addressed the
political aspects of the ban, and personally underwritten, as it were,
the film's moral authenticity, Vigo is ready to take the blame for what
he perceives as the film's evident aesthetic failings:

> Ma responsabilité se trouve entièrement engagée. Certes, je souffre de
> ne pas vous offrir un film meilleur sur un projet qui est tout mon
> cœur. Mais je n'invoquerai nulle excuse. Aucun metteur en scène n'a
> le droit, s'il juge son film imparfait, de se présenter au public pour
> rejeter l'évidence de son échec partiel ou total, l'affirmation de son
> impuissance sur qui ou quoi que ce soit.[18] (Lherminier 1985: 125)

He then proposes, and rejects, three stock excuses that filmmakers
such as himself might offer for their artistic failure. These are, in
turn, lack of creative freedom, censorship and unsympathetic
producers: 'La liberté! Vous n'avez pas été libre de réaliser votre projet
comme vous la sentiez' ('Freedom! You were not free to realise your
project as you wanted it'). To which he replies rather brutally:
'Pourquoi alors choisir ce métier?' ('Why then choose this
profession?'). If you want artistic freedom, then you should not get
involved in a commercial art form in the first place. Secondly, he
claims, it is sheer naivety to complain about the state's interference in
the creative process: 'Pas de fausse excuse en criant: La censure a
mutilé mon film; et regardez: quelle honte!' ('No false excuses, crying
out: The censors have mutilated my film, and look: what a shame!').
You only need to read the newspapers, Vigo points out, to know that
'le service de la censure cinématographique est transféré du Ministère

---

recognise all my friends, Caussat, Bruel, Colin, the cook's son, and Tabard,
known as the girl, who was spied on and persecuted by the administration,
when all he needed was a big brother, since his mother didn't love him [...]
Everything is represented, the refectory smelling of beans, the classroom where
one day one of us said out loud what all of us were thinking. And I shall witness
again the representation of the conspiracy that caused us so much trouble, the
night spent in the loft, the rebellion that took place, the crucifixion of Pète-Sec,
the public celebration that we disturbed on the aptly named day of Sainte-Barbe
[B for 'boredom']. Shall I again set off from that loft, our sole domain, across the
roof and towards a happier sky?'

18 'My responsibility is entirely engaged. Certainly, it hurts me not to be able to
offer you a better film on a project that is close to my heart. But I shall invoke no
excuses. No film director has the right, if he judges his film imperfect, to
present himself to the public in order to reject the evidence of his partial or total
failure, the proof of his lack of power over anybody or anything.'

de l'Éducation Nationale au Ministère de l'Intérieur' ('the film censorship division has been transferred from the Ministry of Education to the Ministry of the Interior'). As he has already explained, this is a political rather than a moral issue, and Vigo as a target of censorship prefers the relative transparency of 'la franchise d'une Censure d'État cynique, mais loyale' ('the frankness of a state censorship that is cynical but honest'). Thirdly, regarding supposedly ignorant or greedy producers, Vigo is neither in the mood nor the position to complain, given the utter generosity and whole-hearted support of Jacques Louis-Nounez and, before him, Hirsch Lozinski: 'Et ne criez pas si fort: "Ce directeur de production est idiot: répondu: Surtout pas de documentaire!"' ('And don't shout so loud: "That director of production is a fool; he told me: Above all no docu-mentaries!"'). In cinema, then, the artist has no excuses for failure, no pretexts for self-pity. If *Zéro de conduite* is politically unacceptable, excessively personal or aesthetically inept, Vigo will not only take full responsibility for those problems, he will also commit himself to the same risks and dangers, all over again, at the first available opportunity.

Thus he finds himself standing alone on a Belgian stage in October 1933. Encouraged and emboldened by Louis-Nounez's unflinching response to the financial disaster of *Zéro de conduite*, Vigo has probably already got the forthcoming adventure of *L'Atalante* in mind, and he finishes his speech in Brussels on the following defiant and optimistic note:

Et puis après!!! Passez-vous à la caisse? Recommencez-vous un autre film? Oui! Ratez-vous celui-là comme le précédent? Oui! Alors taisez-vous et estimez-vous seul responsable. C'est ce que je voudrais que vous reteniez aujourd'hui de ce trop large bavardage. Le coupable est là, ses complices sont solidaires. Personne et rien n'est venu contrarier notre travail. Mais le film traîne le long de ses 1200 mètres de lourds défauts que vous jugerez. J'en souffre un peu. Je m'en excuse beaucoup comme d'une mauvaise plaisanterie faite à des amis.[19] (Lherminier 1985: 126)

19 'And then what!!! Will you go and collect your wages? Will you start another film? Yes? And will you mess it up like the last one? Yes. So keep quiet and consider yourself alone as responsible. That's what I'd like you to retain today from this overly long chat. The guilty man is here, his accomplices stand by him. Nobody and nothing got in the way of our work. But throughout its 1,200 metres the film drags along some heavy mistakes, which you can judge for yourselves. I find that slightly painful. I sincerely apologise, as one would for a bad joke played on one's friends.'

On the contrary, we might reply, if *Zéro de conduite* is a joke, it is an extremely good one, and as such it is arguably Vigo's true signature-film. Utopian and violent, comical and sublime, the highly personal vision and political verve of *Zéro de conduite* perhaps make it a more faithful reflection of Vigo's artistic personality than *L'Atalante*, the film on which he was about to embark and which history has since acknowledged as his undisputed masterpiece.

References

Chardère, B. (ed.) (1961), *Jean Vigo*, Lyons, Premier Plan.

Lherminier, P. (1984), *Jean Vigo*, Paris, Pierre Lherminier/Filméditions.

Lherminier, P. (1985), *Jean Vigo: œuvre de cinéma*, Paris, Cinémathèque française/Pierre Lherminier.

Porcile, F. (1971), *Maurice Jaubert, musicien populaire ou maudit?*, Paris, Éditeurs Français Réunis.

Salles Gomes, P.E. (1988 [1957]), *Jean Vigo*, Paris, Seuil/Ramsay.

Vigo, L. (2002), *Jean Vigo: une vie engagée dans le cinéma*, Paris, Cahiers du cinéma.

1 Jean Vigo directing actors on the set of *Zéro de conduite*

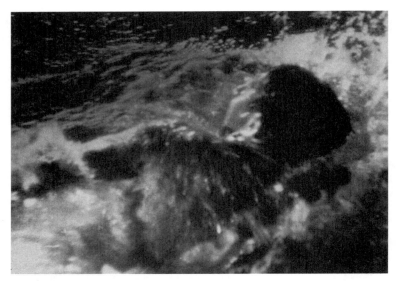

2 Champion swimmer Jean Taris in action

3 Boris Kaufman and Jean Vigo making *À propos de Nice*

4 Preparation of a doll for the Nice carnival

5 Bourgeois lady on the Promenade des Anglais in Nice

6 Young worker at the end of *À propos de Nice*

7 Caussat and Bruel returning to school at the start of *Zéro de conduite*

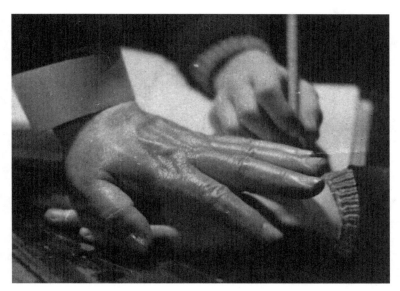

8 The teacher touches Tabard's hand, provoking the boy's rebellion

9 The class is lined up for inspection in the playground

10 The boys' revolt in the dormitory at the climax of *Zéro de conduite*

11 The cast and crew during the filming of *L'Atalante*

12 Juliette and Jean enjoying married life on the barge

13 Juliette goes to Paris in search of adventure

14 Michel Simon in the role of Père Jules

4

An unknown masterpiece

Vigo a emporté son secret, *L'Atalante* porte en lui-même la solution de l'énigme.[1] (*Les Voyages de L'Atalante*, Bernard Eisenschitz, France, 2001)

Why does Louis-Nounez decide to stick by Jean Vigo in the summer of 1933? This simple but essential question remains one of the many unanswered mysteries that inform the extraordinary story of *L'Atalante* and its special place in the French film canon. Given the financial losses incurred with *Zéro de conduite* and the bad reputation of the film's creator, one can imagine that many producers in similar circumstances would rather have looked elsewhere for their next project, or indeed that a novice like Louis-Nounez, with no long-term investment in the film industry, might simply have walked away and pursued another line of business altogether. Perhaps it is precisely because he is an amateur, seemingly motivated by an enthusiasm for the unconventional, and by a personal affection for Vigo, that on the contrary he chooses again to risk his capital and reputation on another film adventure.

What do you want me to do with that?

Before the banning of *Zéro de conduite*, the two men had already discussed a number of options for their next film. These included the dramatisation of the true story of Albert Dieudonné's escape from the

---

1 'Vigo took his secret with him, *L'Atalante* in itself holds the solution to the enigma.'

Guyanese penal colony, *L'Évadé du bagne* (see Chapter 3); a possible collaboration with Blaise Cendrars, *Les Contrebandiers*; and an adaptation of Georges de la Fourchardière's *Clown par amour* ('Clown for Love'), which was going to feature the well-known clown Béby in the principal role (Lherminier 1985: 395–410; Salles Gomes 1988 [1957]: 164). In the summer of 1933, however, Louis-Nounez proposes to Jean, somewhat surprisingly, a rather conventional and uninspiring love-story set on a barge. The synopsis for *L'Atalante* had been registered at the Association des Auteurs de Films in November 1932 by Roger de Guichen, an occasional author known by the pen name Jean Guinée. This one-page outline, which Vigo probably first saw in July 1933, recounts a very simple moral tale about a country-girl who marries a barge-captain, quickly tires of their monotonous life on the canals, and runs away to the big city, only to return to the dull security of marriage after a series of urban misadventures. It is hardly a plot to set Vigo's anarchist heart a-thumping. So why does Louis-Nounez suggest it to him? It seems that the entrepreneur's plan was to get Jean to complete a politically acceptable and financially viable project, which would help re-establish the young director's artistic credentials, as well as the debutant producer's commercial reputation. This is certainly what Louis-Nounez claimed, and Albert Riéra confirmed, in Jacques Rozier's 1964 documentary for French television:

> Un jour Louis-Nounez m'a téléphoné, m'a fait venir, et m'a dit: 'Voilà, j'ai perdu de l'argent avec Vigo, mais ça ne fait rien. Vigo a beaucoup de talent, et je vois ce qu'il faut pour lui. Il faut lui donner un scénario vraiment très anodin; alors il va se dépenser avec tout son génie mais la censure ne pourra pas intervenir. Et c'est ce que je vais faire. J'ai un scénario pour lui. Ça s'appelle *L'Atalante*, je vais le lui donner.' Quand Vigo a lu ce scénario, il m'a dit: 'Mais qu'est-ce que tu veux que je foute avec ça? C'est un scénario pour patronage, enfin il n'y a rien.' Je lui ai répondu: 'Je suis d'accord avec toi, c'est une histoire très banale, mais malgré tout il y a la façon de la raconter.' Il me dit: 'Oui, évidemment.' Et alors, là, son œil s'est allumé. Il a commencé à s'intéresser à la question.[2] (Lherminier 1985: 195)

2 'One day Louis-Nounez called me, asked to see me, and said: "Look, I've lost money with Vigo, but it doesn't matter. He has a lot of talent, and I know what he needs. He needs a really harmless scenario, that way he can express his genius but the censors won't be able to intervene. And that's what I'm going to do. I've got a scenario for him. It's called *L'Atalante*, I'm going to give it to him."

It is unclear here whether Riéra, thirty years after the events in question, is referring to the one-page synopsis written by Jean Guinée in November 1932, or to the more elaborate scenario that Vigo and his co-screenwriter received from Guinée in August 1933, with a view to developing it into a fully operative shooting script, ready for the start of filming that autumn. We shall return to discuss the relationship between these three elements (synopsis, scenario, completed film) later in this chapter, so for now let us focus on the story of L'Atalante's preparation and realisation.

In August and September, then, Vigo and Riéra were working on the script, checking out possible locations on the rivers and canals of the Paris region (with advice from no less an expert than Georges Simenon), and discussing various options for casting the principal roles. Their script was ready by October, at which point Louis-Nounez and Gaumont asked the poet and screenwriter Blaise Cendrars to run a professional eye over it, presumably in the hope of forestalling the kind of incomprehension and outrage that had marked the reception of Zéro de conduite. The author of La Prose du Transsibérien (1913) and assistant director on Abel Gance's La Roue (1923) passed the work of Riéra and Vigo as fit for public consumption, and by mid-November everything was ready for the cameras to roll. On a contractual level, it is worth noting that Louis-Nounez's deal with Gaumont was the same as the one he had struck for Zéro de conduite. This meant that Gaumont would provide the commercial hardware – studios, film-stock and distribution – while the independent producer would cover all running costs, and provide the creative software: the story, the crew, the cast, the costumes and as much loose change (about one millions francs) as it would take to keep the whole circus going for the duration of the shoot (planned for November 1933 to January 1934). Speaking as the chief artistic personality around whom all this business activity was organised, Vigo was clearly very happy with such an arrangement, as he expressed it to a Belgian journalist in October 1933:

L'avenir est aux indépendants. Alors que les grosses compagnies, dont l'équilibre financier se trouve gravement menacé par la crise actuelle,

---

When Vigo read the scenario, he said to me: "What do you want me to do with that? It's trite and moralising, there's nothing in it." I replied: "I agree with you, it's a very banal story, but it depends how you tell it." He said: "Yes, of course." And that's when his eyes lit up. He began to be interested in the idea.'

n'osent plus se risquer dans aucune entreprise en dehors du genre strictement commercial, la production en participation, elle, a au contraire – et de ce fait – la voie libre. Un commanditaire apporte l'argent liquide. Un studio fournit son matériel. Une grande maison se charge de la diffusion sur les écrans de la bande ainsi réalisée. Je vois donc approcher sans la moindre appréhension le moment de commencer *L'Atalante*, que je vais tourner d'après un scénario de Jean Guinée, scénario qui n'est qu'une trame lâche me permettant de mettre en valeur des images du bord de l'eau, dans le monde des mariniers, et l'interprétation.[3] (Lherminier 1984: 102)

In terms of the cast, Vigo retained from *Zéro de conduite* the excellent Jean Dasté, who had become a personal friend and a member of the 'bande à Vigo'. He took the role of Jean, the barge captain. Opposite him, the role of Juliette was given to Dita Parlo, an established German actress, whom Vigo had admired in Joe May's *The Home-coming* (1928), and whose other appearances in French cinema include Julien Duvivier's *Au Bonheur des Dames* (1930), Dimitri Kirsanoff's *Le Rapt* (1934) and Jean Renoir's *La Grande illusion* (1937). The prize of the casting, however, was undoubtedly Michel Simon in the role of 'le Père Jules', the barge's first mate. This is not just because Simon was already a well-known stage and screen actor (Marcel L'Herbier's *Feu Matthias Pascal*, 1926, Jean Renoir's *La Chienne*, 1931, Henri Diamant-Berger's *Miquette et sa mère*, 1933), whose presence was potentially a positive draw for the crowds. More significant was the fact that this encounter between Vigo, the rebel director, and Simon, the eccentric star, would produce for *L'Atalante* a unique collaboration, and for French cinema some of its strangest and most memorable screen moments. Their meeting was facilitated by Riéra, who knew Simon from the theatre, and it was clear from all the eye-witness accounts gathered by Rozier in 1964 that a very

3 'The future belongs to the independents. Whereas the big companies, whose financial stability is severely threatened by the current economic crisis, won't take a risk with a project that isn't strictly commercial, the independents who propose a 'participatory production' have on the contrary a free hand. An independent producer puts up the cash. A studio provides the hardware. A big company takes care of the distribution of the film you've made in this way. So I'm looking forward to starting *L'Atalante*, without any apprehension. It's based on a scenario by Jean Guinée, although I'm using it merely as a loose frame allowing me to work with images of the waterways, the environment of the canal-workers, and the actors.'

special empathy soon came to exist between the young filmmaker and his leading player. As for the role of the Kid, the ship's second mate, Vigo chose to keep Louis Lefebvre, who had played the part of Caussat in *Zéro de conduite*. Finally, the small but essential part of the singing itinerant salesman (or 'Camelot') was given to Gilles Margaritis, whose stage and circus experience suited him perfectly for this semi-vaudeville cameo role.

The crew of *L'Atalante* was largely an extended version of the team that worked on Vigo's previous films. Boris Kaufman and Louis Berger were joined by Jean-Pierre Alphen as third cameraman. Albert Riéra and Pierre Merle continued as assistant directors. Charles Goldblatt wrote the songs and Maurice Jaubert composed the music. The departure of Henri Storck was compensated by the arrival of Almereyda's friend Francis Jourdain as set designer. He was assisted by the young Max Douy, who would later become one of France's best-known designers in the 1940s and 1950s (Robert Bresson's *Les Dames du Bois de Boulogne*, 1945, Claude Autant-Lara's *Le Rouge et le noir*, 1954, Jean Renoir's *French Cancan*, 1955). After the technical problems with sound recording and editing encountered during *Zéro de conduite*, this was clearly an area that required careful attention, especially since *L'Atalante* is a ninety-minute feature film, with considerable amounts of dialogue. Thus, in addition to the sound engineers Marcel Royné and Lucien Baujard, two script assistants were hired, Jacqueline Morland and Fred Matter, as well as an editor with perceived expertise in sound, Louis Chavance. The latter had already worked on Jacques and Pierre Prévert's *L'Affaire est dans le sac* (1932), for example, and he was also personally drawn to Vigo because of their shared left-wing libertarian beliefs, as his involvement in the Prévert brothers' October group demonstrates.

Crew, cast, cash, studios, locations and a script: what else could a gang of independent young people require in order to make a beautiful film? Luck, perhaps, and good weather. In November 1933, when filming started in the village of Maurecourt at the junction of the Seine and Oise rivers, to the north-west of Paris, nobody could have guessed the dramatic events that were to unfold over the next six months, nor the terrible fate awaiting *L'Atalante*, the film and its creator, Jean Vigo.

Fever and improvisation

The shoot of *L'Atalante* lasted a mere eleven weeks, from mid-November 1933 to the end of January 1934. As with *Zéro de conduite*, the clock was running from day one, and the pressure was regularly maintained by Gaumont's 'redoutable trio of functionaries', Anglade, Beauvais, Bedoin (Salles Gomes 1988 [1957]: 170). The decision to film *L'Atalante* during the winter months, like *Zéro de conduite* the previous year, meant that the weather became a crucial factor in the timing and success of operations. This was not just in terms of light and continuity, but also in terms of the sheer practicality and safety of filming outside on barges, canals and riverbanks. Unfortunately, the winter of 1933–34 was particularly harsh, with a good deal of rain, snow and fog. The poor weather added of course to the problems of keeping to the shooting schedule. Frequently, the whole cast and crew had to abandon a planned exterior set-up, and rush back to the Buttes-Chaumont in order to get some filming done in the studios. To some extent, these problems had been encountered during the making of *Zéro de conduite*, but we need to be aware that *L'Atalante* was a much more complicated shoot, particularly in terms of direct sound-recording, both outside and in the studios. Moreover, the sheer number of scenes and locations involved is quite mind-boggling in comparison to the earlier project.

If we look at a map of northern France, and of the 'Île de France' region in particular, we can appreciate more clearly the extent and variety of the terrain covered by Vigo's cast and crew during these eleven feverish weeks. The furthest point north is the seaport of Le Havre on the Normandy coast, where we see a semi-crazed Jean Dasté running wild on the beach, at the height of his suffering provoked by the absence of Juliette. Nearer the capital, to the north-west of Paris, there were a number of scenes shot on the banks of the Seine and Oise rivers, around the villages of Conflans Sainte-Honorine and Maurecourt. The most famous of these are the opening sequences outside the church, after Jean and Juliette's wedding, and the comical welcoming ceremony organised by Père Jules and the Kid for Juliette's arrival on board the barge. Just to the north of the capital, several scenes were filmed along the Canal Saint-Denis and Canal de l'Ourcq. These waterways lead down into Paris, via the Bassin de la Villette in the 19th arrondissement, and thence to the Canal Saint-

Martin. Here we find some of the most celebrated locations of *L'Atalante*: for example, the moment when the barge is negotiating the locks along the Canal Saint-Martin, and Juliette, emerging from below deck, discovers the capital for the very first time. It seems very likely that, if time and money had allowed, Vigo would have shot more scenes in Paris, probably developing further Juliette's experiences in the city, as well as Père Jules's search for her through the streets, at the dramatic climax of the film. We should note, however, that *L'Atalante* is not principally a film about Paris, and the majority of the locations are in fact to be found on or near the canals around the city, in the extended suburban region that we would now think of as the Île de France. The capital itself is more frequently evoked as an exotically 'cruel and marvellous' place of excitement and danger than it is directly represented in its everyday reality. To the south-east of Paris, there are a number of dramatically important locations, notably Charentonneau (the site of the dance-hall or 'guinguette', where Juliette meets the Camelot), Maisons-Alfort (where she decides to run away) and Corbeil (where Jean decides to take the barge, after Juliette's disappearance, rather than wait for her return). Finally, according to Salles Gomes, some of the canal scenes were also shot on 'les premières sections du Canal de la Marne au Rhin' ('the first sections of the Canal de la Marne au Rhin'), in other words, to the east of Paris, leading towards Nancy (Salles Gomes 1988 [1957]: 184). One could, of course, legitimately develop this geographical study of *L'Atalante* much further, since one of the principal sources of the film's realism is Vigo's use of authentic locations at every available opportunity. What this brief itinerary should convey, at least, is the sheer craziness of the undertaking, especially given the time of year, and the severe weather conditions.

In view of the extremely difficult circumstances of the shoot, it is hardly surprising that Vigo's fragile health should quickly shows signs of deterioration. Indeed, it seems clear that it is during these three mad months of intensive shooting and frenetic activity that the filmmaker contracted the illness from which he was eventually to die, just eight months after the end of filming. Given his poor state of health, and no doubt the intuition that something was seriously wrong, it is therefore all the more remarkable that, according to the testimony of the various cast and crew members, it was above all the young director's energy and enthusiasm that kept the whole project driving forward, both on a creative level and in terms of human relations. This is not, however, merely the expression of an understandable sentimentality about a dear friend who died too young. What Kaufman and Riéra, Dasté, Parlo and Simon share in their accounts of the making of *L'Atalante* is their common recollection of Jean Vigo hard at work. Sick maybe, generally good humoured, occasionally a little provocative, but above all inspirational and improvisational in the face of the impossible rigours of the task in hand. This image of Vigo, instilling his headlong enthusiasm into the work of the cast and crew, is powerfully evoked by Boris Kaufman:

> Les trois mois passés sur la péniche et dans les décors construits, à notre demande, à l'échelle exacte des cabines (pour maintenir l'impression du manque d'espace), ne seront jamais oubliés par ceux qui ont participé à ce travail de fièvre et d'improvisation constante. Les canaux glacés, les petits faits de courage accomplis sans en être conscient, Dita Parlo bravant, pieds nus, le pont glacé de la péniche, Jean Dasté se jetant dans le canal parmi les glaçons à la première suggestion de Vigo, créaient le climat moral du film. On utilisait tout: soleil, brume, neige, nuit. Au lieu de combattre les conditions généralement défavorables, on en tirait parti. S'il y avait brouillard on l'augmentait avec de la fumée artificielle, s'il pleuvait on accentuait la pluie avec des projecteurs. On travaillait jour et nuit; le crépuscule venu, on mélangeait la lumière ambiante du jour avec la lumière artificielle; on avait froid, on crevait de fatigue sans s'en rendre compte. On était intoxiqués par les paysages admirables des canaux de Paris et l'on construisait l'action sur l'arrière-fond des écluses, berges, guinguettes et terrains vagues. Au studio, les décors des cabines étaient si petits que l'on démontait un mur ou un plafond pour y pénétrer optiquement et les éclairer. J'ai souvent eu des problèmes techniques paraissant insolubles, mais qui se résolvaient, comme par enchantement, par la passion du travail, dans cette production incroyable.[4] (Chardère 1961: 34)

4 'Those of us who worked on this project full of fever and improvisation will never forget those three months spent on the barge and on the sets that we had constructed exactly to the scale of the cabins (in order to maintain the impression of a lack of space). The frozen canals, the little acts of courage, often unconscious, like Dita Parlo walking barefoot on the frozen bridge of the barge, or Jean Dasté without hesitation diving into the icy canal at Vigo's suggestion, all this created the moral climate of the film. We used everything that came to hand: sun, fog, snow, night. Instead of fighting against the generally unfavourable conditions, we turned them to our advantage. If it was misty, we increased

As for Albert Riéra, it is above all the qualities of imagination and improvisation that he emphasises in his recollection of Vigo during *L'Atalante*:

Ce qui m'a frappé le plus chez Jean Vigo, c'est sa faculté d'improvisation. La fantaisie et l'imagination étaient ses qualités dominantes [...] Cette imagination débordante lui permettait d'improviser avec une facilité surprenante au cours des prises de vue. Le poète venait au secours du metteur en scène. Ce n'était plus les mots mais les visages, les objets et les paysages qui mettaient son imagination en branle. Pour tourner la scène de *L'Atalante* se passant aux guichets de la Gare d'Austerlitz, il avait demandé à des amis d'être des figurants bénévoles. Parmi eux il y avait Jacques et Pierre Prévert. Un de ces figurants, dont je ne me rappelle plus le nom, avait un aspect souffreteux et paraissait toujours avoir faim. Il lui inspira la séquence du voleur lapidé. Une grille sépare le quai de la Gare d'Austerlitz. 'Albert, la grille', me dit-il. Cela me suffit. Je savais qu'il remuerait ciel et terre pour en tirer parti. Ce fut devant cette grille, qui rappelait celle d'une prison, que le voleur fut lapidé [...] La neige n'était pas prévue dans le scénario de *L'Atalante*, pas plus que la file de chômeurs qui piétinent les pieds dans la boue. Un jour il neigea, et Jean Vigo improvisa cette scène. Je le revois à côté de Boris Kaufman choisissant l'angle de prise de vue, sans se soucier du froid, tandis que Pierre Merle et moi, nous persuadions quelques hommes et quelques femmes du voisinage, de vouloir bien, pour quelques maravedis, se mettre à la file devant la porte fermée d'une usine. Pour rien au monde, il n'aurait manqué de tirer parti de ce décor inespéré [...] La glace immobilisa, pendant plusieurs jours, notre péniche sur le canal Saint-Martin, et nous devions tourner une scène se passant sur un canal traversant un paysage verdoyant. C'est alors que Jean Vigo improvisa, pour éviter les maisons et l'eau transformée en glace, cette série de prises de vues de bas en haut découvrant le ciel, et de haut en bas découvrant le pont de la péniche, qui donne au montage un

---

the mist with artificial smoke, if it was raining we accentuated the effect with projectors. We worked night and day. When dusk fell, we mixed the remaining daylight with artificial light. We were cold, we were dead tired without realising it. We were intoxicated by the beauty of the admirable landscapes of the Parisian canals, and we constructed the action of the film against the backdrop of the locks, the barges, the cafés and the wastelands along the riverside. In the studio, the sets for the cabins were so small that we had to take down a wall or the ceiling in order to set up the camera and lights. Often I was faced with seemingly insoluble technical problems, which as if by magic resolved themselves, during this incredible shoot.'

rythme d'autant plus surprenant que les angles en étaient insolites [...]
Je pourrais ainsi multiplier les exemples de la faculté d'improvisation
chez Jean Vigo. Il avait le don de tirer parti d'un détail parfois infime,
et de rendre poétique le plus banal des décors.[5] (Chardère 1961: 36–7)

These testimonies of Vigo's two closest collaborators, Riéra and
Kaufman, together form a particularly vivid picture of the artist at
work, inspiring those around him to enter into the spirit of improvisation and playfulness that was his creative response to the
impossibly harsh conditions of the shoot. It is a portrayal that is as
authentic in its sources as it is free of sentimentality. We could easily
provide further evidence of this kind from Pierre Merle, Jacques
Louis-Nounez, Gilles Margaritis, Charles Goldblatt and Jean Painlevé,
all of whom were interviewed by Jacques Rozier for his remarkable
television film of 1964.

5 'What struck me most about Jean Vigo was his faculty for improvisation.
Fantasy and imagination were his two principal qualities [...] This abundant
imagination enabled him to improvise with a surprising facility during the
shoot. The poet came to the aid of the director. It was no longer words that
inspired his imagination, but rather faces, objects, and landscapes. In order to
film the scene in *L'Atalante* that takes place at the ticket office of the Gare
d'Austerlitz he had asked some friends to perform as extras for free. Among
them were Jacques and Pierre Prévert. One of the extras, whose name I forget,
had a sickly aspect and looked like he was always hungry. He inspired Vigo for
the sequence with the thief who gets beaten up. There are railings down the
middle of the platform at the Gare d'Austerliz. "Albert, the railings", he said to
me. That was enough. I knew he would move heaven and earth to use these
railings to his advantage. So it was in front of the railings, which looked like the
bars of a prison-cell, that the thief was beaten up [...] There was nothing about
snow in the scenario, nor was there mention of the line of unemployed people
waiting in the mud. One day it was snowing, and Vigo improvised the scene
outside the factory. I can still see him next to Boris Kaufman choosing the
camera angle, unconcerned by the cold, while Pierre Merle and I were persuad-
ing some men and women from the area to get into line in front of the closed
factory gates, in exchange for a few coins. For all the world he wouldn't have
missed the opportunity to turn this unexpected setting to his advantage [...]
During several days, the ice blocked our barge on the Canal Saint-Martin, when
we were meant to be shooting a scene taking place on a canal surrounded by
beautiful countryside. This is where Vigo improvised, in order to avoid showing
the houses and the frozen water, the series of shots of the sky seen from below,
and of the barge seen from above, which edited together give a surprising rhythm
to the scene, all the more so with those unexpected angles [...] I could give many
such examples of Vigo's faculty of improvisation. He had a gift for getting the
best out of even a tiny detail and for making poetic the most banal of settings.'

A slightly different angle, however, is provided by the accounts of *L'Atalante*'s three principal actors, not because their testimonies contradict those of the crew, but simply because the nature of the relationship between director and performer implies a different type of artistic collaboration. Jean Dasté, for whom this was his second experience of working with his close friend, stresses the collaborative and improvisatory spirit in which *L'Atalante* was made, thus confirming the accounts of Kaufman and Riéra. But he adds that the director could also be extremely demanding, even a little cruel, and that he expected those around him to have the same absolute commitment to the cause of cinema as he had, even to the point of physical danger or mental exhaustion. For her part, Dita Parlo speaks of Vigo with a certain awe, as an exceptional human being whose mystery cannot be explained. But she adds to this rather pious image some interesting remarks about the working method for directing a young but established actress such as herself. She describes his directorial manner as uncomplicated and direct, instinctive rather than intellectual, always happy to demonstrate an action and discuss its effectiveness over a series of rehearsals, rather than to verbalise his instructions in advance, or prescribe a set method for the way a scene should be played. Like Dasté, she confirms that Vigo was willing to repeat the same scene a number of times, until he decided that it was intuitively right. The director's relationship with Michel Simon, however, seems to have been significantly different, possibly because of the actor's status and famously sensitive personality, possibly because Vigo had sensed from their early encounters that he would gain more than he would lose from the exchange, if he let Simon do things his own way:

> Je l'ai surtout vu dans ma loge, quand il venait pendant le spectacle, au théâtre du Gymnase. Je lui racontais des histoires vaudoises et c'est là que, petit à petit, le personnage de *L'Atalante* s'est dessiné. Dans ma loge, parce que je racontais des histoires. Je lui disais: 'Je connais un personnage, à Leysin, le père Isaac, qui était un personnage très extraordinaire, très extravagant, un personnage hoffmannesque.' Ça séduisait Jean Vigo et finalement le personnage s'est créé comme ça, tout seul.[6] (Lherminier 1984: 111)

6 'I saw him mainly in my dressing room, where he came to see me during the show, at the Théâtre du Gymnase. I told him some stories about the Vaud region of Switzerland, and that's how little by little the character of Père Jules for

During the filming itself, Vigo seems to have been able to handle quite effectively Simon's emotional highs and lows. The young director no doubt benefited from the spiritual complicity that the two men had quickly established, while Simon realised that with Vigo he could enjoy the same kind of collaboration that he had known with Jean Renoir (*Tire-au-flanc*, 1928, *On purge bébé*, 1931, *La Chienne*, 1931, *Boudu sauvé des eaux*, 1932), and that he would later experience with Sacha Guitry (*La Poison*, 1951, *La Vie d'un honnête homme*, 1953):

> Je lui avais dit: 'Je déteste répéter deux fois une scène, la seconde fois elle est fatalement mentie.' Eh bien, il y a peu de gens qui ont compris ça, il y a Vigo, il y a Renoir, il y a Sacha Guitry, il y a très peu de metteurs en scène qui ont compris que la deuxième fois, c'était déjà un mensonge.[7] (Lherminier 1984: 114)

From a technical point of view, this remark about using the first take is especially interesting, since it confirms that Vigo's directorial method with Simon was different from the more demanding manner that he adopted with the other performers. Whatever the method or the manner, the result of their collaboration in *L'Atalante* is astonishing, and we can only regret that they would never have the opportunity to work together again.

I killed myself with *L'Atalante*

By the end of January 1934, the filming of *L'Atalante* was complete, except for the final shot, an aerial view of the barge sailing down the canal, which the exhausted Vigo entrusted to the faithful Kaufman:

> Je me rappelle les dernières prises de vue, en avion. Vigo était déjà malade, au lit, et m'avait demandé de survoler la péniche, très bas, et de monter ensuite pour obtenir les deux rives dans le cadre. J'ai rempli la première partie mais pas la deuxième, l'avion, au lieu de monter,

---

L'Atalante took shape. In my dressing room, because I told him some stories. I said to him: "I know a character, from Leysin, Père Isaac, he's a very extraordinary character, very extravagant, like a character from the tales of Hoffmann." This appealed to Vigo, and the character created itself, on its own.'

7 'I said to him: "I hate doing a scene twice, the second time it's necessarily a lie." Well, very few people understood that, apart from Vigo, Renoir and Guitry. Very few directors understood that the second time it's already a lie.'

était tombé dans un champ de poireaux. Le soir je racontais à Vigo cet incident. Il était souffrant mais souriant, heureux de me voir sain et sauf, essayant de visualiser cette dernière image du film, qu'il n'a jamais vu, hélas![8] (Chardère 1961: 34)

In February, having seen an initial edit of the film prepared by Chavance, the director left Paris for Villard-de-Lans in the Vercors region, where he took a much needed break with family and friends. Despite the rest, however, when he returned to Paris in March, his health had taken a turn for the worse. Henceforth, in reality, Vigo was far too ill to take a fully active role in the complicated and conflictual post-production of *L'Atalante*. It was Chavance therefore who spent the next few weeks working on the first complete edit, notably incorporating Maurice Jaubert's music, and regularly consulting Vigo if he was in any doubt about the director's precise intentions. In early April, this version was shown at a technical preview for the cast and crew, as well as Louis-Nounez and, of course, the producers from Gaumont. As for Vigo himself, we do not know for sure if he actually attended this screening. Whereas Salles Gomes claims that he was present for the projection, Lherminier suggests that the filmmaker was already too ill to attend (Salles Gomes 1988 [1957]: 196; Lherminier 1984: 175). What is certain is that the critical reaction of the film's financial backers was divided. Louis-Nounez was very happy with the result of Chavance's work, and supported the film wholeheartedly. But the Gaumont people found this version too long, incoherent and commercially unattractive. They asked for cuts to be made accordingly. The Vigo gang resisted, and Louis-Nounez negotiated a compromise very much in their favour. Only a few shots were cut from the end of the film. According to Chavance's later testimony, these showed Père Jules searching for Juliette in Paris, near the Bassin de la Villette (Chavance 1955: 55). It was with Vigo's approval therefore that the editor made these minor changes, in time for the trade screening of *L'Atalante* on 25 April 1934, at the Palais-

8 'I remember the final shots, taken from a plane. Vigo was already ill, in bed, and he'd asked me to fly over the barge, very low, and then to climb in order to get both riverbanks into the frame. I managed the first of these tasks but not the second, because the plane, instead of climbing, fell into a field of leeks. That evening I recounted the incident to Vigo. He was in pain but smiling, happy to see that I was safe and sound, trying to visualise this final image of the film, which he never saw, alas!'

Rochechouart, 56 Boulevard de Rochechouart, in the 18th arrondissement.

Although this occasion was nothing like as dramatic or confrontational as the trade premiere of *Zéro de conduite* a year earlier, the reactions of the distributors and the cinema-owners present that day were extremely negative. As a result, Gaumont increased the pressure on Louis-Nounez and the ailing Vigo to accept more significant cuts and alterations, which would make the film in their eyes more commercially viable. Despite some positive reviews of *L'Atalante* appearing in the film press after the trade screening, it was Henri Beauvais of Gaumont who eventually won the argument. He persuaded Louis-Nounez to agree to a major re-edit of the film, and from that point the project was taken out of the hands of Vigo and his supporters. Did Vigo approve Louis-Nounez's decision to let the film go? Again, there exist conflicting accounts of who exactly conceded what, when and why. For many years, there was an unfortunate tendency to blame Louis-Nounez's supposed weakness or self-interest. But this facile image of the greedy producer abandoning the dying artist does not stand up to a close examination. All the eye-witness accounts, on the contrary, insist on Louis-Nounez's good faith and his sincere desire to protect Vigo's interests. If the filmmaker had lived, after all, his producer's decision to concede a strategic defeat to Gaumont would probably have allowed Vigo to fight another day. Ultimately, he may well have been able to pursue the kind of semi-independent artistic career, within the commercial system, which typifies the trajectory of so many French filmmakers of the period (Marcel Carné, René Clair, Julien Duvivier, Jacques Feyder, Jean Renoir). Concerning Vigo's response to the pressure from Gaumont, Claude Aveline and Charles Goldblatt recall him vigorously resisting the proposed alterations to *L'Atalante*, while Riéra and Louis-Nounez maintain that in the end the filmmaker gave his consent, albeit as unwillingly as the other defenders of the film (Lherminier 1984: 175). It is unlikely that we will ever know for sure exactly what happened, but we should not exclude the possibility that Vigo was simply too weak to put up much of a fight, and (who knows?) maybe too ill at this stage even to care. His reported comment to Fernand Després, 'Je me suis tué avec *L'Atalante*' ('I killed myself with *L'Atalante*'), certainly suggests that by the summer of 1934 he was resigned to his own tragic destiny, as well as to the unhappy fate of his final film (Lherminier 1984: 175). As for Louis-Nounez, it is not impossible to understand why an inexperienced and isolated producer, having lost money on *Zéro de conduite* and now facing the prospect of losing a great deal more on *L'Atalante*, should eventually give in to the pressure exerted by the hardened negotiators of the second biggest studio in France at the time. What is clear is that the people at Gaumont then took over the project entirely, and they were responsible for its final form and commercial release. Having significantly re-edited the film, and even changed its title, Gaumont thus launched *Le Chaland qui passe* (as *L'Atalante* had now been renamed) in September 1934, at the Colisée cinema, on the Champs-Élysées in Paris. In commercial terms, however, the film did not have much success with the public, and in spite of some favourable reviews it soon disappeared from the screens, after a brief run at the Colisée.

On 5 October 1934, three weeks after the unsuccessful release of *Le Chaland qui passe*, Jean Vigo died at the age of 29. He was buried at the same Bagneux cemetery where his father Miguel Alemereyda had been buried seventeen years earlier, and where his young wife Lydu would join him on 24 April 1939, herself only 30 years old. It is said that on the afternoon of Vigo's burial, 8 October 1934, a screening of *Le Chaland qui passe* took place at the Adyar cinema, as part of a Michel Simon retrospective. Thus the creator of *L'Atalante* disappeared, his passing largely ignored and soon forgotten by the majority of the film world. As for his unknown masterpiece, *L'Atalante* now embarked on an odyssey of loss and restoration, whose peregrinations were to last for the next fifty-five years.

The voyages of *L'Atalante*

In Chapter 5, we shall examine in detail the posthumous career of Jean Vigo, and his long-term reputation in French cinema culture. For now, in order to launch our analytical discussion of *L'Atalante*, we must first briefly explain the complex history of the film's successive versions and restorations, from *Le Chaland qui passe* in 1934 to the Gaumont restoration of 2001. For one of the most striking paradoxes of *L'Atalante*, so rich in many aspects as an allegory of the love of cinema, is surely that this classic film, which has inspired generations of filmmakers and cinephiles, was until the 1990s only known in a series of incomplete versions of poor technical quality. The film that we shall analyse here is the second Gaumont restoration of *L'Atalante*, supervised by the eminent cinema historian Bernard Eisenschitz, and released on DVD as part of *L'Intégrale Jean Vigo* in 2001. As we can see from the table below, however, this latest and no doubt optimal restoration of the work is just one in a long line of versions, dating back to the original edit approved by Vigo himself in April 1934.

Date	Description	Remarks
1934	*L'Atalante* as approved by Vigo and shown at the trade screening, April 1934.	Never released commercially in France but was seen by critics in Paris and shown in London.
1934	*Le Chaland qui passe*, the retitled, re-edited, and rescored version of *L'Atalante*.	Commercially released in September 1934, but withdrawn after an unsuccessful three-week run.
1940	A first and partial restoration of *L'Atalante* by Henri Beauvais, the former producer at Gaumont.	Favourably received by critics in October 1940, this version was seen by the post-war generation of French cinephiles who built Vigo's critical reputation.
1950s	Henri Langlois's enhanced version of the above, with additional material from Beauvais.	The founder of the Cinémathèque française incorporated rushes from *L'Atalante* to produce the most complete version of *L'Atalante* at the time.
1990	Gaumont's restoration of *L'Atalante* supervised by Jean-Louis Bompoint and Pierre Philippe.	This version benefited from the discovery of a copy of *L'Atalante* deposited at the British Film Institute in the 1930s.
2001	The version now available on Gaumont's DVD *L'Intégrale Jean Vigo*.	Bernard Eisenschitz and Luce Vigo revised the 1990 Gaumont restoration, correcting some errors of interpretation.

The very first version of *L'Atalante*, the ideal film that the restorers have been trying to reconstitute ever since, was of course never commercially released in France. Its status is therefore slightly ambivalent, insofar as it is rightly presumed to be the most faithful to

Vigo's intentions, and yet it was only ever seen by a handful of unsympathetic distributors and exhibitors, and a few divided critics. In stark contrast to this original version of the film, there is *Le Chaland qui passe*. This film was substantially shorter than *L'Atalante*, and Vigo's friends were scandalised by the loss of narrative rhythm and thematic coherence. Moreover, Maurice Jaubert's musical score had been replaced at several points in the film by a popular song of the time, 'Le Chaland Qui Passe', written by Cesare Andrea Bixio for the performer Lys Gauty. It is worth noting that when *Le Chaland qui passe* was shown at the Bologna 'Il Cinema Ritrovato' film festival in 2001, some observers claimed that the film was far less of a betrayal or massacre of *L'Atalante* than cinema historians had commonly maintained for many decades (Waintrop 2001). In terms of the story of *L'Atalante*'s peregrinations and transformations, however, *Le Chaland qui passe* would later provide an important source and reference point for the Gaumont restorations of 1990 and 2001, as fortunately a decent copy of the truncated and retitled film had been conserved at the Cinémathèque Royale de Belgique.

In 1940, the first serious attempt at restoring *L'Atalante* came from an unlikely source. Henri Beauvais, the principal culprit responsible for the mutilation of the film six years earlier, had meanwhile left Gaumont in 1937 and set up his own company, Franfilmdis. He then bought the rights to a significant number of Gaumont films, including *Taris ou la natation*, *Zéro de conduite* and *L'Atalante*. We can only imagine that Beauvais must have regretted his previous actions, since in October 1940 – at the same time as the Vichy government was publishing the first of its vicious anti-Semitic decrees excluding undesirables from the cinema industry – he released a much improved copy of *L'Atalante*, whose title and original music had notably been restored, along with several sequences missing in *Le Chaland qui passe*. The film enjoyed a modest three-week run at the Studio des Ursulines in Paris, and was favourably received by the critical press at the time. After the war, this was the version of *L'Atalante*, far from complete and technically of rather poor quality, which for the next four decades was seen by the vast majority of spectators who fell in love with Vigo's cinema during those years. Some of them would also have had the opportunity to see the 1950 restoration conducted by Henri Langlois, which incorporated extra materials deposited by Beauvais at the Cinémathèque française.

In the late 1980s, the voyages of *L'Atalante* (as Bernard Eisenschitz calls them in his elegant and fascinating documentary for *L'Intégrale Jean Vigo*) would take another unexpected and slightly miraculous turn. The directors of Gaumont, having reacquired Beauvais's Franfilmdis catalogue, decided to pay for the sins of their fathers by financing a major restoration of Vigo's film, which by then had become one of the classic jewels in their collection. The aim of the project was to produce the most complete version of *L'Atalante* possible, as well as to apply the latest restoration techniques in order to clean up the image and clarify the sound. As part of the process, the restorers Jean-Louis Bompoint and Pierre Philippe assembled and compared as many different copies of the film as they could find, and it was during a trip to the National Film and Television Archive (NFTVA) in England that Bompoint discovered by chance an overlooked copy of *L'Atalante*, dating from 1934. This marvellous piece of good fortune changed the scope and ambition of the project, and it meant that a much more significant restoration of the film became possible (Bompoint 1993). It would seem that, for reasons that nobody can really explain, Gaumont had sent a copy of *L'Atalante*, rather than *Le Chaland qui passe*, to London some fifty-five years earlier. This is probably the copy that, having found its way into the vaults of the NFTVA warehouse at Berkhamstead, would later serve as the key element in the restoration of 1990, considered at the time as the most faithful version of *L'Atalante* imaginable. However, in 2001, Bernard Eisenschitz and Luce Vigo made some changes and improvements to the earlier Gaumont restoration. Notably, this 2001 version, available on *L'Intégrale Jean Vigo*, corrects what some critics judged as the overenthusiastic tendency of the 1990 team to include in its 'complete' version-of-versions every piece of material available (Magny and Tesson 2002: 62–71). This had led to certain anomalies, such as the bizarre shots of Jean Dasté licking a huge lump of ice, which did not meaningfully fit into the film's narrative structure. Other critics of the 1990 restoration felt that at times it appeared to contradict Vigo's intentions, for example by including a dramatically inappropriate version of the song that Juliette plays in the recordshop (Bretèque 2002: 7–13; Porcile 2002: 15–16). All in all, the story of *L'Atalante*'s journey through the film business and into cinema history, from mutilation to restoration, from oblivion to glory, is at times quite as moving and strange as the film's romantic narrative.

Indeed, one could say that in retrospect the tale of love lost and miraculously found, which we watch on the screen, seems almost to foresee and project the film's future destiny as a lost cinephile fetish, magically restored to our hearts and senses. With those thoughts in mind, let us now turn to our analytical discussion of *L'Atalante*, focusing in particular on three areas: the film's narrative structure, the representation of its key themes and the creation of its principal characters.

Poetry applied to prose

Writing about *Zéro de conduite* and *L'Atalante* in *The Nation*, 5 and 12 July 1947, the American film critic and screenwriter James Agee expressed his preference for the former in the following terms:

> *Zéro de conduite* seems to me all but unblemished inspiration, moving freely and surely in its own unprecedented world from start to finish, one of the few great movie poems. I admire *L'Atalante* less; it is only the best French movie since the best of René Clair. *Zéro* seems to have been made, as all the best work has to be, from the inside out; *L'Atalante*, on the whole, is put together from the outside inward. It is very good, spasmodically great poetry applied to pretty good prose; a great talent trying, I judge, to apply itself so far as it can stand to, conventionally and commercially [...] But for all its quality *L'Atalante* suggests the strugglings of a maniac in a straitjacket; whereas in *Zéro de conduite* he moves freely, and it turns out that he is dangerous only to all the world that most needs destroying. (Feldman and Weinberg 1951: 15–16)

There is nothing grandly theoretical about Agee's distinction between film poetry and prose. He deploys the terms rather to express his preference for Vigo's personal signature-film, as we described it earlier, over the more culturally conventional form of *L'Atalante*. Like all good critics, Agee 'works from the inside out', insofar as he starts from the strict appreciation of a work – or in this case the comparison of two works – and develops his empirical observation into a more general idea of cinema, as he conceives it. He acknowledges thereby that his point of view is culturally and historically limited. Here, for example, his identification of 'the best French movie since the best of René Clair' suggests the references available to a New York critic writing just after the Second World War. Agee's preference and theory thus modestly advanced, the reader can take it or leave it, choosing to agree or disagree with his judgement of the two films, and at the same time to ignore or develop his rhetorical distinction between poetry and prose. What we propose to do in the following pages is precisely to extend Agee's remark about 'spasmodically great poetry applied to pretty good prose', towards a more detailed analysis of *L'Atalante*, Vigo's unique attempt at a regular fiction film. Notably we shall examine in some depth the formal 'straitjacket' of the narrative feature film that *L'Atalante* certainly remains, as well as discussing the poetic 'strugglings' that Vigo attempts to induce in that prosaic form. We shall do this principally by focusing on *L'Atalante*'s narrative structure, especially its relationship to the original scenario written by Jean Guinée. We shall also examine how Vigo deals with other conventional aspects of the mainstream feature film, such as thematic development and the creation of fictional characters. In order to make our analysis easier to follow, we shall refer to a schematic breakdown of the film into twenty-three narrative segments, as presented in the table below.

	Number	Timing	Description
	0	0.00–1.30	Opening credits.
I Union. Introduction and exposition.	1	1.30–8.10	Wedding party leaves church and walks through village to barge at riverside. Père Jules and Kid welcome Jean and Juliette on board.
	2	8.10–10.10	First evening on *L'Atalante*, Jean and Juliette's first night together.
	3	10.10–17.30	First day on *L'Atalante*, Juliette discovers her new life and companions. Singing of 'Le Chant des Mariniers'. Juliette explains legend of seeing your beloved's image in the water.
		[First major temporal ellipsis]	
II Disunion. Development. Complication and conflict. Crisis.	4	17.30–20.10	Night: first signs of Juliette's boredom and of tension between characters; dispute over 'Radio-Paris'.
	5	20.10–24.30	Fog: sulking, Juliette 'disappears' in the fog. Père Jules 'fed up' with couple, but reconciliation around dinnertable.

	Number	Timing	Descripton
	6	24.30–28.20	Père Jules and Juliette alone in dining room: Juliette gets Père Jules to model the skirt she is making; their game gets out of hand.
	7	28.20–29.50	Arrival in Paris: L'Atalante negotiates locks at Canal Saint-Martin; Juliette very excited.
	8	29.50–36.50	Père Jules's cabin: curiosity and intimacy develop between Père Jules and Juliette. Jean interrupts them, very angry. Père Jules's 'haircut'.
	9	36.50–39.20	Jean and Juliette, reconciled, decide to go out for the evening; but Père Jules wants to go for his 'consultation'. Juliette disappointed and resigned to never seeing Paris.
	10	39.20–45.40	Père Jules at the clairvoyant's, where she gives him 'le grand jeu'. He gets drunk, steals a phonograph speaker, disturbs everyone on L'Atalante. Jean decides to leave Paris.
	11	45.40–53.00	Jean and Juliette go dancing at the 'guinguette'. The Camelot sings and flirts with Juliette. Jean gets angry and the couple leave.
	12	53.00–55.30	Juliette alone on L'Atalante, the Camelot comes and offers to take her to Paris. Jean returns unexpectedly and sends Camelot packing.
	13	55.30–58.40	Tempted by the Camelot's promises and frustrated by Jean's oppressive jealousy, Juliette escapes from L'Atalante at night. Jean refuses to wait for her to return and the barge leaves for Corbeil.
III Reunion. Consequences and reactions. Climax.	14	58.40–61.00	Curious and amazed, Juliette discovers the wealth of shops in the city. She returns to the canal, but the barge has left.
Resolution.	15	61.00–62.20	Juliette alone in Paris: her handbag is stolen at the railway station, the thief is attacked by the crowd.

Number	Timing	Description
16	62.20–63.30	Juliette looking for work in Paris. Unemployed workers outside factories. A man propositions her in the street. Meanwhile, Jean and L'Atalante sailing further north.
		[Second major temporal ellipsis]
17	63.30–71.00	Jean's depression caused by absence of Juliette. Père Jules tries to distract him with game of draughts and phonograph. Underwater sequence in which Jean 'sees' his beloved, as predicted by Juliette.
18	71.00–72.30	In parallel, Juliette desperately searching for Jean in Paris, Jean looking out for Juliette from the barge. Separated at night, each dreams of making love with the other.
19	72.30–74.50	The barge arrives at Le Havre. Half-mad, Jean runs towards the sea, looking for Juliette. A crowd gathers around him on the quay, but Père Jules comes to the rescue.
20	74.50–77.50	Summoned to the Offices of the Waterways Company, Père Jules is questioned by the Manager about Jean's erratic behaviour. He decides that the only way to resolve the situation is to find Juliette.
21	77.50–79.30	Père Jules looking for Juliette in Paris around the Bassin de la Villette and the Canal Saint-Martin.
22	79.30–81.20	Juliette is working at the 'Palace-Chansons' music shop. She plays the record of 'Le Chant des Mariniers', which Père Jules hears from outside the shop in the street. He puts her over his shoulder and carries her off, back to L'Atalante.
23	81.20–84.00	Informed by the Kid that Père Jules has gone to get Juliette, Jean smartens himself up. Juliette and Père Jules return. Jean and Juliette are reunited. Final aerial view of L'Atalante.

The basic story of *L'Atalante* can be summed up in the phrase 'love lost and found'. We can express this more abstractly by the three terms 'union' 'disunion' and 'reunion'. These correspond in our table to the three narrative movements of the film: I Union, segments 1–3, 1.30–17.30 minutes; II Disunion, segments 4–13, 17.30–58.40 minutes; III Reunion, segments 14–23, 58.40–84.00 minutes. The couple of Jean and Juliette are united by love and marriage. Then they are disunited by the rigours of canal life and their conflicting desires. Finally, they are reunited by Père Jules as the agent of love's destiny. This simple narrative structure, we should note, is already present in the one-page synopsis by Jean Guinée, dating from November 1932 (Lherminier 1985: 329). Looking at this preparatory document, we can get an initial sense of the narrative 'straitjacket', in which Vigo's genius will have to struggle. So what does Guinée's story look like? The Skipper of a barge marries a country-girl, Juliette, and the young couple begin their life on board *L'Atalante*, in the company of an Old Sailor, a Kid and a Dog. Although she is warned against 'the unhealthy pleasures of the City', Juliette is tempted by a sweet-talking Young Sailor, and escapes from the barge one night, with the help of the Kid. The Skipper refuses the Old Sailor's offer to go and look for her. Juliette experiences the 'honest pleasures' as well as the corrupt morals of the city, before finding a job as a waitress in a restaurant, where she is bullied by her boss and pursues a solitary urban existence. Some time later, the Old Sailor disobeys the orders of the Skipper and goes to look for Juliette in the city. He searches in vain. However, on the way back to *L'Atalante* he stops outside a church, intuitively looks inside, and there he finds Juliette, whose little hands he recognises as she says her rosary. Back on board, the Skipper accepts Juliette's return without emotion, 'as if she had left him that morning'. The barge resumes its course, 'but Happiness has fled the vessel'.

Although we can identify a number of significant differences between this initial synopsis and the resulting film, especially in terms of its major themes and secondary characters, it is nonetheless clear that Vigo and Riéra retained the basic narrative structure of Guinée's storyline for the script that they elaborated together in late summer 1933. Between Guinée's synopsis and the Vigo-Riéra script, however, there is an intermediary stage of the screenwriting process for *L'Atalante*, namely the detailed scenario that Guinée produced for the filmmaker and his assistant, possibly after some discussion of the synopsis had already taken place between the various parties that summer. This document, comprising approximately fifty scenes, takes the form of a literary description of *L'Atalante* as Guinée envisaged it eventually appearing on the screen (Lherminier 1985: 331–49). It contains extensive dialogue, some of which survives in the film word for word, as well as fairly precise indications of time, place and action, which Guinée has substantially developed from the earlier synopsis, and much of which we can again recognise in *L'Atalante* as we know it today. Likewise, the protagonists of the film have been expanded from the brief sketches of the synopsis, into more clearly defined fictional characters. Thus the Skipper is now called Jean, the Old Sailor has become Père Jules, and the seductive Young Sailor has been replaced by the Camelot. Finally, however, it is important to remark that Guinée's scenario is neither a technical shooting-script (despite the occasional suggestion of the way he thinks a particular scene might be filmed), nor even a 'screenplay' in the sense that we would normally understand the term (in other words, a fairly rigorous dramatic version of the film, notably with dialogue and action written scene by scene, as in a stageplay). If we now compare Guinée's text more closely with the finished film, we shall see how the narrative structure of *L'Atalante* emerges from this written document in a fairly recognisable shape, but also how much Vigo and Riéra have cut, altered, added, and replaced in the transposition from page to screen.

I Union: introduction and exposition

Guinée's scenario opens with a series of shots of the barge, establishing the title of the film and the situation of the story. Then we discover Père Jules and the Kid hurriedly leaving the church, followed by the wedding-party making its way towards the barge. Several guests are overheard discussing Juliette's choice of husband and future prospects. At the riverside, Père Jules and the Kid are awaiting the couple with flowers and preparing their humble welcoming reception – 'Heureuse vie à bord de *L'Atalante!*' ('Happy life on board *L'Atalante!*') – which passes off without incident. The barge departs at once, following the strict itinerary ordered by the Company, and in the following scenes we witness the early blissful days of the young couple's happily married life. These first dozen or so scenes described in Guinée's scenario correspond to segments 1–3 of our table. What is striking about the comparison is that Vigo and Riéra's introduction and exposition of the story is much neater and more economical. Notably it dispenses with quite a significant amount of 'character-building' dialogue and action, which Guinée includes in order to tell us what the characters are like (for example, we know that Juliette is 'happy' because Jean asks her if she is happy and she 'considers him lovingly and nods her head gravely in agreement'). Having cut this superfluous material, much of which concerns Père Jules and the Kid, Vigo and Riéra introduce instead a number of simple narrative elements that are much more efficient in terms of telling a story on screen. These include descriptive motifs, such as the cats and the dirty washing, which establish an immediate sense of the ramshackle lifestyle on board *L'Atalante*. The audience also receives key narrative signals for important events occurring later in the film. For example, the singing and playing of 'Le Chant des Mariniers' – by Père Jules, the Kid, Jean and Juliette, in various combinations – sets up the scene in the Palace-Chansons at the end of the film (segment 22). Just as importantly, Juliette relates to Jean the legend of seeing your beloved's image in the water, which will later trigger the famous underwater scene (segment 17). If the narrative exposition of the film is generally much shorter and sharper than it is in the scenario, we can also identify a major transformation in the tone of certain sequences. Here, instead of cutting material entirely, Vigo and Riéra have rather subtly changed its manner of presentation. Thus, in the scenario, the opening sequences at the church and the riverside look broadly similar to the corresponding scenes in the film, but in fact Vigo and Riéra have reworked the tone of Guinée's material entirely. For example, the representation of the wedding guests now take on a distinctly satirical flavour, while the welcoming ceremony organised by Père Jules and the Kid descends from a rustic expression of family values into irreverent slapstick and subversive comedy.

II Disunion: development – complication and conflict – crisis

Turning to the second movement of the narrative, here we can see how Vigo and Riéra have given themselves a much freer hand than they did in the first movement. From a structural point of view, this vital second phase of the story develops our interest in the initial dramatic situation established at the beginning of the film. It elaborates more complex relationships between the characters, as well as introducing elements of conflict between them, and eventually it brings the story to its major dramatic crisis (in this case, the departure of Juliette). In Guinée's text, this is probably the weakest section of the story. In fact, the essential role of the middle phase of the narrative is neglected, as if the screenwriter wanted to get to the dramatic crisis as soon as possible, without preparing the necessary ground. Thus Guinée signals that time is passing by showing us the years (1930, 1931, etc.) superimposed over the movement of the barge through the water. To this he adds a voiceover: 'Et ainsi passèrent des jours et des jours, dans une monotonie heureuse que les hommes nomment la vie, mais que le destin appelle le bonheur!' (Lherminier 1985: 334).[9] We then witness a long dialogue between Jean and Juliette, from which we gather that she wants to experience life in the city, whereas he thinks that it is just an expensive waste of time. This is followed by a scene in a working-class riverside café, where Juliette is approached by a Camelot, who presents his wares and performs a song, before Jean punches him out for flirting with his wife. The Camelot, however, turns up at the barge the next day and tries to persuade Juliette to run away with him to the city. But Jean interrupts their conversation and angrily chases off his rival. That evening, we hear the inner thoughts of Jean and Juliette as they reflect on the day's events. Finally, Juliette decides to leave.

If we compare this section of the scenario to the second narrative movement of the film, we can see that Vigo and Riéra have kept very little of Guinée's material, apart from the scene at the 'guinguette'. Even this sequence, in fact, they transform beyond recognition, cutting some rather stereotypical representation of 'low-life' that Guinée had conceived, and injecting a comical, even carnivalesque, tone into the character of the Camelot and his narrative role as romantic rival. What is most impressive about this central section of *L'Atalante* is the dynamic that Vigo and Riéra create between continuous narrative momentum (the relationships developing between the three principal characters, the conflict of desires gradually escalating

9 'The days passed in a happy monotony that men call life but that destiny calls happiness!'

between Jean and Juliette), and a series of formal set-pieces (the dress-making scene, Père Jules's cabin, the visit to the clairvoyant). These latter scenes require a slower, more episodic pace, in order to allow the audience time to get to know the characters and generally to enter into that mysterious atmosphere for which *L'Atalante* is rightly celebrated. In terms of narrative rhythm, Vigo and Riéra achieve this balance between momentum and atmosphere by the simple trick of rolling each scene into the next, with an incidental overlap. This means that as spectators we have the impression that the forty or so minutes from the first signs of Juliette's boredom (segment 4) to the critical moment of her departure (segment 13) have passed in one flowing and progressive movement. After the implicit temporal ellipsis between segments 3 and 4 (no calendar pages or voiceover), each scene is dramatically linked to its successor by a simple narrative indicator of 'what's going to happen next'. Thus, when the couple argue over the choice of radio stations (segment 4), Jean immediately leaves their cabin, because he has to guide the barge through the thick fog, into which Juliette will symbolically 'disappear' in the next scene (segment 5). Once Juliette is retrieved, all the characters gather around the dinner table, but Jean and the Kid have to return to duty, thus leaving Père Jules and Juliette alone for their first dramatic duet in the dress-making scene (segment 6). In turn, this bizarre exchange of gender roles and physical intimacy is interrupted by the Kid, who announces the barge's arrival in Paris. There follows the brief montage sequence of images shot around the Canal Saint-Martin (segment 7), which ends with an excited Juliette descending into Père Jules's cabin, carrying the clean clothes that she had tried to give him earlier (in segment 6). And so on, through segments 8 to 13, the narrative rhythm and continuity is maintained, all the way up to the fifty-eighth minute and beyond (in fact, the second and final major temporal ellipse comes in the sixty-third minute, at the end of segment 16). It is this linking together of sequences into a steady temporal flow of action that prevents *L'Atalante* from becoming a mere accumulation of discrete dramatic episodes. It also enables the story to take its time when necessary, particularly in those scenes of a rare intensity (such as the visit to the clairvoyant and his drunken return to the barge), where Michel Simon as Père Jules has the freedom to construct one of his richest and funniest roles. However, if *L'Atalante* consisted solely of formal set pieces and Simon's marvellous turns, there is no doubt that it would be a lesser film as a result. Notably, it would forfeit the fine tension between 'poetry' and 'prose' that James Agee so precisely identified in his article. Slightly adjusting Agee's use of these terms, we could claim that the poetic 'strugglings' of *L'Atalante* in fact require the prosaic 'straitjacket' of its narrative continuity in order for the film's magic to be fully realised on screen.

III   Reunion: consequences and reactions – climax – resolution

The third narrative movement of *L'Atalante* takes us from the dramatic consequences of Juliette's departure (segment 14) to the final reconciliation of the lovers at the end of the film (segment 23). The route to reunion, however, is difficult for all concerned, and each of the three principal characters will react differently to the crisis. Thus Juliette will experience the harshness and solitude of urban life in an economically depressed and socially divided France. Jean will encounter psychological depression and near madness, as well as the prospect of professional ruin. And Père Jules will evolve from the rough-and-ready embodiment of scarred masculinity towards a more caring and ultimately 'salvational' role at the film's climax. In purely narrative terms, we know as spectators that, once Juliette has run away from *L'Atalante*, the question left in suspense is 'How will the crisis be resolved?' – in other words 'How will Juliette get back to the barge?'. In Guinée's scenario, the answer to this question is quite neatly and effectively constructed. Indeed we could argue that, on paper at least, the third movement of the story is more balanced and better proportioned than in the film (which does not mean to say that *L'Atalante* would be better if Vigo and Riéra had stuck more closely to Guinée's text). Notably Juliette's experience of life as a single woman is afforded more time and attention in the scenario. After leaving the barge, she takes a train to the city, and we witness her dreams and nightmares about the dangerous and exciting turn that her life is taking. Once she gets over her initial amazement at the wealth and diversity of city life, she confronts the urban realities of looking for work and accommodation, in a world where single women are sexual and economic prey for the dominant patriarchy. As a good country-girl, however, she neither succumbs to the advances of a cabaret-owner offering her work as a dancer, nor revolts against the oppressive behaviour of her boss at the restaurant, where she eventually finds a job as a cleaner. As for life back on *L'Atalante*, in Guinée's text we are given to understand that Jean is 'too proud' to go and look for Juliette, and so Père Jules and the Kid attempt to fill the domestic void caused by Juliette's absence, while exchanging philosophical dialogue on the mysteries of human behaviour, especially in matters of the heart. After five months of this separation and disharmony, Père Jules decides to go and look for Juliette, against the express wishes of his skipper, Jean. We follow him through a number of scenes and incidents in the city, but he fails to find Juliette. Then, on his way back to the barge, he stops at a country church, instinctively decides to go in, and there discovers Juliette saying her rosary. They return to *L'Atalante*, where Jean, concealing his inner joy, accepts Juliette back, but only if she swears to him that sexually 'there was nobody else' during her absence, and, of course, that she will never run away again. 'On va être heureux, maintenant?' ('Are we going to be happy now?'), asks the Kid. 'On repart, on repart, c'est la vie, ça!' ('We embark once more, and that is life!)', the philosophical old sailor replies.

It will be clear from this brief summary that Vigo and Riéra kept very little of Guinée's scenario in the third movement of *L'Atalante*, and that film culture is infinitely richer as a result of their decision. What is important to note, however, when we compare the scenario to the film, is that 'the application of great poetry to pretty good prose' is less elegantly realised here than in the second narrative movement. In particular, we can remark a certain imbalance in the narrative structure between a number of episodes that seem in rhythmical terms extremely condensed, even rushed (Juliette in Paris, segments 14–16; Jean at Le Havre, segment 19; Père Jules searching for Juliette, segment 21), and a couple of outstanding 'bravura' sequences that require the story's flow temporarily to be suspended (Jean swimming under water, segment 17; the parallel fantasies of the separated couple, segment 18). The whole of Juliette's encounter with the charms and perils of Paris, for example, occupies no more than five minutes of screen time. This includes her discovery of consumer capitalism, her unsuccessful return to the barge (Jean has already decided to embark for Corbeil), her encounter with urban crime and police brutality, her failure to find work at the factory gates, and her initiation into sexual harassment. By contrast, the astonishing sequence that Vigo and Riéra construct around Jean's dive into the canal lasts almost eight minutes on its own (segment 17). Here, after a significant temporal ellipsis between segments 16 and 17, we discover Jean below deck in the company of Père Jules and the Kid, playing a rather desultory game of draughts. Jean looks haggard, dirty, unshaven, his psychological distraction reflecting the physical absence of Juliette. Suddenly he gets up, sticks his head in a bucket of water (in the hope of seeing Juliette's image), then goes out on deck and dives headlong into the canal. Back inside, Père Jules somehow manages to get his old phonograph working, which he hopes will cheer up Jean with a little musical entertainment. But when the Kid informs him that 'le Patron s'est foutu à l'eau' ('the Skipper has gone overboard'), Vigo's subtle use of Jaubert's music transforms the tone of this famous scene. The direct sound from Père Jules's phonograph (we recognise the lovers' theme-tune) becomes the musical accompaniment to Jean's miraculous 'vision' of Juliette in her wedding gown. By the magic of montage, she appears to be 'swimming' before his amorous submarine gaze. The astounding beauty of this passage, its lyrically unreal intensity, is a perfect illustration of L'Atalante's poetic qualities. No less typical of Vigo's artistic signature, we might add, is the comical twist at the end of the scene, when Jean resurfaces on the other side of the barge and we see him politely enquiring of Père Jules and the Kid what it is they are looking for in the water. Vigo's cinema is often sublime, but he always enjoys the ridiculous. Immediately following on from Jean's underwater vision, a second poetic sequence shows us Jean and Juliette's separate experiences of romantic estrangement (segment 18). The scene is constructed in parallel sequences. Firstly, we see Jean on deck, looking out for Juliette along the riverside. This is alternated with images of Juliette wandering the streets and bridges around the canals, looking for the barge. Then the parallel editing attains a more intense degree of alternation, switching between images of the two lovers in their respective beds, as they fantasise about making love to each other. This is one of the most memorable passages of L'Atalante, and a uniquely intense expression of desire and longing in French cinema. In Agee's terms, one could almost take this scene as emblematic of 'the strugglings of a maniac in a straitjacket', since what we see here is the mad body of a conventionally unrepresentable passion (whether that be for aesthetic or moral reasons) struggling to find a form of expression. It is precisely in such instances that Vigo's poetic instincts, his openness to formal experimentation, can stretch the prosaic restrictions of codified film language, and (to paraphrase Agee), 'seek to make the rest of the alphabet available, so that enjoyment may be enlarged'.

It is in counterpoint to these two highly lyrical sequences that we can better appreciate the apparent structural imbalance of the third movement of *L'Atalante*. Apart from the neatly functional scene in the Office of the Waterways Company, where Père Jules is summoned by the rather brutal Manager to answer for Jean's increasingly erratic and irresponsible behaviour (segment 20), the rhythm of the action throughout this movement is hurried and even fragmented. In particular, we should note that, from the crucial turning point of Père Jules's decision to go and look for Juliette, which from a structural point of view 'inverts' Juliette's earlier decision to leave (segment 13), the whole dramatic finale of *L'Atalante* takes barely seven minutes of screen time. By contrast, Guinée's scenario had played out the suspense of Père Jules's search ('How will he find her?'), by taking the spectator through a series of digressive incidents and false leads, even fooling us into thinking that he has failed in his mission, before springing the melodramatic counter-surprise of Juliette's salvation in the rustic chapel. In the film, we see Père Jules wandering around the Bassin de la Villette and the Canal Saint-Martin, looking rather disconsolately at a few shop fronts and hotel entrances, and catching the attention of an elegant Parisian woman (clearly not Juliette) as she passes by. On this point, it is worth noting that Vigo and Riéra's shooting script does in fact indicate some extra material for this sequence, which presumably was never filmed. Notably they planned a series of 'mistaken identities', where Père Jules at first 'recognises' Juliette in a number of different guises (run over by a car; cleaning windows up a ladder; begging in the street), then realises that in each case it is not Juliette at all, but someone else whom he has imagined in her place (Lherminier 1985: 320–3). In addition, we know from Louis Chavance's testimony that, with Vigo's consent, he cut a couple of 'redundant' shots from the search sequence, before the film was shown at the trade screening in April 1934 (Chavance 1955: 55). It is reasonable to speculate, therefore, that if Vigo had disposed of more time and money, during the filming and editing of *L'Atalante*, he may well have preferred a more sustained and suspenseful build-up to the film's dramatic climax, i.e. the moment when Père Jules miraculously discovers Juliette working in a music shop called the 'Palace-Chansons'.

In the film as we know it, however, it is precisely the miraculous improbability of Père Jules's discovery that makes the climax so engaging and unique. We first see a timid and troubled Juliette handing out the tokens that the clients have to buy from the shop's cashier, if they want to play and listen to a record (all this information we quickly infer from the few brief shots of Juliette's workplace). Then we watch her sneaking a look at her boss, who is fortunately asleep at the till. Juliette uses one of the tokens herself, in order to listen to 'Le Chant des Mariniers', the song that is the theme-tune of her love for Jean, as well as a successful enough hit to feature in the music shop's play-list. She slips on the headphones, and we hear on the soundtrack 'Le Chant des Mariniers', sung by the same male and female voices that performed the song earlier in the film, at the time when Jean and Juliette were first discovering their love and passion (segment 3). By a subtle transposition, similar to Vigo's use of the gramophone record in the underwater scene (segment 17), it is this music 'in Juliette's head', as it were, that Père Jules hears relayed by a loudspeaker onto the street, outside the Palace-Chansons. Recognising not just the song, then, but also the magical voice of Jean and Juliette's love projected into the harsh social climate of Paris during the economic depression, Père Jules enters the music-shop. He then rescues Juliette triumphantly, if rather comically, by putting her over his shoulder and carrying her out of the shop, much to the alarm of her customers and colleagues. Once again, this is Vigo's poetically intense and ingenious solution to the prosaic problem of resolving the film's melodramatic crisis. At the climax of the film, this improbable but lyrical staging of the restoration of love transcends both the mediocrity of Guinée's original story, and the structural awkwardness of the film's third narrative movement. Thus love really does conquer all, providing the poetically just form for the film's happy ending, and in the process revealing Michel Simon as cinema's most unlikely Cupid.

The final scene of resolution must logically take place on the barge, where Jean is informed by the Kid that Père Jules 'est allé chercher la Patronne' ('has gone to get the Boss's wife'). We see Jean hurriedly attempting to smarten himself up, washing and shaving quickly before Père Jules and Juliette return. From a narrative point of view, the improbably condensed timing of this action is irrelevant, since all we are awaiting now is the imminent catharsis – or release of tension

– that the couple's reunion will communicate to the spectator. Thus when Père Jules duly delivers Juliette back to Jean, Vigo cleverly inserts a few brief but delicious instants of further suspense, as the separated lovers face each other silently and nervously across the cabin. Suddenly they fall into each other's arms, and tumble to the floor in one of cinema's most beautifully realised and tenderly joyful embraces. The very last shot of L'Atalante is the famous aerial view of the barge sailing once more along the canal. As we know from Kaufman's testimony, this shot was filmed from a plane, more or less according to Vigo's instructions, but after the main filming of L'Atalante had been completed. By that time, of course, the filmmaker was already extremely ill, and Kaufman is acutely aware of the historic irony of his anecdote, whereby we interpret retrospectively the film's final shot as somehow prefiguring Vigo's tragic absence from his most celebrated work. If, however, this emblematically eternal image appears to be shot from a heaven in which the atheist filmmaker certainly did not believe, at least we can be equally sure that Vigo the artist would have found this unintended closing enigma as comical as it is poignant, as incredible as it is both haunting and strange.

Merely a loose frame

Speaking to a journalist just before filming started on L'Atalante, Vigo remarked:

> Je vais tourner d'après un scénario de Jean Guinée, scénario qui n'est qu'une trame lâche me permettant de mettre en valeur des images du bord de l'eau, dans le monde des mariniers, et l'interprétation.[10] (Lherminier 1984: 102)

As our preceding discussion has demonstrated, this statement by Vigo is only partly justified. From a narrative point of view, we can agree that Vigo and Riéra 'loosely' adapted Guinée's text, insofar as they had no hesitation in cutting and replacing material from the existing scenario and adding new ideas as they saw fit. We have also seen, however, that they retained the solidity of the basic narrative

10 'The film's based on a scenario by Jean Guinée, although I'm using it merely as a loose frame allowing me to work with images of the waterways, the environment of the canal-workers, and the actors.'

'frame' inherited from Guinée, and indeed in certain sections of the film they appear to have considerably 'tightened' its structure and rhythm, especially in the second movement. It is this play of looseness and structure, we have argued, this dynamic of poetic digression and formal bravura contrasting with narrative structure and dramatic rhythm, which ultimately makes *L'Atalante* such an extraordinary, perhaps unique, achievement. It is no surprise, then, that Vigo's unknown masterpiece of 1934 should over the years come to be celebrated equally as a classic French feature film of the 1930s, alongside the works of Marcel Carné, Julien Duvivier, Jacques Feyder and Jean Renoir, and at the same time as an experimental work that draws on the invention of the 1920s avant-garde, while looking forward to the innovations of the New Wave in the late 1950s and early 1960s. Having focused thus far primarily on what James Agee identified as the film's distinctive dynamic of poetry and prose, we shall now turn our attention briefly towards two further aspects of *L'Atalante* – thematics and characterisation – which Vigo also mentions in his comments to the journalist quoted above.

Firstly, let us consider more closely the film's dominant themes, in other words the ideas and motifs that Vigo was intending to embroider onto the 'merely loose frame' of Guinée's scenario. To the journalist he mentions in particular his desire to film the canals and riverside as well as the working environment of the bargemen. This ambition is both painterly and documentary, and in this respect we should not underestimate the filmic vision of Boris Kaufman. The cinematographer not only lent his eyes and experience to Vigo for *L'Atalante*, as he had earlier done for their 'documented point of view' about Nice. He had also previously worked on Jean Lods's *La Seine ou la vie d'un fleuve* (1931), as well as other socially conscious and formally elegant depictions of modern life, including his own *Les Halles centrales* of 1927. What is remarkable about *L'Atalante* is the simplicity and ease with which Vigo and Kaufman succeed in incorporating these documentary elements and their left-wing values into the fictional structure of the film. The social realism of *L'Atalante* comes essentially from the decision to shoot on location. This difficult choice implies a certain ethical as well as aesthetic rigour, which respects the physical setting of the dramatic action within the routines of everyday working life. If the film avoids the twin dangers of social realism – either miserabilist preaching or stereotypical representation of 'the people' – it is because Vigo and Kaufman inject a certain documentary spirit of openness and improvisation into the fictional parameters of storytelling and characterisation. They never seek to illustrate with 'authentic' images a fixed ideological discourse, nor merely to locate cardboard characters in natural landscapes. Thus, as the film's narrative unfolds, we absorb indirectly the distinctive atmosphere of the canals, the working conditions and routines of the barge folk, the stop–start rhythm of their itinerary along the Seine and Oise rivers, and their intermittent encounters with the people and social customs of the riverside world.

There are moments in the film, however, when we can feel a more explicit insistence on a particular social theme that is personally important to Vigo's belief-system. The scene in the Manager's Office (segment 20), for example, reveals the kind of libertarian anger against all figures of authority that we recognise from *Zéro de conduite*. Here the contrasting characters of the downtrodden bargeman, who describes himself as 'un rien du tout' ('a complete nobody'), and the bullying and disrespectful Manager, all pompous bluster and banging fists, are perhaps getting close to the kind of ideological caricatures that *L'Atalante* generally avoids. In a similar vein, the scene in the railway station, when Juliette's handbag is stolen, feels like an illustration of Vigo's political views about social injustice. Thus the vulnerable woman, Juliette, is the victim of an impoverished thief who is simply more desperate and hungry than she is. For Vigo, the greater ill is the violent reaction of the petty bourgeois mob and the cowardly complicity of the forces of order. Finally, we can identify signs of Vigo's political intolerance for the intrinsically conservative tendencies of mainstream society, notably in the portrayal of the wedding-guests at the church (segment 1), and in the scene at Le Havre where the gathering bystanders express their moral disapproval of Jean's apparent 'drunkenness' (segment 19).

Given Vigo's profound aversion to this popular but petty-minded ideology of common sense and traditional morality, it is understandable that, on a thematic level, he and Riéra should have transformed the conventional values of Guinée's conservative world-view into their own left–libertarian vision of progressive politics. The simplest way of achieving this was to cut all the tedious speechifying about evil city ways and simple rustic rectitude, which Guinée had written for the male characters in particular, as well as the long stretches of dialogue that the screenwriter had composed, in order to explain what the characters are thinking, and the moral codes that motivate their behaviour. In the film, there remains little or no trace of the conservative family values, and passive respect for the existing social order, which originally had caused an exasperated Vigo to exclaim: 'Mais qu'est-ce que tu veux que je foute avec ça? C'est un scénario pour patronage.'[11] There is no sense in *L'Atalante*, for example, that Juliette has done anything morally wrong by fleeing the oppressive boredom of her domestic existence. Indeed, if we can hear any sign of an authorial opinion in the film, regarding the morality of her situation and of bourgeois marriage in general, it is probably expressed by the Camelot's sarcastic exhortation to Jean and Juliette: 'Amusez-vous bien en famille, tas de rigolos!' ('Have a good time with the family, you bunch of jokers!'). Since Juliette has committed no offence (she may well regret her decision, but an error is not a crime), she does not need therefore to be 'punished' for her misdeeds (the fact that she has such a hard time in the city is not a punishment for her rebellion). Nor is she 'saved' from moral or physical danger by Père Jules, who rescues her in the name of love rather than the law. Nor is she 'forgiven' by Jean, who welcomes her back because he loves her, because he cannot live without her. In Vigo's world there is no sin, except for those who refuse to be free. It is these twin themes of love and freedom that give *L'Atalante* a precociously post-war, post-Vichy and 'liberated' feel, in terms of its politics and moral vision, despite the film's undeniable anchoring in the harsh social realities of France in the early 1930s. The representation of the couple's passion is remarkably simple and frank. They love each other deeply, but the relationship goes wrong (work, routine, boredom). Eventually, the strength of their common desire overcomes these obstacles and limitations, and transports the reborn lovers onto a higher plane. If *Zéro de conduite* ends on the emphatically anarchistic assertion of revolt and destruction as transcendental values, then in *L'Atalante* it is the uplifting power of love that can change the world, by its passionate embodiment of freedom and its infinite renewal of the human experience.

11 'What do you want me to do with that? It's trite and moralising.'

Working with the actors

Let us now conclude this analysis of *L'Atalante* with a brief discussion of characterisation, the second area of filmmaking that Vigo declared he was looking forward to exploring, thanks to the 'loose frame' of Guinée's scenario. The phrase that he employed when talking to the journalist was in fact 'mettre en valeur l'interprétation', which literally means 'bring to the fore the performance' of the actors. Between characterisation and performance, there is a whole domain of thinking where film theory has feared to tread. One could seek to distinguish, for example, between firstly, the 'characters' of a film as they are conceived on paper by the screenwriter, much like characters in a novel or a play; secondly, the 'interpretation' that the actors and the director then give to those roles, as they would if they were working in the theatre; and thirdly, the specifically filmic dimensions of recording the human body in 'performance', its movements and gestures, its rhythms and textures of speech. For the purposes of the following discussion, however, we shall talk about characterisation and performance as essentially part of the same creative process. In particular, we shall focus on the portrayal of 'Jean' (Jean Dasté), 'Juliette' (Dita Parlo) and 'Père Jules' (Michel Simon), as they evolve from the textual sketches that Guinée wrote for the scenario, into those tangible screen presences through whom we live *L'Atalante*. In each case we shall see that the characters may well begin the process as little more than fictional stereotypes – a name, an age, a gender, an occupation, a milieu, a set of basic behavioural codes – and yet somehow the end result is a dramatically interactive group of contradictory, complex and changing human beings. We shall probably never know to what extent the credit for that transformation should go to Guinée, Vigo and Riéra, to Kaufman and the technical craft of the crew; or whether we should rather praise the talent of the cast, and their working responses to the script and to Vigo's direction.

The character of Jean starts on paper as a pretty uninteresting cliché of immature masculinity, his social function and power an effective shield for psychological insecurity and boyish fears. He is married to his barge, as it were, and when he sees that Juliette is struggling to adapt to her new role, his reactions are insensitive at best and bullying at worst. Faced with the reality of his wife's escape, he goes into moody denial, and even when Juliette is returned to his arms his main concern is to reassert his rights of sexual possession. By contrast, the Jean portrayed by Dasté is a much more open and complex figure. Perhaps it is because we remember him from *Zéro de conduite*, where the character of Huguet struggles to assume a position of male authority, but there is something that does not quite fit, as it were, between the innocent, wide-eyed, sensitive Dasté, and the macho role of the Skipper as it was originally conceived. Even his clothes seem a little too big for him, and the clean, hairless and relatively undeveloped body that he reveals in the film's more intimate or athletic sequences hardly suggests the bullish power of working-class masculinity, as exemplified (to the point of caricature) by Jean Gabin in films of the same period. In comparison to the male stereotype with which he began, Dasté's Jean is loving, passionate, sensitive, sharing, playful, and – perhaps the key quality in all of Vigo's characters – open to change. Given the melodramatic frame of the story, Jean's persona fluctuates and evolves quite significantly, both from scene to scene and over the whole stretch of the film. Obviously this psychic flow does not exist in isolation, it is always in response to the evolving circumstances of the drama, and in particular it interacts with the equally dynamic and open character of Juliette. It is Jean's immaturely excessive desire to please his new wife that causes his inappropriate and insecure reactions to her growing boredom and frustration. He tries to find the means to make her life more interesting and varied, but jealousy and resentment get in the way of his best intentions, firstly, when he 'discovers' Père Jules seemingly getting intimate with his wife in the old sailor's cabin, and secondly, when the Camelot displays his worldly charms and sexy palaver to the curious and enquiring gaze of Juliette. The most intriguing aspects of Jean's personality, however, are revealed by the crisis of his wife's departure and absence. After his initially brutish denial of the new situation ('Je ne voudrais pas d'elle si elle revenait dans cinq minutes' ['I wouldn't take her back if she turned up in five minutes']), the young husband falls apart psychologically. He is lost without her love, depressed, dysfunctional and desperate enough to throw himself overboard and plunge into the dirty canal – not in order to kill himself, it is true, but certainly to undergo some kind of magical resourcing in the depths of his desire and erotic imagination. In symbolic terms, Jean's watery 'death' is in fact the extreme expression of the utter passivity to which he has fallen victim, since

Juliette left the barge. It is from this paralytically unmasculine and damsel-like state of distress that only Père Jules's miraculous intervention can save him. At the end of the film, Jean suddenly returns to life from his depressive torpor, having magically been given a second chance to start his love for Juliette all over again. We have no idea what will happen next, nor how he will respond to future challenges and desires, but it is perhaps through Jean's character more than any other that we feel in the final images the excitement of that uncertainty, and the prospect of life flowing forward again, after the near-fatal error of the couple's unhappy separation.

Like the principal masculine role of *L'Atalante*, the figure of the film's leading lady begins life as a rather one-dimensional gender stereotype. On paper, Juliette is the simple woman-as-child par excellence. Unable to assume her proper responsibilities, as wife to Jean and surrogate mother to the crew, she allows herself to be distracted by the shiny baubles of a travelling salesman, whose seductive description of city life is so much more gratifying than her husband's prudent conservatism. Foolishly deciding to run away from home, she soon falls victim to urban evils, and can only be rescued from moral corruption by taking refuge in religion. Even when she returns to the barge, according to the scenario, she will continue to be punished for her irresponsibility by the guilt of nearly having wrecked a home. In comparison to this stereotype, what is immediately striking about Dita Parlo's incarnation of Juliette on screen is that, although she is physically quite girlish in build and look – she is neither a curvaceous vamp nor a busty matron – her behaviour from very early in the film is largely that of a responsible, intelligent and active adult woman. Although she appears to have some childlike qualities, we should remember that in Vigo's world these are considered positive personality traits rather than character defects. To retain your childhood is to retain your sense of becoming. Thus Juliette is open, funny, enthusiastic, sensual and generally willing to engage in married love and life more as an adventure than as a merely social contract. On the barge she assumes the role of 'Patronne' (or 'Boss's wife'), which obviously means acting to some extent as mother to the men on board (despite their reluctance to let her do their washing). But this dimension of her role is relatively insignificant in the film, compared to the frank equality of her loving camaraderie with Jean, and the complex exchange of knowledge and sensations that marks her relationship with Père Jules. Like the other main characters of *L'Atalante*, Juliette is not a fixed recipe of character traits but an openly shifting set of feelings, emotions, reactions and, most importantly, questions. Thus her relationship with Jean changes unevenly and zigzaggedly over the course of the film. It is a dynamic of amorous advances, tentative questions and emotional setbacks. We see the awkwardness and joys of their first days together, the surprises and compromises, disappointments and tensions of their early married life, their dramatic separation and painful absence from each other, and finally their beautiful yet inconclusive reunion, with its unspoken and open-ended renewal of their vows. Throughout this complex process, it is Juliette who is by far the more active partner in the couple. It is her inquisitiveness and desire that makes things happen, because she asks the questions and takes the initiative. In this respect, one of the most important if subtle changes to the plot that Vigo and Riéra introduced was the idea of transforming Juliette's blindly melodramatic flight, as it was written in Guinée's text, into a calculated risk that simply goes wrong. Thus she leaves the barge only for an hour or so, in order to go and satisfy her curiosity about life elsewhere, and no doubt intending to return later. Her dramatic 'error' is merely not to have foreseen Jean's angry and impetuous decision to leave for Corbeil, as soon as he realises that she has gone. Her action is not a fault that she commits, it is rather a risk that she runs and whose consequences she must assume.

Juliette's sense of exploration and curious exchange is presented most memorably in *L'Atalante* by the two long scenes that Dita Parlo plays opposite Michel Simon's Père Jules. Again it is she who takes the initiative with the old sailor, carefully and playfully encouraging him to respond to her questions, and to open up his vastly disorderly memory bank of experiences and emotions. In the first scene, she invites him to show her his skills on her sewing machine, then to act as her model for the skirt that she is making. It is this ludic advance that enables Père Jules to talk about and, more powerfully, to re-enact some of his infinite travels and troubles across the globe. At one point literally pricking him into reaction with her sewing-needle, she eventually pushes him too far, or rather her probing and cajoling of Père Jules incites the old sailor to get a little carried away, and Juliette quickly decides to make a tactical retreat from her front line of enquiry. The investigation resumes, however, in the famous cabin-scene, where the encounter becomes much more intimate, and therefore more intense and more dangerous, both in terms of what Père Jules is willing to show Juliette – his loves and losses, his trophies and relics – and in terms of what she is prepared to expose of herself, and to risk emotionally in the exchange. The strongest and strangest moment here is perhaps when Père Jules deliberately cuts himself with his 'navaja' in order to show Juliette that 'it really cuts'. For a second, we think that she is going to lick the old sailor's blood from the back of his hand. Clearly overcome and astonished by what she finds in Père Jules's private universe, Juliette is brutally returned to her humdrum life by the jealous interruption of her husband. Jean violently breaks their intimate spell, which momentarily has bound together this most improbable of screen couples, Vigo's Beauty and the Beast. But the dramatic effects of Juliette's exchanges with Père Jules are carried over into her meetings with the Camelot (who is Père Jules but younger and better-looking). More significantly, they inform both her decision to leave the barge, and the difficult consequences and new experiences deriving from the chances that she takes. No longer an irresponsible girl, led astray by dreamy guys and flashy trinkets, the Juliette that Dita Parlo makes her own is an enquiring and exciting young woman, who is ready to take the risk of discovering the world.

Finally, then, what shall we say of Michel Simon and Père Jules? It will be clear from the preceding pages that Simon's contribution to *L'Atalante* is much more than a series of brilliant thespian turns. Whatever his remarkable skills as an actor – and we need only to look at Jean Renoir's *Tire-au-flanc* (1928), *La Chienne* (1931) and *Boudu sauvé des eaux* (1932) to confirm that Simon was enjoying an extraordinarily rich vein of form during these years – there is something else going on in *L'Atalante*. Something that is deeper and more paradoxical than the mere recording of a theatrical genius performing a finely crafted role (as is certainly the case in so many of Simon's other films from the 1930s and 1940s). The figure of Père Jules is profoundly resonant at every level of the film, his presence is vital to its story, its development, its complexity, its charm. And yet he is neither one of the heroes of *L'Atalante* – that is clearly the twin task of Jean and Juliette – nor even the central focus of its action or attention. We cannot rightly say that he hogs the camera, nor that he steals all the best lines. The paradox is that Père Jules thus becomes the film's decentred centre, everywhere and nowhere, palpably dispersed in every sound and image, as if Simon's body and voice had somehow got integrated into the grain of the filmstock. By a strange chemical process, whose exact composition and reactions we can only analyse in these metaphorical terms, Père Jules becomes the whole film, not in terms of its critical meaning or historical reputation, but in much more physical and material terms, as if the secrets of *L'Atalante*'s enduring mystery were written on Simon's tattooed and perforated skin.

Like Jean and Juliette, however, the character played by Simon was originally conceived by Guinée as a bundle of cultural clichés, a mixture of the faithful old servant, the salty sea dog and the country elder purveying the eternal wisdom of the land. In the scenario, he never stops talking, indeed he seems to perform the function of the story's busy narrator, guiding us through the action, commenting on its progress and significance, and ultimately intervening in its course, in order to bring Juliette back to the barge and the story to its conclusion: 'On repart, c'est la vie, ça!' ('We embark once more, and that is life!'). By stark contrast, Simon's Père Jules is deprived of all eloquence and discursive wisdom, and the earthy common sense of Guinée's old sailor becomes a kind of poetic nonsense, cut up into rhythmically repetitive chunks of popular language, or even reduced to a barely comprehensible babble. Questions without answers, assertions without logic, injunctions without address, Père Jules's speech is self-referentially idiomatic to the point of idiocy. Its wisdom emerges backwards like a sailor's slang, in the form of exclamations, sarcasms, obscenities, jokes, oaths and superstitions. As a linguistic performance, it corresponds to the 'decentred centre' that we evoked earlier in order to describe Père Jules's screen presence. This is in part a regional issue, since Simon is effectively drawing on his stock of gestures and inflections recorded in the Vaudois region of his native Switzerland. But the creation is more a poetic act than a socio-linguistic exercise. It looks and sounds like an actor performing dialogue, but as if the words and gestures had been imploded into the substance of the image, so that its effects are everywhere eminently palpable, and yet nowhere graspable in a conventionally meaningful way. We can extend this notion of Simon's role as an 'informal' form – an unreadable composition of recognisable parts – to other aspects of the character of Père Jules. Thus his personal interaction with the other characters is always decidedly off-centre. It is never very clear to what extent he is actually listening and responding to the other's words, or whether he is just talking to himself anyway, and occasionally tuning in (and out again) to normal human conversation. When the context demands that he must communicate clearly, he soon gets frustrated and angered by the additional linguistic effort that is required. This happens with the Kid, for example, at the beginning of the film, when they try to organise a welcoming party for Juliette; with Jean at various points, for technical reasons to do with their work and the progress of the barge; and with the unsympathetic Manager at the Waterways Company office, where Père Jules tactically deploys his performance of idiocy, as a working-class ruse against the hated bosses. The exceptions to this rule are significant, notably his easy conversation with the 'gypsy' Raspoutine about the purchase of a second-hand gramophone, and his semi-magical, semi-sexual transaction with the clairvoyant, who reads his 'sensual' palms and offers him 'le grand jeu' ('the full works') as a bonus attraction. This happy communication with the socially exotic is an important part of what Simon's character brings to the film.

As Juliette begins to realise in the two scenes previously discussed, there is a whole new world of experiences to discover in Père Jules's randomly accessible memory, if only she can succeed in coaxing and cajoling him into showing her some of his secrets and treasures. His cabin is a cabinet of curiosities, an imaginary museum of voyages and locations (without a readable map), of memories and stories (without a comprehensible history), and of knowledge and know-how (without a coherent science). The informal composition of the cabin's exhibits is reproduced on the sailor's scarred and tattooed body ('comme ça on n'a pas froid' ('that way you don't get cold')). Encouraged by Juliette, Père Jules decides to display his body-art by performing a tarantella on the accordion, while smoking a lighted cigarette in his navel. How could Juliette desire a more eloquent demonstration of Père Jules's hidden depths? How can she resist, aesthetically and epistemologically, this dancing collage of cuts and drawings, names and scars, places and graffiti? It is as if he were projecting an avant-garde travel film directly onto his body, and for her eyes only ... But the erotic and artistic promise of this extraordinary improvisation is deferred indefinitely, and the spell between Père Jules and Juliette is rudely broken, by Jean's violent misreading of their intimate situation. All he can see in his rage is an old faun having his hair combed by the woman that he loves. He starts smashing up the cabin and reproaching Père Jules for the uncivilised conditions in which he lives. 'Et cette photo?' ('And what's that photo?'), Jean cries, angrily pointing at a photograph of a young African woman. 'C'est moi quand j'étais petit' ('It's me when I was little'), Père Jules replies, non-sensically but understandably returning to his natural idiom of miscommunication. As Henri Langlois is reported to have said, 'Vigo a emporté son secret, *L'Atalante* porte en lui-même la solution de l'énigme' (*Les Voyages de L'Atalante*, Bernard Eisenschitz, France, 2001).[12] If that is true, then the character of Père Jules, both in terms of what he shows and what he conceals, is certainly part of the solution. Likewise, Simon's enigmatic performance is one of the film's unspeakable charms, which always bring us back to *L'Atalante*, each time ready for a new discovery.

References

Bompoint, J.-L. (1993), '*L'Atalante* de Jean Vigo: l'histoire d'une restauration', Centre culturel français de Groningen, Netherlands, September 1993, available at http://perso.club-internet.fr/bompoint/jl_bompoint.htm

Chardère, B. (ed.) (1961), *Jean Vigo*, Lyons, Premier Plan.

Chavance, L. (1955), 'Encore un mot sur *L'Atalante*', *Cahiers du cinéma*, 53, December, 55.

de la Bretèque F. (2002), 'L'histoire sans fin du "texte" filmique: que nous apprend la comparaison des diverses versions de *L'Atalante*?', *Archives*, 90–1, March, 7–13.

Feldman H. and J., and Weinberg, H. (eds) (1951), *Jean Vigo*, London, British Film Institute/New Index Series.

Lherminier, P. (1984), *Jean Vigo*, Paris, Pierre Lherminier/Filméditions.

Lherminier, P. (1985), *Jean Vigo: œuvre de cinéma*, Paris, Cinémathèque française/Pierre Lherminier.

Magny, J., and Tesson, C. (2002), 'Le paradoxe de *L'Atalante*', *Cahiers du cinéma*, 565, February, 62–71.

Porcile, F. (2002), 'La musique de *L'Atalante*', *Archives*, 90–1, March, 15–16.

Salles Gomes, P.E. (1988 [1957]), *Jean Vigo*, Paris, Seuil/Ramsay.

Waintrop, É. (2001), 'La double vie de *L'Atalante*', *Libération*, 9 July.

12 'Vigo took his secret with him, *L'Atalante* in itself holds the solution to the enigma.'

5

Visions of Vigo

> La légende qui auréole d'un halo romanesque et mystérieux les héros morts jeunes les emprisonne aussi comme un suaire.[1] (Chardère 1961: 89)

In this final chapter of our study, we shall consider how the critical reputation and historical status of Jean Vigo and his work have evolved in French cinema culture since the filmmaker's premature disappearance in 1934. We shall show that, within a decade or so of his death, this virtually unknown artist, whose modest corpus had at the time of its production scarcely made a mark in the spirit of the film-going public, was already on his way to becoming a vital legend of French cinephilia, as well as an inspirational hero for the younger generation of filmmakers and critics emerging in the post-war years. Indeed, as early as 1951, Vigo's unexpected posthumous glory – which we can only imagine would have raised an ironic smile from its irreverent beneficiary – was sufficiently well established to serve as the target of Gilles Jacob's respectfully sceptical article, first published in *Raccords*, spring 1951, 'Saint Jean Vigo, patron des ciné-clubs' ('Jean Vigo, Patron Saint Of Film Clubs'). Here the author observed that 'en moins de vingt ans, le massacreur d'idoles, le révolté, l'insulteur public numéro un, l'anti-conformiste, le guillotineur des valeurs établies est devenue une institution nationale aussi permanente que Louis Jouvet [...] à la Comédie Française' (Chardère 1961: 89).[2] For Jacob, the

---

1 'The legend that crowns with a fictional and mysterious halo those heroes who die young imprisons them also like a shroud.'

2 'In less than twenty years, the destroyer of idols, the rebel, the public insulter number one, the anti-conformist, the guillotiner of established values, has

romantic myth of Vigo as a *cinéaste maudit*, 'un génie mort trop tôt, avant d'avoir achevé son œuvre' ('a genius who died too young, leaving his work unfinished'), represents an intellectual obstacle to an accurate appreciation of the work's artistic merit. In fact, according to Jacob, Vigo was paradoxically 'lucky' to have made such an exceptional feature as *L'Atalante*, and then to have suddenly disappeared without having had time to disappoint his admirers with poorer films in later years. Thus while fortunately preserving him from subsequent mediocrity, Vigo's precocious death has led historians and critics to create a falsely perfect image of what is in reality, Jacob claims, an admirable but uneven legacy.

There is a good deal of wit and common sense in Jacob's sharply worded call to order and critical reassessment. In the following pages, however, we shall advance a more nuanced and, we hope, more generous vision of Jean Vigo's posthumous career. Chiefly we shall argue that 'the myth of Vigo' is neither a factual error nor a critical misinterpretation, which would therefore need to be corrected, but is rather a historical form that demands to be understood in the broader context of French cinema culture since the 1930s. A myth, then, for the purposes of this discussion, we shall define in these fairly neutral terms: 'a set of stories, ideas, desires and images, which gather around the name of an artist and together form an enduring cultural memory'. What is it about Jean Vigo that persists and insists in the collective consciousness of the French film world? What qualities does his name represent, what values does it embody, what dreams does it incite? How has Vigo's relationship to French cinema evolved in the last seventy years? And does it have a future? Is Jean Vigo still 'the Cinema incarnate', as Henri Langlois claimed so boldly in 1956? Or is his name merely the symbolic expression of a period of film culture that has definitively disappeared? These are some of the questions that we shall now address, as we pass through the impressive gallery of 'Visions of Vigo', which several generations of critics, historians and filmmakers have successively built for our collective remembrance and contemplation. Let us start by looking at three documents from 1934, the year of Vigo's death: a review, an obituary and a petition. We shall use these together to establish the three basic

---

become a national institution as permanent as Louis Jouvet [...] at the Comédie Française.'

elements of the Vigo myth – the aesthetic, the social and the political – which although encompassing the figure of the *cinéaste maudit*, as Gilles Jacob remarked somewhat sarcastically, in fact brings so much more than that cultural stereotype to post-war French cinema.

Forgotten, forbidden, foreclosed

One of the most interesting articles ever written about Jean Vigo was published by the great French art historian Élie Faure, in the film magazine *Pour vous*, 31 May 1934, shortly after he had seen the full-length and uncut version of *L'Atalante* at the film's trade screening. It is important to recall that Faure was not just a well-known art historian, whose multi-volume *Histoire de l'art* (1909–27) was for decades considered essential reading for anyone interested in the visual arts in France. He was also a major left-wing intellectual who from the earliest days of cinema had taken a genuine and well-informed interest in the emergence of this new, dynamic and popular form of expression. His portrayal of the filmmaker in this review of *L'Atalante* gives us therefore a particularly suggestive introduction to the story of Vigo's representations in French film culture:

> Les Français, a dit René Clair, le plus constamment heureux sinon le meilleur de nos cinéastes, ne comprennent rien au cinéma. C'est vrai. Pourquoi? Peuple plus loquace, sinon écouteur, que visuel. Bavard, ou plutôt aimant le bavardage, et le bavard. Éprouvant toujours le besoin de traduire l'image en mots, chose assez choquante, et probablement impossible, quelque peu sotte par surcroît. D'abord sensible au développement dialogué d'une intrigue romanesque, et par là indifférent à la beauté d'un éclairage, d'un rythme, d'un contraste, d'un volume, d'un passage, réalités pourtant nécessaires et suffisantes à définir le cinéma.
>
> C'est pourquoi les vrais cinéastes français sont rares, ou trop vite découragés. En voici un. Et son bilan devrait suffire à le classer. Jean Vigo? Un film oublié, parce qu'inattendu. Un film interdit, parce que d'une pensée trop amère, et subversive. Un film non encore projeté. Pourquoi? *À propos de Nice, Zéro de conduite, L'Atalante.*[3] (Lherminier 1984: 123)

3 'The French, said René Clair, the most consistently felicitous if not the best of our filmmakers, understand nothing about cinema. This is true. But why? As a people, they are loquacious (if not attentive), rather than visual. Talkative, or at

What is very striking about Faure's account of Vigo is the manner in which he situates the young filmmaker as both exception and example, in relation to the rest of French cinema and even in relation to the French as a people. Vigo is held up as an example precisely because he is an exception. He is rare, different, unexpected. And as such he can provide a model for filmmakers, now and in the future. Whereas the French understand nothing about cinema, Vigo is 'un cinéaste né' ('a born filmmaker'). Whereas the French, who like to talk a lot, therefore prefer a cinema of words and theatricality, Vigo intuitively grasps the essential virtues of the image and its silent language. In the early days of sound, then, Faure presents Vigo as an artist who is still in touch with the origins of film and its first three glorious decades of invention and expansion, but who is also young and bold enough to take French cinema forward, and into the unknown terrain of modern art and new social realities. As a cultural historian, Faure has a broad and ambitious vision of cinema's future evolution, and it is clear that he foresees therein a potentially important role for the young Jean Vigo, this 'born filmmaker' (as the title of the article proclaims). A role that is, precisely, to embody cinema's potential. What Faure could not have known in May 1934, of course, is that this debutant filmmaker would never have the chance to realise his early promise, and that his symbolic function would therefore be subtly transposed into something more ambiguous: an image of what cinema can still become, but also the image of what cinema might have been ... Perhaps Faure already knew that Jean was seriously ill, perhaps he was aware of the forthcoming mutilation of *L'Atalante*, but certainly we can detect a sense of foreboding in the art historian's triple résumé of Vigo's short career to date: 'un film oublié ... un film interdit ... un film non encore projeté'. Forgotten,

---

least liking talk and talkers. They always feel the need to translate the image into words, a fairly shocking thing, and probably impossible, as well as a little stupid. Primarily interested in the dramatic development of a novelistic intrigue, they are thereby indifferent to the beauty of lighting, of rhythm, of contrast, of depth, of movement, even though these realities are necessary and sufficient to define cinema. This is why true French filmmakers are rare, or are quickly discouraged. But here is one. And his record should speak for itself. Jean Vigo? A film that has been forgotten, because it was unexpected. A film that was banned, because its ideas were too harsh and subversive. And a film that has not yet been projected. Who knows why? These are *À propos de Nice*, *Zéro de conduite* and *L'Atalante*.'

forbidden, foreclosed. When we read these words, it is difficult to avoid the feeling that Élie Faure was intuitively projecting a vision of Vigo as already the *cinéaste maudit*.

As we shall see from our next document, the obituary for Vigo written by the journalist Frédéric Pottecher, it is the filmmaker's tragic death that will provide the second fundamental aspect of this profoundly suggestive and resonant myth. To the image of Vigo as an exceptional and exemplary artist is added, or superimposed, a 'phantom image' of the filmmaker as victim of society and martyr for the cause of art. Here then is Frédéric Pottecher's fine obituary for the filmmaker, which appeared with the title 'Jean Vigo est mort' ('Jean Vigo Is Dead') in the magazine *Comœdia* on 7 October 1934, just two days after Vigo's demise:

Hier, dans la soirée, nous avons appris la mort, à l'âge de 29 ans, des suites d'une affection septicémique, de Jean Vigo. Cette nouvelle inattendue, navrante, a tristement ému tous ceux qui connaissaient Vigo. Il commençait à peine à nous donner des preuves de son talent, non pas de metteur en scène, mais de poète des images vivantes. On a discuté beaucoup de la valeur de son dernier film, *Le Chaland qui passe*, film étrange où se trouve le meilleur et le pire. Vigo était surtout un poète, un lyrique. Il *voyait* ce que le commun des mortels ne distinguait pas, et il n'est pas étonnant qu'on l'ait si peu compris. Mais ceux qui ont eu la chance d'approcher ce garçon maigre, à la voix un peu sourde, d'une délicatesse de pensée et de manières exquises, ont pu apprécier les trésors que contenait cette âme d'élite, trésors irremplaçables et que Vigo sut parfois communiquer aux films qu'il tournait. Il y avait en lui quelque chose de neuf, une sensibilité, une pénétration des ambiances que seul il avait su tirer du néant. Pour exercer son art si personnel, si délicatement *novateur*, Vigo s'est tué de travail, car il cherchait sans cesse, dans tous les domaines, visions, techniques, jeux d'ombres et de lumières, tout était de lui, et ne pouvait être que de lui. C'est un artiste admirable qui disparaît. C'est une conscience d'artiste probe qui nous quitte. L'homme était charmant, très lettré, très raffiné, tendre et fort, sensible et direct, il savait vous toucher, et l'on sentait que tout ce qu'il disait, que tout ce qu'il faisait, jaillissait de son âme pure comme celle d'un enfant, et de son cœur d'artiste solide et sincère. Avant *Le Chaland qui passe*, Jean Vigo avait tourné *Zéro de conduite*, un film plein de trouvailles, et deux documentaires remarquables, qui eurent un grand retentissement (notamment celui qu'il consacra à la nage). À sa compagne, à Riéra, son plus fidèle ami, nous adressons l'expression de notre profonde et très émue affliction.[4] (Lherminier 1985: 29)

As is often the case when we read retrospectively the obituary of a famous person, this description of the recently deceased Vigo at first seems uncannily timeless, since our sense of the subject's immortality has long ago removed all traces of death's heavy hand. It is important therefore to recall the context in which this touching article was first written, and to acknowledge how the simple facts of Pottecher's journalistic report have become so familiar to us that it is hard to imagine what their impact might originally have been. Who would actually have read the obituary with anything other than the vaguest knowledge of who Jean Vigo was? Who would have really cared, for that matter, beyond those close friends and rare admirers, necessarily all too aware of the terrible news? For in talking of the eternal filmmaker's death, we should not forget that the mortal Jean Vigo really did pass away on 5 October 1934, and that 29 really is a terribly tender age to die. Nor should we undervalue Vigo's actual

---

4 'Yesterday evening, we learned of the death of Jean Vigo, aged 29, as a result of a septicemic ailment. This unexpected and deplorable news has moved to sadness all those who knew Vigo. He was only beginning to prove to us his talents, not just as a director but as a poet of living images. The merits of his final film have been much debated, *Le Chaland qui passe*, a strange film in which one finds both the best and the worst. Vigo was above all a poet. He saw what common mortals could not distinguish, and it's hardly surprising he was so misunderstood. But those who had the good fortune to meet this slender boy, with his slightly muted voice, his delicacy of thought, and his exquisite manners, were able to appreciate the riches that this elite soul contained, irreplaceable riches that at times Vigo succeeded in transmitting to the films he made. There was something about him that was new, a sensibility, a feeling for atmospheres that only he was able to rescue from nothingness. In order to exercise his highly personal and delicately *innovative* art, Vigo killed himself through work, for he was always searching, in every domain, visions, techniques, effects of light and shade. Everything came from him, and could only come from him. An admirable artist has disappeared. An honest artistic conscience has left us. As a man he was charming, well-read, very refined, tender and strong, sensitive and direct. He knew how to touch you, and you felt that everything he said, everything he did, sprang from his soul, pure like a child's, and from the robust heart of a sturdy and sincere artist. Before *Le Chaland qui passe*, Jean Vigo had made *Zéro de conduite*, a film full of discoveries, and two remarkable documentaries that had drawn much comment (especially the one he devoted to swimming). To his partner, and to Riéra, his most faithful friend, we should like to express our deep and heartfelt grief.'

achievement of having made four such films in such a brief life, a fact that repetition and familiarity can lead us to underestimate and neglect.

As for the human likeness drawn by Pottecher, it is perhaps more sombre than the generally upbeat testimony of Vigo's contemporaries. While it is true that he was physically slight, effectively haunted by a fatal illness, and that he was sensitive both to the world's suffering and in respect of his personal history, we should not forget that he was also tough, driven and determined. Moreover, the memoirs of his friends and associates tend to emphasise that Vigo was equally full of life, warm, outgoing, childlike, playful, even provocative. Little of the filmmaker's gaiety is conveyed by Pottecher's portrait, although this is hardly surprising in the circumstances. But otherwise we can already identify in the obituary most of the essential traits that would soon come to represent Vigo as an emblematic figure in French film mythology. The brutal prior fact of premature death. The real achievement and the impossible promise. The vision, the innovation, the risk. The unique signature, the interrupted work as an unrepeatable exception. The sense of a personal sacrifice for the greater glory of art ... In terms of French cultural history, many of these features derive from the Romantic archetype of the *poète maudit*, the poet condemned to social exclusion and early demise. This figure of the damned or cursed poet is of course represented in the English Romantic tradition by Keats, Byron and Shelley, each of whose prodigious poetic works was cut short by a tragic death. The French Romantic models include Alfred de Vigny's theatrical creation Chatterton in the stageplay of that name (1835), Alfred de Musset's literary self-portrait in *La Confession d'un enfant du siècle* (1836) and perhaps most powerfully the ultra-gifted and hyper-sensitive Gérard de Nerval, author of *Les Filles du feu* and *Les Chimères* (1854), whose brief life ended in madness and suicide. In the second half of the nineteenth century, Charles Baudelaire's literary translation and cultural transposition of Edgar Allan Poe became an ethical and aesthetic model for a second generation of *poètes maudits* (including Baudelaire himself, Paul Verlaine and a host of symbolists and decadents). This tendency culminated in the most hauntingly modern expression of the myth, Arthur Rimbaud, whose violent and rebellious life and intensely sibylline writings were to become the absolute reference point for experimental French literature throughout the twentieth century. It is thus the poet Rimbaud's ungraspable but imposing shadow that we may discern, not just behind Pottecher's highly typical representation of Vigo (which as a text is unique only because of its date and circumstances), but also across the whole spectrum of cultural visions of the filmmaker in general, especially as these developed in the 1940s and 1950s.

In terms of the broader evolution of French film culture, then, this persistent sense of Vigo as 'a poet of living images', via the link with Rimbaud, will provide the symbolic foundations for the post-war consecration of filmmakers as authentic and autonomous creators – or, to use the vocabulary of the New Wave critics twenty years after Vigo's death, as *auteurs* who are entirely and ethically responsible for the artistic creation of their works. It is paradoxical, to say the least, that cinema's modern specificity as an art form should derive from a literary model of authorship, when its earlier theorists had spent so much furious energy in the 1920s repelling the prior claims of liter-ature, both high and low, along with the despised theatre, and other logocentric forms. Yet the Vigo we begin to perceive in Pottecher's portrait is already the product of just such a cultural transformation. The ideal filmmaker will henceforth be considered a poet and not a mere 'director', since the term 'metteur en scène' is devalued by its theatrical overtones and its connotations of functionality. He will be a visionary like Rimbaud's *voyant*, with a personal creative vision that is discernible in his artistic signature. He will be an original thinker, an inventor of forms and a discoverer of truths. But this modern-day alchemist will be prepared to sacrifice all worldly goods, and ulti-mately his own life, thus becoming an exemplary martyr for the cause of art in general, and independent cinema in particular. In the French tradition, no single filmmaker has fulfilled this role of the *cinéaste maudit* with such mythical efficacy and historical good timing as Jean Vigo. Thus Gilles Jacob's critique of the 'saintly' image of Vigo as an impediment to a true appreciation of the filmmaker's work is accurate in its choice of target, but limited in its effective range. The stereotype of the *cinéaste maudit* certainly restricts our understanding of Vigo, if we only see its Romantic and melancholic aspects. What Jacob fails to grasp, writing in 1951, is the inspirational promise and creative potential which remain fully active in Vigo's after-image, and which therefore at any moment can return to life and energise French cinema in its next wave of renewal.

Give us his film!

Back in 1934, of course, Vigo's close friends and admirers had a very different sense of the significance of the filmmaker's death. Their personal sentiments of loss were mixed with feelings of anger at what they saw as the injustice with which their friend had been treated during his brief life. A fascinating illustration of this can be found in our third document, Claude Vermorel's 'Open Letter to the President of the Board of Film Control', published by *Pour vous* on 22 November 1934. The writer demanded that the ban on *Zéro de conduite* should be lifted, as immediate material reparation for the damage suffered by Vigo and his battered work, at the hands of the film industry and the cultural establishment:

> Nous venons vous prier très gentiment, Monsieur le Président, d'user de votre haute influence pour faire lever l'interdiction de *Zéro de conduite*, de Jean Vigo. Nous ne faisons pas d'illusion sur la difficulté de l'entreprise, car *Zéro de conduite* est un film subversif. On y voit des enfants fumer dans les cabinets alors que c'est interdit, un autre demander s'il peut 'y aller', ce qui n'est vraiment pas convenable. Le principal du collège, représentant l'Autorité est, hélas, un nain, à belle barbe noire il est vrai, mais bien qu'il le soit terriblement, on ne peut le prendre au sérieux. Il y a même un répétiteur de fantaisie qui suit les femmes dans la rue et qui va jusqu'à prendre un ecclésiastique pour une dame à cause de sa robe. On dira en effet ce qu'on voudra, et qu'il ne l'a pas fait exprès, et que c'est un poète, ce ne sont pas les choses à donner en exemple à des enfants. On voit pire, Monsieur le Président. À la fin du film, un sous-préfet et un capitaine des pompiers reçoivent des boites de conserves et de vieux livres de classe sur leur bel uniforme de cérémonie. Si l'on se met à se moquer des sous-préfets, où allons-nous? [...] Tout cela est intolérable, Monsieur le Président, et fort capable d'inciter des citoyens paisibles à descendre dans la rue ou à renvoyer leurs feuilles d'impôts. Déjà, des jeunes gens de très bonne famille avaient sifflé le film à sa présentation, usant ainsi à juste raison des droits de la critique. Mais, Monsieur le Président, Jean Vigo est mort. Il ne se moquera plus des sous-préfets, des ecclésiastiques et des principaux de collège. Donnez-nous son film![5] (Lherminier 1984: 119–20)

5 'We have come to ask you very kindly, Mister President, to use your considerable influence in order to have the ban lifted on *Zéro de conduite*, by Jean Vigo. We have no illusions about the difficulty of the task, for *Zéro de conduite* is a subversive film. One sees children smoking in the toilets, although this is

In this remarkable document, both vitriolic and grief-stricken, we can see the emergence of an explicitly political dimension to Vigo's mythological function. Whereas Élie Faure identifies the long-term aesthetic significance of the myth – Vigo exemplifying cinema as modern art – and Pottecher's text initiates its socio-cultural tendency – Vigo fulfilling the role of cinema's sacrificial victim – here we can see Vermorel introducing the third fundamental element, which is the idea that the filmmaker's work is ideologically dangerous and his martyrdom the symbol of a political struggle. Thus the personal grief of a friend is translated into the dark humour and sarcastic raillery so typical of the anarchistic tradition, into which Jean had of course been born, and to which Vigo and his gang had remained intellectually faithful. Along with his caustic tone, Vermorel's choice of targets is therefore familiar to us from the left–libertarian films of his late friend. The trappings of civil authority, in all its manifestations, the church, the state, the army, thus constitute the enemy against which liberty must fight in order to define itself, and to affirm its alternative cultural values. It is the pettiness of the bourgeoisie, its conservative ideology rather than its economic domination, which draws the sarcastic fire of Vermorel's anger. Similarly he targets the educational establishment, rather than the capitalist system, as the social citizen-factory that fabricates docile adults from raw and rebellious children. Looking at this ideological dimension of the Vigo myth in an historical perspective, we can already see in Vermorel's public letter of 1934 a reverse image of that triple-headed monster of conservative

---

forbidden, another child asking if he can 'go', which is really not acceptable. The college principal, representing authority, is, alas, a dwarf, with a nice black beard, it is true, but one cannot take him seriously, even though he certainly does. There is even a fanciful teacher, who follows women in the street, and even goes so far as to mistake a priest for a lady because of his robes. One can say what one likes, that he did not do it on purpose, that he is a poet, but these are not things to be shown as examples to children. There is worse, Mister President. At the end of the film, we see tin cans and old schoolbooks being thrown at a local government official and a captain of the fire brigade, in their fine ceremonial uniforms. If one starts disrespecting government officials, where will it end? All of this is intolerable, Mister President, and capable of inciting peaceful citizens to demonstrate in the street or to refuse to complete tax returns. Already, young people of good family have booed the film, exercising their legitimate rights to criticism. But, Mister President, Jean Vigo is dead. He will no longer laugh at officials, churchmen or college principals. Give us his film!'

France – 'Travail, Famille, Patrie' ('Work, Family, Fatherland') – which six years later was to take full advantage of the German invasion of 1940 in order to install its viciously repressive and ultimately murderous regime under Marshall Pétain. However, what Vermorel's choice of sarcastic tone and easy targets equally illustrates, again seen from a historical angle, are the serious political limitations of the libertarian left, not just in the 1930s, but beyond the Second World War, and into the 1950s and 1960s, when of course Jean Vigo and his films would become cultural symbols of youthful rebellion and utopian revolution. Thus Vermorel's petition, well intentioned but ineffectual, sarcastic but pleading, is symptomatic of a left-wing tradition that historically has preferred to remain within the politics of protest and gesture, unwilling or unable to fix a coherent strategy or assume responsibility for its ideals. Three decades after Vigo's death, this tendency reached a spectacular climax with the North American counter-culture of the 1960s, and in France with the legendary 'events' of May '68. Never a politically viable revolutionary project, the long-term influence of this libertarian left has been far more significantly expressed through cultural evolution. As an emblem of utopian idealism, and as an exemplary victim of 'the system', it is therefore historically appropriate that Vigo should become an important cultural vector of such an ideology.

Apart from these points of historical and political interest, Vermorel's text is also significant to our discussion of Vigo's posthumous reputation because of the heart-felt demand that it issues for the immediate liberation from censorship of *Zéro de conduite*. This 'Open Letter to the President of the Board of Film Control' is therefore the first symbolic act in the long and complex story of the restitution and restoration of the filmmaker's censored and mutilated works. We have already discussed this matter at some length in Chapters 3 and 4, but it is worth recalling here that in November 1945 the ban on *Zéro de conduite* was finally lifted, thus marking in material terms the symbolic rebirth of Jean Vigo into post-war French film culture. We can gather a sense of what the release of the film meant at the time, by turning to our fourth 'vision of Vigo', namely the review of *Zéro de conduite* published by the critic and screenwriter Pierre Bost in *L'Écran français*, 28 November 1945. Beyond its intrinsic value as a sympathetic analysis of the film, Bost's article is pertinent to our discussion because it poses the paradox of Vigo's 'future anteriority',

in other words the ambivalent sense in which this young filmmaker
of the past is perceived as a vital part of cinema's future:

> On présente enfin au public *Zéro de conduite*, de Jean Vigo, film
> célèbre et inconnu. L'œuvre date de plus de dix ans, elle fut interdite
> par la censure dès sa naissance, et depuis ce jour, les amis de Jean Vigo
> et du cinéma, qui se trouvaient être aussi les ennemis de la censure, se
> montraient le film en cachette et en parlaient beaucoup. Nous avions
> raison d'en parler. Maintenant, tout le monde peut le voir. Je ne dirai
> pas que la bataille soit gagnée, d'abord parce qu'il est trop tard: Jean
> Vigo est mort à vingt-neuf ans, après une carrière difficile, qui ne fut
> guère soutenue que par l'amitié, ce qui ne suffit pas au cinéma.
> Ensuite parce qu'on ne juge pas bien un film vieux de dix ans (la copie
> est, semble-t-il, imparfaite et incomplète), et surtout parce que nous ne
> saurons jamais ce que Jean Vigo aurait fait par la suite, les bénéfices et
> les leçons qu'il aurait tirés de sa propre victoire. Mais, justement, dans
> *Zéro de conduite*, ce qui est le plus émouvant, c'est peut-être, mieux
> encore que l'œuvre elle-même, mieux encore que cette découverte d'un
> passé, l'image d'un avenir qui ne s'est pas réalisé. L'avenir de Jean
> Vigo, d'abord. On l'a dit cent fois: il était l'un des mieux doués parmi
> les metteurs en scène de son âge, et il aurait bien fini par trouver les
> commanditaires et le public qu'ont trouvés les autres. Mais aussi, dans
> une certaine mesure, l'avenir du cinéma français.[6] (Chardère 1961: 72).

Despite the deceptively modest tone of Bost's remarks, this is quite a
remarkable claim that the critic is making for Vigo's strategic importance

6 'A famous and unknown film, Jean Vigo's *Zéro de conduite*, is finally presented
to the public. More than ten years old, the work was banned at birth by the
censors, and since then the friends of Jean Vigo and of cinema, who it so
happened were also the enemies of censorship, have secretly shown each other
the film and have talked about it a good deal. We were right to talk about it. Now
everyone can see it. I won't say that the battle is won, firstly, because it's too late:
Jean Vigo died at 29, after a difficult career that was barely even sustained by
friendship, which is insufficient in the cinema. Also because one cannot really
judge a film that's ten years old (apparently the print is imperfect and
incomplete), and above all because we shall never know what Jean Vigo would
have done subsequently, the advantages and lessons that he would have drawn
from his own triumph. But, precisely, what is most moving about *Zéro de
conduite* is perhaps, more than the work itself, even more than this discovery
from the past, the image of a future that never happened. The future of Jean
Vigo, firstly. It's been said a hundred times: he was one of the most gifted
directors of his generation, and he would have eventually found the backers and
the audience that others have found. But also, in a certain sense, the future of
French cinema.'

to French cinema in 1945. The path that Vigo would have taken is the path that French cinema can still take. Where French cinema will go, Jean Vigo will already have been. Two major points characterise this possible route for cinema: a critical attachment to the real, and the notion that cinema is an instrument of thought. Firstly, it is Vigo's documentary spirit and political verve that Bost identifies as those outstanding qualities of his work that can serve as a model for filmmakers. Thus *Zéro de conduite* is described as developing the earlier documentary research of *À propos de Nice*: 'Ce film, qui se déroule dans un internat de jeunes garçons, est presque, lui aussi, un documentaire, mais vivant, riche, chargé de sens, lourd d'amertume et d'ironie' (Chardère 1961: 72).[7] Here we can recognise one of the most important theoretical ideas in post-war French cinema, running from André Bazin, a contemporary of Bost's, right through to Serge Daney in the 1980s and 1990s: namely, the belief that film realism is not just a set of formal and narrative conventions, but that it implies an ethical duty to the real, regardless of whether it is labelled as 'documentary' or 'fictional' cinema. From the early 1950s, it is this ethical spirit of the real, this formal openness onto the world, which, following Vigo's example, many young socially conscious filmmakers, such as Chris Marker, Alain Resnais, Jean Rouch and Agnès Varda, would develop and illustrate in their early films. At the same time, their less politically committed comrades of the New Wave, such as Claude Chabrol, Jean-Luc Godard, Jacques Rivette and François Truffaut, were also drawing inspiration from *À propos de Nice*, *Zéro de conduite* and *L'Atalante*, for what they saw as their critical mission to revitalise the flagging forms of French narrative cinema. Apart from Vigo's concern for the real, which combines his documentary and political ambitions, Bost also makes an intriguing claim for the filmmaker's work as philosophical thought. Speaking of *Zéro de conduite*, he suggests that the satirical force of the film stems from an instability or volatility of tone, rather than from the precise nature of its targets: 'La censure ne s'y est pas trompée: elle ne tolère que la satire souriante, anodine, c'est-à-dire, finalement, un peu complice. Or *Zéro de conduite* est un film brusque, sans politesse, et qui passe, sans avertir, de

7 'This film, which takes place in a school for young boys, is almost, like *À propos de Nice*, a documentary, but lively and rich, loaded with meaning, heavy with bitterness and irony.'

l'aimable à l'acerbe'[8] (Chardère 1961: 72). This volatility is 'troubling',
according to Bost, not just for the censors but for any spectator:

> Et pourtant, il y a à travers tout le film un ton insolite, une dureté dans
> l'ironie, une lucidité découragée qui font un film très différent de
> toutes les autres histoires de collège. Ce n'est pas parce que les gamins
> se révoltent, ce n'est même pas parce qu'ils viennent chahuter,
> pendant la fête du collège, le principal, le préfet et l'abbé, que ce film a
> été interdit. On en a vu bien d'autres. Ce n'est même pas à cause de
> telle ou telle image: non; rien n'est violent dans ce film; rien n'est
> vraiment cruel. C'est à cause de l'auteur; non pas de Vigo person-
> nellement et nommément, mais parce que derrière ce récit il y a un
> homme qui pense à quelque chose, au-delà de ses images. Ce n'est pas
> fréquent. Et cela fait toujours un peu peur.[9] (Chardère 1961: 72)

In terms of the history of film theory, we should note that the term
'auteur' is used here by Bost in the fullest sense of 'artistic personality'
and 'embodiment of cinema as art', i.e. with exactly the same force
and value as it would soon come to acquire in the pages of the *Cahiers
du cinéma*. What is more important, however, is the fact that for Bost
there is something volatile and unsettling about this authorial figure,
this shady presence of thought, which is lurking behind the habitual
forms of cinema, ready to shake or frighten us out of our merely functional expectations as film consumers. This philosophical cinema,
then, is neither a cinema about philosophy, nor even a didactic cinema
of intellectual themes and big ideas. It is simply a cinema that makes
us think, that is prepared to run the risk of disrupting our illusions
and disturbing our consciences. In Vigo's name, Bost is thus advancing
a model of cinema that the *auteur* personally guarantees (whatever the

---

8 'The censors were not mistaken: they only tolerate satire that is funny, anodyne,
   i.e. somewhat complicit ultimately. But *Zéro de conduite* is a brusque film,
   without manners, that changes from the likeable to the acerbic, without
   warning.'

9 'And yet, there is throughout the film an unusual tone, a toughness in the irony,
   a disheartened lucidity that make it different from all other college stories. The
   film wasn't banned because the kids rebel, nor even because during the college
   festival they insult the headmaster, the government official and the bishop.
   Many other films have done as much. It's not even because of such and such an
   image: no, there's nothing violent in this film, there's nothing really cruel. It's
   because of the *auteur*; not Vigo personally or by name, but because there is
   behind the story a man who is thinking about something, beyond these images
   of his. It's uncommon. And it is always a little frightening.'

cost) as an art of discovery and interrogation. Is it an art of living, perhaps, as much as an art of representation and communication? If so, then in that sense alone it is a 'philosophical' cinema, a cinema of life.

There is surely a historic irony, however, in Bost's positioning of Vigo at the forefront of French cinema in 1945. How is it that, ten years after his death, the name of Jean Vigo can represent to Bost, and to many critics and filmmakers who would follow his example, the current state of French cinema as a lively, thinking art form? Does not Vigo rather represent a missed opportunity, a lost hope, which is made all the more evident and poignant by his tragically early demise? At the end of his piece, Bost comes to recognise that in temporal terms it is paradoxically, but precisely, *what Vigo will have been* that counts in the grander scheme of things, in the perspective of film history and cinema's future evolution. He sees that Vigo was (in the past) ahead of his time (part of the future). So today, Bost observes, while Vigo can certainly serve as an encouragement to filmmakers, an inspiring example for cinema's new movers and shakers, he is also necessarily a model that we must always regard with a backward glance, with a certain regret or sense of loss: 'J'avais tort de dire que Jean Vigo n'avait pas eu son avenir. Il l'a maintenant. Son avenir, c'est le passé des autres'[10] (Chardère 1961: 73). In this simple review, then, Bost foresees by a decade the whole problematic of modern cinema in France, especially as typified by the New Wave. From the late 1950s, and into the 1960s, French cinema embarks on a mission to rejuvenate and reinvent itself. Faced with the new realities of television, radio, music and advertising as the younger, more dynamic and expanding cultural forms, cinema's unquestionable primacy as the cutting-edge popular art form can no longer be taken for granted. So this modern cinema is born from an explosive tension between the old and the new, between tradition and adventure. On the one hand, a critical interrogation of film history, a formal re-actualisation of its silent masterpieces and Hollywood classics. On the other, an absolute headlong leap into the contemporary unknown, a new world where nothing is decided and everything is still possible. In one emblematic figure, the myth of Jean Vigo brings together such living images of the past and moving intimations of cinema's many futures.

---

10 'I was wrong to say that Jean Vigo had not had a future. He has it now. His future is the past of others.'

I dream of Vigo

For Vigo's critical reputation and cultural image, the 1950s and 1960s represent a period of consolidation and consecration. In 1950, Henri Langlois showed his restored version of *L'Atalante* at the 'Festival du Film de Demain' ('Festival of Films of Tomorrow'), an important stage in the long-term process of salvaging Vigo's masterpiece from abuse and neglect (see Chapter 4). At the same time, film historians began to take a more studious interest in Vigo's story, and a series of books and special issues, typically combining documents and testimonies with critical evaluations, appeared in France, England, Italy, the USA: *Ciné-Club* in 1949, *New Index Series* in 1951, *La Cittadella* and *Controcampo* in 1952, *Positif* in 1953, *Premier plan* in 1961, *Jeune cinéma* and *Études cinématographiques* in 1966. Most significantly, the curator of the Brazilian cinematheque, Paolo Emilio Salles Gomes, had by 1952 completed his immense scholarly quest to locate and reconstitute all the surviving personal, textual and photographic traces of Vigo's brief work and existence. This research eventually resulted in his 1957 study, *Jean Vigo*, which not only remains the simplest and best reference book on the subject, but also has come to be considered a classic of the genre. The double effect of Salles Gomes's biography was to demystify the image of Vigo as 'saint and martyr of the film clubs' (to paraphrase Gilles Jacob), without in any way destroying the positive and inspirational aspects of the Vigo myth. In other words, the rigorous research and documentary detail of the study returned Jean Vigo to the real world, to the social and political history of France in the early twentieth century, to the cultural context of the French film industry in the 1930s. As such, the book is neither a hagiographical 'life of the saint', nor a tragic account of the death of a *cinéaste maudit*. All Salles Gomes's love and admiration for Vigo and his films is expressed through the sheer hard work of trying to reconstitute an artist's life. As a result, the myth of Vigo – in the sense of an enduring and enriching cultural presence – is reinforced, deepened and rendered more tangible for future generations, thanks to Salles Gomes's remarkable endeavour.

If proof were required that the positivist researches of the historian are far from incompatible with the fervour of the cultural myth, one need only turn to Henri Langlois's memorable text of 1956, with which we began our study (see Chapter 1). Salles Gomes and Langlois were of course colleagues in the small but influential universe of international film conservation, and the Brazilian biographer even dedicated his *Jean Vigo* to the founder of the Cinémathèque française. Whereas Salles Gomes's contribution to the myth of Vigo, however, comes from the patient accumulation and analysis of documents, facts and testimonies, Langlois remains the master of the grand vision, imbued with an almost mystical sense of cinema's artistic mission, and of Vigo's exceptional place in that story:

> À voir ses films, on se rend compte qu'il est beaucoup plus qu'un metteur en scène, qu'il ne se contente pas d'épeler, qu'il n'explore pas une terre étrangère. Il y est né. C'est pourquoi il fait des films comme on respire. Il voit, il rêve, il pense, il écrit, il vit cinéma. Il est le résultat de trente-cinq ans d'images. Son premier film est le dernier des films muets et, là où chacun se trouvait déconcerté par la fin du silence, Vigo réussit d'emblée à prouver que le cinéma parlant c'est le cinéma à la puissance quatre. La magnificence visuelle de l'œuvre de Vigo s'explique: pour la première fois, l'image n'est pas telle que l'œil la voit, ni telle que l'objectif la voit, ni telle que l'objectif l'enregistre, mais telle qu'elle serait si l'objectif avait une vie propre, un cerveau. D'où cette féerie, cette transfiguration, cette découverte perpétuelle; l'inédit d'*À propos de Nice*. Mais personne n'a réussi encore à s'expliquer comment Vigo a su créer une photographie du dialogue et donner aux mots, sans qu'ils perdent leur signification, la valeur des sons. Nous le constatons dans *Zéro de conduite* ou *L'Atalante*, mais nous n'arrivons pas encore à comprendre à quoi cela tient et comment il a fait. Si le cinéma est un art du sommeil, il n'y a qu'un homme qui ait la clef des songes: Jean Vigo.[11] (Langlois 1986: 283–4)

11 'Seeing his films, one realises that he is much more than a director, that he wasn't content just to learn the language [of cinema], that he wasn't exploring a foreign country. He was born there. That's why he makes films as easily as breathing. He sees, he dreams, he thinks, he writes, he lives cinema. He is the result of thirty-five years of images. His first film is the last of the silent films and, whereas others were disconcerted by the end of silence, Vigo succeeded from the start in proving that talking pictures are cinema to the power of four. The visual magnificence of Vigo's work can be explained: for the first time, the image is not as the eye sees it, nor as the lens sees it, nor as the lens records it, but the image as it would be if the lens had a life of its own, a brain. Hence that fairyland, that transfiguration, that perpetual discovery; the unique work that is *À propos de Nice*. But nobody has yet succeeded in explaining how Vigo was able to create a photography of dialogue and give to words, without depriving them of their meaning, the value of sounds. We can witness this in *Zéro de conduite* or *L'Atalante*, but we can't understand yet how it works or how he did it. If the cinema is an art of sleep, there's only one man who holds the key to dreams: Jean Vigo.'

This brief but evocative text was written by Langlois for a catalogue accompanying the celebration of the Cinémathèque française's twentieth anniversary. It is worth noting that Vigo had played an important symbolic role in the founding of that venerable institution, since Langlois claimed that it was after seeing *L'Atalante* that he had decided to devote his life to film conservation rather than filmmaking. On the one hand, the impact of Vigo's inimitable work had made him realise that by comparison he would never amount to much as a creative artist (a rare case of Vigo discouraging someone from becoming a filmmaker), while on the other he saw that, if a great film like *L'Atalante* could be mistreated and discarded so brutally, then someone would have to fight for the protection and conservation of cinema, against the ravages of time and the indifference of the film industry. Perhaps it is this key role played by Vigo in his personal destiny that accounts for the extreme and exceptional importance that Langlois affords the filmmaker who in his eyes is 'the Cinema incarnate'. Indeed we could argue that Langlois's brilliant vision of 'the man who holds the key to dreams' represents in 1956 both a summary and summit of the Vigo myth to date, after which the cultural representations of the artist will generally assume a more prosaic form, with less grandiose ambitions. This is not to suggest that Langlois's vision is inflated or pretentious. It is just that few mortals have ever been possessed by quite such an overwhelming love and knowledge of cinema as the fervour that ran through Langlois's veins, and so to compete or take issue with the founder of the Cinémathèque is like telling Saint John that his gospel needs toning down a little. What this text conveys so boldly are three of the fundamental truths about Vigo's significance in French film culture. Firstly, we can identify the sense that for Langlois Vigo's work is deeply in touch with the very origins of filmmaking, an idea that he evokes through the marvellous image of cinema as a country, into whose language and habitat Jean Vigo was born, just as Mozart was no doubt born in music, and Picasso in painting. But the difference between cinema and these other arts is of course that its own birth is relatively recent, and thus Vigo is one of those rare artists who can exceptionally say that he is the same age as his art. What this means for Langlois, and for generations of French filmmakers and historians, is that Vigo is thus connected to the twin sources of cinema's invention and authenticity: Lumière and Méliès, documentary and fiction, the recording of the real and its transfiguration through magic and storytelling. As Langlois knew perfectly well, this vision of cinema's founding fathers is historically false (or at least a gross simplification), but for him the benefits of its mythical force far outweigh the inconvenience of factual inaccuracy. What matters for Langlois is the idea that Vigo embodies in one art a cinema of the real and a cinema of the imagination. Equally, and this is the second major point that Langlois raises, Vigo's work is crucially positioned at the transition to sound, in the late 1920s and early 1930s. Thus, just as Vigo has historical connections with cinema's origins as well as its modernity, so the four films that he made can be seen to straddle those critical years (in the sense of crisis and decision), when the 'loss' of silent film would for some be briefly mourned, while others (like Vigo) were already translating its visual powers into the new art of sound. There is no melancholy, therefore, in Langlois's extreme declaration that *À propos de Nice* is 'the result of thirty five years of images'. While it is clear to him that Vigo's whole experience of cinema was acquired in the silent era, Langlois insists very strongly that in *Taris ou la natation*, *Zéro de conduite* and especially *L'Atalante*, Vigo was ready to exploit and enjoy the fresh opportunities of recorded sound. In the longer term, following Langlois's vision, one could reasonably hypothesise about what Vigo might have done with colour, with 16mm cameras, with lightweight sound equipment, with video and, of course, with television. Thirdly, then, leading on from this speculation, Langlois poses the question of the unknown, the notion that Vigo's premature disappearance should make us aware of necessary limitations of our historical knowledge and critical understanding. Thus 'we can witness *Zéro de conduite* and *L'Atalante*, but we can't understand yet how it works or how he did it'. This sense of cinema's mystery, the secret of Vigo's art that we cannot understand, is an essential part of Langlois's vision, and a humble counterweight to his grandiosity and exaggeration. Twenty years later, he would return to this theme of the unknown, in the series of interviews that he granted a team of Canadian filmmakers in 1976. Nobody knows, he repeatedly insists, how a novice like Vigo managed to blend the materials of sound and image so perfectly as he did in *L'Atalante*, no more than art historians can explain how the artisans of the cathedral at Chartres obtained the perfect blue of their stained-glass windows (*Parlons cinéma: les anti-cours de Henri Langlois*, H. Fischbach, Canada, 1976). This is not, however, a reason for intellectual pessimism, nor an excuse for cultural melancholy. For Langlois, as for any true film-lover, the mystery of Vigo's unknown art is an incitement to further research and a promise of future discoveries.

Between the historical positivism of Salles Gomes and the poetic vision of Langlois, we can situate the last of our visions of Vigo, namely the study written by Pierre Lherminier in 1967 for the popular 'Cinéma d'aujourd'hui' ('Cinema of today') series, published by Pierre Seghers. In terms of French film culture, Vigo's inclusion in this collection reflects the continued importance of his reputation into the 1960s and beyond, since the series included only the most significant figures from film history and contemporary cinema. It is also important to note that a parallel collection by Seghers, 'Poètes d'aujourd'hui' ('Poets of today'), was devoted to the greatest names in classic and modern pœtry. The juxtaposition of filmmakers and poets in this way (the design and format of these books is identical) tells us a good deal about the equal cultural standing of these two arts, at the end of the New Wave and on the verge of May '68. If poetry was thus seeking to market itself for a broader readership, perhaps the *auteur* cinema that Vigo's name had come to symbolise was by now defini-tively moving in the opposite direction, away from the general film-going public and towards a more self-consciously motivated spectator, who would be willing to read a book about 'Bresson' or 'Vigo', as he or she might study 'Aragon' or 'Éluard'. Who can say what Jean's ghost might have said or done at the sight of such social advancement? The volume written by Lherminier is particularly relevant at this point of our discussion, precisely because it both confirms and questions Vigo's cultural assimilation, as a minor but significant 'national insti-tution' (to use Gilles Jacob's phrase). The late 1960s was a time when the traditional humanist values of the free-thinking left were under attack from a formidable army of Saussurian structuralists, Althus-serian marxists and Lacanian psychoanalysts. In contrast to this heady intellectual climate, Lherminier's book features all the classic pedagogical virtues of the Seghers series: the simple prose and ample illustrations, the semi-biographical and semi-critical portrait of the artist and his work, the invaluable documents and testimonies at the back of the book, and the detailed filmography and guidance for further reading. Likewise, the vision of Vigo projected by Lherminier is easy to recognise:

Aimer Vigo et l'admirer, c'est le plus souvent aimer et admirer quelque chose de plus que lui-même. Au même titre qu'aimer Rimbaud et l'admirer, c'est aimer et admirer quelque chose de plus que ce qu'il fut. C'est que leur destin à tous deux [...] a sa valeur et son sens propre, non pas en dehors ou au-delà de leur œuvre, mais de surcroît. Le destin de Rimbaud est pour nous aujourd'hui la source d'une certaine grande idée de la littérature, tout comme celui de Jean Vigo est déjà à son tour celle d'une certaine grande idée du cinéma. Mort à vingt-neuf ans après avoir vécu dangereusement et mis difficilement au jour une œuvre presque aussitôt soustraite à son public, Vigo a pris rang parmi ces artistes foudroyés qui donnent à l'art qu'ils ont illustré une caution irremplaçable, en le plaçant dès lors sous le signe de Prométhée. Plus encore que l'auteur d'une œuvre émouvante, belle, et fragile, Jean Vigo est dans l'histoire du cinéma une victime exemplaire, qui l'honore et qui le flatte, l'encourage à toutes les ambitions, et aide ceux qui placent très haut le septième art à se persuader qu'ils ont raison de le faire.[12] (Lherminier 1967: 5–6)

Although the passage succinctly rehearses some key elements of the myth (youth, loss, Rimbaud, sacrifice, promise), Lherminier also seems concerned in the late 1960s that this consensual image of Vigo, as exemplary exception and social martyr, will eventually obscure the beauty and complexity of the work, or at least will weaken our appreciation of its original and caustic qualities. In response to this danger, Lherminier expresses a modestly iconoclastic desire to strip Jean Vigo of his mythological accoutrements, and examine the man and the films for what they are truly worth:

12 'To love Vigo, and to admire him, is usually to love and admire something more than Vigo himself. In the same way that to love Rimbaud and to admire him is to love and admire something more than what Rimbaud was. Their destiny in both cases [...] has its own value and its own meaning, not outside or beyond their work, but in addition to it. Rimbaud's destiny is for us today the source of a certain grand idea of literature, just as Jean Vigo's destiny is already in its turn the source of a certain grand idea of cinema. Dead at 29, after having lived dangerously and having with difficulty given birth to a work which was almost immediately removed from its public, Vigo has taken his place among those thunder-struck artists who give the art-form in which they have excelled an irreplaceable legitimacy by henceforth placing it beneath the sign of Prometheus. Even more than the author of a moving, beautiful, fragile work, Jean Vigo is in the history of cinema an exemplary victim, who honours and flatters cinema, encourages it in all its ambitions, and helps all those who place the seventh art very high to convince themselves that they are right to do so.'

> Je rêve en somme d'un Vigo démythifié, c'est-à-dire vivant, présent,
> charnel; dont la brève existence pèserait le poids d'une vie d'homme,
> pas moins, mais pas davantage; dont l'œuvre imparfaite apparaîtrait
> telle qu'elle est, confidence et création d'un certain homme, à un
> certain moment de l'histoire d'un art encore occupé à chercher sa
> direction et ses moyens. Un Vigo sans magie, et sans 'mise en scène',
> dans la lumière crue de la simple vérité.[13] (Lherminier 1967: 6)

To some extent we share this dream, insofar as we have endeavoured
in this study to examine the films in their cultural context, to speak
simply of their genesis, their production, their formal and thematic
complexities, as if the myth of Vigo did not exist to interfere with our
critical perceptions and historical enquiries. But as Lherminier's
phrase perhaps unwittingly reveals, that ideal of demythification is
already itself an illusion: 'I dream in the end of a Vigo ...'.

The fact is that, as lovers of French cinema, we cannot just rid
ourselves of this important cultural myth, since Vigo's example is part
of the very reason why we love cinema in the first place. Indeed it
would be perverse to try to eliminate the myth, since the cultural
values that Vigo represents – political commitment and ethical
realism, formal experiment and playful humour – are as vital to the
healthy memory of French cinema, as they are to its future artistic
evolution. To Lherminier's great credit, the subsequent works of this
cinephile historian have illustrated the persistent paradox of the Vigo
myth with lucidity and devotion. Not only did Lherminier produce in
1984 a revised and, one might say, slightly 'demythified' version of
his 1967 text, he is also responsible for one of the most detailed and
rigorous historical tributes ever devoted to a single filmmaker, the
splendid *Jean Vigo: œuvre de cinéma*, published with the Cinémathèque française in 1985. This beautifully illustrated, 500-page volume
contains shot-by-shot descriptive scenarios of the four films, and
reproduces Vigo's extant theoretical writings. It even includes all the
available textual evidence of the synopses and scripts that the film-

13 'I dream in the end of a Vigo who has been demythified, that is to say who is
   living, present, flesh and blood; whose brief existence would be judged as the
   life of a man, no less, but no more; whose imperfect work would appear for what
   it is, the confession and creation of a certain man, at a certain moment in the
   history of an art-form which was still in the process of searching for its direction
   and its means. A Vigo without magic, and without "mise en scène", in the crude
   light of simple truth.'

maker is known to have worked on, thus providing the contemporary reader with a fascinating insight into the films that the young artist might one day have gone on to make. Along with Salles Gomes's biography (some of whose minor factual errors Lherminier corrects in his later work), the *Œuvre de cinéma* is one of the three fundamental pieces of film scholarship that have given real historical substance to the myth of Vigo, to those multiple stories and visions of the artist that we have presented and discussed in this concluding chapter. The third element, of course, is the long and patient work of restoration, at first carried out by individuals such as Henri Beauvais, Henri Langlois and Salles Gomes, but more recently taken into the realm of institutional sponsorship and the latest scientific techniques, notably through the persistent endeavours of Gaumont, since the late 1980s, to redeem themselves for their original sin of nearly destroying *L'Atalante*. These three modes of historical activity – contextual research, critical scholarship and film restoration – have combined to give Vigo's once fragile and ghostly image a solidly material presence in the world of contemporary cinema. Not only have their findings informed our current study at every stage of its progress, they also provide today an inspiring example for students and scholars, curators and cinephiles, indeed for anyone who is interested in the memory of cinema and its continuing creative evolution as a modern art.

The films of my life

In 1975, François Truffaut wrote in *Les Films de ma vie* ('The Films Of My Life') a text that has become the most frequently quoted account of the discovery of Vigo's cinema:

> J'ai eu le bonheur de découvrir les films de Jean Vigo en une seule séance un samedi après-midi de 1946 au Sèvres-Pathé grâce au ciné-club de 'La Chambre Noire' animé par André Bazin et les autres collaborateurs de *La Revue du cinéma*. J'ignorais jusqu'au nom de Jean Vigo mais je fus pris aussitôt d'une admiration éperdue pour cette œuvre dont la totalité n'atteint pas 200 minutes de projection. Bien que n'étant pas accoutumé à voir les films tournés avant 1942, j'ai d'abord sympathisé avec *Zéro de conduite*, probablement par identification. Ensuite, à force de voir et revoir les deux films, j'en suis venu à préférer définitivement *L'Atalante*, qu'il me sera toujours impossible

d'oublier lorsque je suis amené à répondre aux questionnaires du type: 'Quels sont, selon vous, les 10 meilleurs films du monde?'[14] (Lherminier 1985: 15)

If we choose to cite this brief extract from Truffaut's substantial article, here, in the closing pages of our study, it is not for the intrinsic value of the great French filmmaker's thoughts about Vigo, nor indeed for the insight that the passage offers into the film-club culture of post-war France. It is rather because it will help us to pose an important question, which has remained invisible until now. Namely, 'What direct influence has Jean Vigo had on other filmmakers?'. Apart from the cultural presence of Vigo, his role as a historical precursor and artistic example, where can we actually locate the tangible traces of his films in the work of his followers and fans? This is potentially a vast new area of investigation, whose limits would depend on the definitions and parameters that one imposes on the notoriously vague notion of 'influence'. So here we shall restrict ourselves to a few brief remarks, which we hope will provide the basis for further research. Four possible categories of traces of Vigo's influence spring to mind: (a) quotations; (b) remakes; (c) portraits; (d) the Vigo prize. Let us look at them one by one, and discuss some significant examples of each type of influence.

Quotations

In the first category, we could include all those films, or rather those moments of films, where there exists a clear citation of a work by Vigo, or an implicit allusion to one of his works. We recall how Boris Kaufman described as 'a quotation from Chaplin' (see Chapter 3) the moment in *Zéro de conduite* when Jean Dasté imitates Chaplin's walk in the school playground, and the children watch him from behind, as

14 'I had the good fortune to discover the films of Jean Vigo in a single screening, one Saturday afternoon in 1946, at the Sèvres-Pathé cinema. It was thanks to the film-club run by André Bazin and his colleagues at *La Revue du cinéma*. I did not even know who Vigo was, but I was immediately seized by a boundless admiration for this work, whose total length was less than 200 minutes. Although I was not used to watching films made before 1942, I was drawn at first to *Zéro de conduite*, probably by identification. Later, having watched both films repeatedly, I came to prefer *L'Atalante*, definitively. The latter film will always come to mind whenever I am asked to reply to one of those questionnaires: "Which are, according to you, the ten greatest films in the world?".'

in *Easy Street* (1917). We find numerous examples of such quotation from Vigo in Truffaut's *Les Quatre cents coups* (1959): for example, when the children's outing in Paris with the sports teacher reproduces the comic disorder of *Zéro de conduite*'s promenade in Saint-Cloud. The function of this homage to Vigo is symbolic for those who recognise the connection, but it is not in anyway necessary to the clear understanding of the film's narrative or thematic development. It establishes a communal link between the *auteur* François Truffaut and his spiritual precursor, Jean Vigo, very much in the manner of a dedication. In Truffaut's case, as he explained in *Les Films de ma vie*, the initial connection that he felt with the Vigo of *Zéro de conduite* was an emotional identification (via their shared experience of an unhappy childhood) rather than a desire for artistic emulation. This would come later for Truffaut, notably through his 'definitive' admiration for *L'Atalante*, which served as an absolute standard against which he could measure himself as a creative artist. In the cinema of the last fifty years, we can identify a number of similar instances of quotation of Vigo. For example, in Bernardo Bertolucci's *Last Tango in Paris* (1972), when Jean-Pierre Léaud is filming his girlfriend Maria Schneider around the Canal Saint-Martin, he gives her a lifebuoy with 'L'Atalante' written on it. She then throws it into the water, and we watch it sink, as a presage of the film's tragic ending. On the contrary, at the end of Jean-Charles Tacchella's *Travelling avant* (1985), the young cinephile couple return to the church at Maurecourt from the opening of *L'Atalante*, as a way of symbolically sealing their love. In Leos Carax's *Les Amants du Pont-Neuf* (1991), the romantic couple of marginals plunge into the waters of the Seine, and when they resurface a barge called *L'Atalante* passes by, as if to signal that Vigo is watching over their filmic and amorous destiny. Finally, in Emir Kusturica's *When Father Was Away on Business* (1985), there are repeated allusions to the sleepwalking boy from *Zéro de conduite*, while the same director's *Underground* (1995) extensively reworks the famous underwater scene from *L'Atalante*. In each case, one would need to look closely at the exact form of the quotation or allusion, its place in the narrative and thematic structure of the film, and also the external connections between the filmmaker in question and the work of Vigo (all the filmmakers mentioned here, it so happens, have made explicit statements about their love and admiration for the master's cinema).

Remakes

The most celebrated example of Vigo's direct influence on a film-maker is no doubt Lindsay Anderson's *If...* (1968), which is a dramatic transposition of *Zéro de conduite* to an English private boarding school at the end of the 1960s. Here the term 'remake' does not imply a shot-for-shot reconstruction (as in Gus Van Sant's *Psycho*, 1998), nor even a faithful reproduction of a classic film for contemporary audiences (Todd Haynes's *Far from Heaven*, 2002). What Anderson does so powerfully in *If...* is to invent a form of creative criticism. He takes the broad narrative outline of *Zéro de conduite*, the basic dramatic premise, the 'instability of tone' identified by Pierre Bost in his review, and above all the film's rebellious fervour. Then he re-ignites the whole explosive ensemble of inflammable parts in a new social setting and for a different political era. Made in 1968, the film is often cited for its end-of-an-era spirit of joyous nihilism. Its tone is certainly darker and more pessimistic than the upbeat revolutionary transcendentalism of *Zéro de conduite*, thirty-five years earlier. The question that Lindsay Anderson poses most critically for film historians is: 'What kind of a film would Vigo have made in the late 1960s?'. Would the innocent kids of *Zéro de conduite* have swapped their schoolbooks for machine guns? Would the psychedelic distortions of *If...* have replaced the transcendental utopia of the 1930s? Does a post-revolutionary heaven really lie just over the horizon? Or is there a darker vein of violence in the desire for social upheaval? Inspired and interrogative, Anderson's remake thus becomes a historical and aesthetic critique of Vigo's classic work.

An equally suggestive, but very different, variant of the remake is provided by Manoel de Oliveira's *Nice, à propos de Vigo* (1983), which was commissioned by INA (the French National Audiovisual Institute), as part of a television series about France's diverse immigrant communities. Oliveira, it should be noted, was born in 1908, just three years after Vigo, and is officially considered the oldest living filmmaker active in the world. As such, the very idea of the veteran Portuguese director remaking a film by cinema's most famous young fatality is particularly touching and thought-provoking. It serves to remind us that Vigo belonged to the same French generation of film-makers, for example, as Marc Allégret (1900), Yves Allégret (1907), Claude Autant-Lara (1903), Jacques Becker (1906), Robert Bresson

(1907), Marcel Carné (1909), Henri-Georges Clouzot (1907), Jean Delannoy (1908), and so on. In international terms, one can briefly pause to reflect that Vigo's career would have run in historical parallel to that of Luis Buñuel (1900), John Huston (1906), David Lean (1908), Vincente Minnelli (1906), Max Ophüls (1902), Yasujiro Ozu (1903), Michael Powell (1905), Otto Preminger (1906), Roberto Rossellini (1906), George Stevens (1904), Luchino Visconti (1906) and Billy Wilder (1906). It is a vertiginous idea to think that most of these great names were making their finest work in the 1950s and 1960s, twenty or thirty years after Vigo's death. As for Oliveira's remake of *À propos de Nice*, it is a very subtle and evocative updating of Vigo's experimental documentary. Partly it restages certain shots and sequences of the original in a modern city that now looks, sounds, and feels so different fifty years later, partly it refocuses the entire enquiry on the specificity of Nice's Portuguese community and residents. In this way Oliveira, like Anderson, produces a work of critical imitation, retesting Vigo's premises and methods for a different age. The film closes on a long and very moving shot of Luce Vigo, now 52 years old in 1983, who ironically evokes both the honours that she has received because she is Jean Vigo's daughter, and the dishonour and injustice experienced by her father, and by Miguel Almereyda, during their brief lives. Finally, in this category of remakes, we should mention *À propos de Nice, la suite*, the highly ambitious and multi-authored tribute to Vigo, produced by François Margolin in 1995. The list of directors is as impressive as it is diverse: Catherine Breillat, Costa-Gavras, Claire Denis, Raymond Depardon, Abbas Kiarostami and Parviz Kimiavi, Pavel Lungin and Raoul Ruiz. Most of the episodes take Vigo's original as a springboard for formal remotivation and thematic speculation. Some redirect *À propos de Nice* towards contemporary fictional sketches set in the city (Denis 'Nice, Very Nice', Ruiz's 'Promenade'), while others remain faithful to the experimental documentary spirit of their model (Breillat's 'Aux Niçois qui mal y pensent', Costa-Gavras's 'Les Kankobals'). Perhaps the most intriguing and intelligent episode is 'Repérages', written by Kiarostami for Kimiavi, in which the latter plays a Franco-Iranian film director looking for Vigo's original locations in Nice. He discovers one of the women who, sixty-five years earlier, had appeared in *À propos de Nice*, frenetically dancing the cancan with Vigo at the end of the film. Kimiavi finds her working in a bar, and the two characters, artist and model, watch the film on video, and discuss the issues raised by Vigo's participation in his own work. Thus 'Repérages' cleverly combines those qualities of ethical realism, ludic experiment, and social contextualisation, which in this instance Vigo's ghost seems successfully to have transmitted to the younger generation.

Portraits

In our third category, films explicitly about Jean Vigo, there is one work that stands out as one of the most fascinating and poignant documentaries about a filmmaker ever made. This is Jacques Rozier's contribution to the famous 'Cinéastes d'aujourd'hui' ('Filmmakers of today') television series, produced by Janine Bazin and André S. Labarthe in 1964. We have drawn on this film repeatedly in the course of our study, and it remains an invaluable resource for anyone interested in Vigo's work. But Rozier's documentary should also be celebrated for its intrinsic qualities as a film in its own right. Beyond the documentary's evident subject, *Jean Vigo* captures a significant moment in French audiovisual culture, when television and cinema were briefly promiscuous partners, rather than divorced enemies or pimp-and-prostitute. The opening scene of Rozier's documentary takes place in a TV studio, where we see Vigo's former collaborators, Gilles Margaritis and Pierre Merle, directing a popular variety show, which is about to go out live. These exciting and energetic sequences could be lifted straight from Rozier's fictional New Wave feature, *Adieu Philippine* (1963), which also take place in the milieu of early French television. Thus Rozier's dynamic documentary is a pure product of technological miscegenation in the early 1960s. As such, it provides a fascinating glimpse of where Vigo's artistic career might have led him, in the age of television.

Thirty years later, at the other extreme of artistic excellence, we find Julien Temple's sincere and sentimental biopic, *Jean Vigo: a Passion for Life* (1997). This melodramatic reconstitution of the filmmaker's life reproduces every conceivable cliché about Jean Vigo as the *cinéaste maudit*, with no critical distance and little sense of history. As for the film's political content, *Jean Vigo: a Passion for Life* presents a caricature of Almereyda's anarchist ideology. 'Imagine a world', opines one character, 'in which teachers can learn from children, in which cobblers can be kings, in which parents can no longer tell children what to do!'. In response to which a young child cries: 'Mummy, I want to be an anarchist!'. However, despite all the film's faults, it is impossible not to feel sympathy for Temple's good intentions, which he expresses in a written message at the end: 'Jean Vigo opened my eyes to cinema. In telling my version of his story, I hope in some way to repay my debt to him and encourage others to find their own inspiration in his films.'

Between Rozier's admirable documentary and Temple's mediocre fiction, there exists a third manifestation of this portrait category, best illustrated by the place that Vigo has come to occupy in the historical video works of Jean-Luc Godard. It is worth noting that Godard's *Les Carabiniers* was dedicated to Vigo in 1963, a fact that should probably make us include the film as a 'homage' in our quotations category. However, the more intriguing and persistent signs of Vigo's presence in Godard's creative imagination are to be found in the great director's later works. For example, in *Grandeur et décadence d'un petit commerce de cinéma* (1986), the cultural memory of Vigo is represented by the comical character of the disabused film producer, 'Miguel Almereyda', played by Jean-Pierre Mocky. In real life, Mocky is of course the kind of maverick independent filmmaker that Vigo might have become in later years, struggling to sustain a career in the margins of the industry. Ten years later, we find a more lyrical image of Vigo in *2 fois 50 ans de cinema français* (1995), a video work commissioned by the British Film Institute for its 'Century of Cinema' series. This historical essay, co-directed by Godard and Anne-Marie Miéville, closes on a sustained double elegy to the twin 'angels' of French cinema: Henri Langlois, its guardian angel at the Cinémathèque française, and Jean Vigo, its angelic messenger, announcing the second coming of the New Wave. The anarchist singer and composer, Léo Ferré, provides a politically resonant accompaniment to this moving tribute. Also from the 1990s, we can remark a similar passage in chapter 3B of *Histoire(s) du cinema*, 'Une Vague Nouvelle'. Here Vigo appears as a more ambiguous national emblem of French cinema. In this case, it is difficult to tell whether he is the angel announcing the good news of French cinema's future rebirth, or if his symbolically early demise rather represents a melancholic foresight of the New Wave's failures and broken promises. In Godard's historical videos, as in Philippe Garrel's film essay, *Les Ministères de l'art* (1988) – a sombre meditation on the world-weary state of the post-New Wave generation of filmmakers at the end of the 1980s, in which Vigo appears as a symbol of loss and despair – we can feel the full historical ambivalence of the Vigo myth, profoundly experienced and eloquently expressed. For both artists, he incorporates a powerfully melancholic image of mourning for the death of an art form, while at the same time conveying the promise of cinema's renaissance from the ashes.

The Prix Vigo

Our final category of influence, the Prix Jean Vigo ('the Jean Vigo prize'), although the least directly connected to Vigo's films in material terms, is perhaps the most culturally significant manifestation of the filmmaker's abiding presence in French cinema. The prize was founded in 1951 by the writer Claude Aveline, whom Vigo had met in the Font-Romeu clinic in the late 1920s, and who would later act both as the executor of the filmmaker's estate, and as legal guardian to Luce Vigo, after her mother's death in 1939. Alongside filmmakers Jacques Becker and Jean Cocteau, as well as the critic and screenwriter Pierre Bost, Aveline assembled an impressive committee for the adjudication and attribution of the Prix Vigo, including the film historians Paul Gilson and Georges Sadoul, and the critics Maurice Bessy and Georges Charensol (Marie 1991: 9–11). The aim of the prize is to identify young talent and reward those filmmakers who are ready to take risks, both with the experimental form and the political content of their work. The official citation declares that the Jean Vigo prize will be awarded to 'films produced in France which are characterised by their independence of spirit and the originality and quality of their realisation'. Films, in other words, which reflect the artistic values and ethical commitment of Jean Vigo's legacy to French cinema. When we look at the role-call of prize-winners since 1951, we therefore discover not just a rich inventory of independent cinema in France in the last fifty years, but also a vividly suggestive and, alas, virtual filmography of all the works that Vigo might have signed in his impossible later career. How would a mature Vigo, for example, have dealt with the violent contradictions of France's post-war decolonisation? Perhaps with an ironic pamphlet such as Alain Resnais and Chris Marker's *Les Statues meurent aussi* (1953). How would he have responded to France's responsibilities in the

Holocaust, and to cinema's impossible duty to render the horror of the concentration camps? Maybe with a lyrically restrained essay like Alain Resnais and Jean Cayrol's *Nuit et brouillard* (1955). Would Vigo, at the age of 50, have encouraged the New Wave to adopt a more explicitly political direction? We can ponder this question as we review Claude Chabrol's *Le Beau Serge* (1957) and Jean-Luc Godard's *À bout de souffle* (1959). Would he have recognised elements of his own *Zéro de conduite* in Yves Robert's popular and more sentimental children's film *La Guerre des boutons* (1961)? Would he have followed Chris Marker's *La Jetée* (1962) down the path of narrative experimentation and post-nuclear allegory? Or would he have turned to the historical montage of Frédéric Rossif's Spanish Civil War documentary *Mourir à Madrid* (1962)? Might he have embraced the playful Pop Art satire of William Klein's *Qui êtes-vous, Polly Magoo?* (1965)? Or might he rather have pursued the savage realism of Maurice Pialat's *L'Enfance nue* (1967)? We can follow this speculative line all the way through to the present day, when the committee for the Prix Jean Vigo is led by filmmaker Agnès Varda, with Luce Vigo remaining its honorary president. But such speculation is not just a party game for cinephiles. What these hypothetical questions make us realise is something much more fundamental. In fact, Jean Vigo's talent was so versatile and inventive that he could probably have made any or all of the ninety or so features and shorts, fictions and documentaries, which have thus far received the prize that bears his name. The award is not only a great honour for each year's promising recipient, therefore, it is also an enduring expression of the diversity, openness and resplendent freedom that Jean Vigo has donated to the filmmakers who have followed his unique example. With this gift, may cinema remain for ever young.

References

Chardère, B. (ed.) (1961), *Jean Vigo*, Lyons, Premier Plan.

Langlois, H. (1986), *Écrits*, Paris, Cahiers du cinéma/Cinémathèque française.

Lherminier, P. (1967), *Jean Vigo*, Paris, Seghers.

Lherminier, P. (1984), *Jean Vigo*, Paris, Pierre Lherminier/Filméditions.

Lherminier, P. (1985), *Jean Vigo: œuvre de cinéma*, Paris, Cinémathèque française/Pierre Lherminier.

Marie, M. (1991), 'Préface', *Prix Jean Vigo 1951–1991*, Paris, Ramsay, 9–11.

Filmography

Films by Jean Vigo

À propos de Nice, 1930, France, 23 mins, 35mm, b/w, silent

Direction: Boris Kaufman and Jean Vigo
Scenario: Jean Vigo
Camera: Boris Kaufman
Editing: Boris Kaufman, Jean Vigo
Filmed February–March 1930 in Nice
Premiere: 28 May 1930, Théâtre du Vieux-Colombier, Paris
Notes: the version available on *L'Intégrale Jean Vigo* (Gaumont, 2001) features musical accompaniment by Marc Perrone. Some sources give the length of the film as up to 42 mins.

Taris ou la natation, 1931, France, 9 mins, 35mm, b/w, sound

Production: GFFA
Artistic director for *Le Journal vivant*: Constantin Morskoï
Direction: Jean Vigo
Assistant: Ary Sadoul
Scenario: Jean Vigo
Camera: G. Lafont, Lucas
Editing: Jean Vigo
Cast: Jean Taris (as himself)
Filmed January 1931, mainly at swimming pool of Racing-Club de France, Paris.
Notes: also known as *Taris, roi de l'eau* and *La Natation par Jean Taris, champion de France*

Zéro de conduite, 1933, France, 42 mins, 35mm, b/w, sound

Produced by Jacques Louis-Nounez (Argui Films) and GFFA
Direction: Jean Vigo
Scenario: Jean Vigo
Assistants: Albert Riéra, Pierre Merle
Production manager: Henri Storck
Camera: Boris Kaufman, Louis Berger
Sound: Marcel Royné, R. Bocquel
Editing: Jean Vigo
Music: Maurice Jaubert
Song lyrics: Charles Goldblatt
Make-up: Massard
Cast: Jean Dasté (Huguet), Robert Le Flon (Parrain, 'Pète-Sec'), Blanchar aka
    Du Verron (General Supervisor, 'Bec-de-Gaz'), Delphin (College
    Principal), Léon Larive (Chemistry Teacher), Madame Émile (Mother
    Beans), Louis de Gonzague-Frick (Government Prefect), Louis Lefebvre
    (Caussat), Gilbert Pruchon (Colin), Coco Golstein/Constantin Kelber
    (Bruel), Gérard de Bédarieux (Tabard), Louis Berger (Correspondent),
    Henri Storck (priest), Rafaël Diligent, Félix Labisse, Georges Patin,
    Georges Vakalo (Firemen), Michelle Fagard (Little Girl), Albert Riéra
    (Watchman), Georges Belmer, Émile Boulez, Maurice Cariel, Jean-
    Pierre Dumesnil, Igor Goldfarb, Lucien Lincks, Charles Michiels,
    Roger Porte, Jacques Poulin, Pierre Regnoux, Ali Ronchy, Georges
    Rougette, André Thille, Pierre Tridon, Paul Vilhem, Natale Bencini,
    Leonello Bencini (Children)
Filmed 24 December 1932 to 22 January 1933 at college and in streets of
    Saint-Cloud; also at Belleville-La Villette railway station, and at
    Gaumont studios, Buttes-Chaumont, Paris
Premiere: banned after its trade premiere 7 April 1933, the film was first
    shown commercially in France in November 1945, at the Panthéon
    cinema, Paris

L'Atalante, 1934, France, 85 mins (2001 version), 35mm, b/w, sound

Production: Jacques Louis-Nounez and GFFA
Direction: Jean Vigo
Scenario: Jean Vigo, Albert Riéra (original synopsis and scenario by Roger
    de Guichen, aka Jean Guinée)
Assistant directors: Albert Riéra, Pierre Merle
Production manager: Henri Arbel
Camera: Boris Kaufman, Louis Berger, Jean-Paul Alphen
Sound: Marcel Royné, Lucien Baujard
Editing: Louis Chavance

Script assistants: Jacqueline Morland, Fred Matter
Music: Maurice Jaubert
Song lyrics: Charles Goldblatt
Design: Francis Jourdain, Max Douy
Make-up for Michel Simon: Chakatouny
Stills photographer: Roger Parry
Cast: Jean Dasté (Jean), Dita Parlo (Juliette), Michel Simon (Père Jules), Louis Lefebvre (the Kid), Gilles Margaritis (the Camelot), Fanny Clar (Juliette's Mother), Raphaël Diligent (Raspoutine), Maurice Gilles (Manager of Waterways Company)
Also appearing: Claude Aveline, Sylvia Bataille, René Blech, J.-B. Brunius, Paul Grimault, Genia Lozinska, Gen Paul, Jacques Prévert, Pierre Prévert, Lou Tchimoukoff, Lydu Vigo
Filmed November 1933 to January 1934 at Gaumont studios, Buttes-Chaumont, Paris; Le Havre, Maurecourt, Conflans Sainte-Honorine, Charentonneau, Maisons-Alfort, Corbeil, and other locations along the Seine and Oise Rivers, the Canal Saint-Denis, Canal de l'Ourcq, Canal Saint-Martin and the Canal de la Marne au Rhin
Premiere: after trade premiere 24 April 1934, the film was re-edited by Gaumont and released as *Le Chaland qui passe*, 12 or 13 September 1934, at the Colisée cinema, Paris
Notes: different versions of *L'Atalante* have existed since 1934 (see Chapter 4), notably the Beauvais version (1940), the Salles Gomes-Langlois version (1950), the Bompoint-Philippe version (1990) and the Eisenschitz version (2001)

Films cited in this study

À bout de souffle, Jean-Luc Godard, France, 1959
À nous la liberté, René Clair, France, 1932
À propos de Nice, la suite, Catherine Breillat, Costa-Gavras, Claire Denis, Raymond Depardon, Abbas Kiarostami and Parvis Kimiavi, Pavel Lungin, Raoul Ruiz, France, 1995
Adieu Philippine, Jacques Rozier, France, 1963
L'Affaire est dans le sac, Jacques and Pierre Prévert, France, 1932
L'Âge d'or, Luis Buñuel, France, 1930
Les Amants du Pont-Neuf, Leos Carax, France, 1991
Au Bonheur des Dames, Julien Duvivier, France, 1930
Aujourd'hui/24 heures en 30 minutes, Jean Lods, France, 1928
Baby Doll, Elia Kazan, USA, 1956
Le Beau Serge, Claude Chabrol, France, 1957

La Belle Nivernaise, Jean Epstein, France, 1923
Berlin, a City Symphony, Walter Ruttmann, Germany, 1927
Boudu sauvé des eaux, Jean Renoir, France, 1932
The Bridge, Joris Ivens, Netherlands, 1928
Les Carabiniers, Jean-Luc Godard, France, 1962
Champs Élysées, Jean Lods, France, 1928
La Chienne, Jean Renoir, France, 1931
Cinema-Truth, Dziga Vertov, USSR, 1925
La Coquille et le clergyman, Germaine Dulac, France, 1928
Daïnah la métisse, Jean Grémillon, France, 1931
Les Dames du Bois de Boulogne, Robert Bresson, France, 1945
Le Dernier milliardaire, René Clair, France, 1934
2 fois 50 ans de cinéma français, Jean-Luc Godard, France, 1995
Drôle de drame, Marcel Carné, France, 1937
Easy Street, Charlie Chaplin, USA, 1917
L'Enfance nue, Maurice Pialat, France, 1967
Espoir, André Malraux, France, 1939
Far from Heaven, Todd Haynes, USA, 2002
La Femme de nulle part, Louis Delluc, France, 1922
Feu Matthias Pascal, Marcel L'Herbier, France, 1926
Fièvre, Louis Delluc, France, 1912
La Fin du jour, Julien Duvivier, France, 1939
French Cancan, Jean Renoir, France, 1955
La Glace à trois faces, Jean Epstein, France, 1927
La Guerre des boutons, Yves Robert, France, 1961
La Grande illusion, Jean Renoir, France, 1937
Grandeur et décadence d'un petit commerce de cinéma, Jean-Luc Godard, France, 1986
Les Halles centrales, Boris Kaufman, France, 1927
Histoire(s) du cinéma, Jean-Luc Godard, France, 1998
The Homecoming, Joe May, Germany, 1928
Hôtel du Nord, Marcel Carné, France, 1938
If..., Lindsay Anderson, UK, 1968
Images d'Ostende, Henri Storck, Belgium, 1929
Jean Vigo, Jacques Rozier, France, 1964
Jean Vigo: a Passion for Life, Julien Temple, UK, 1997
La Jetée, Chris Marker, France, 1962
Le Jour se lève, Marcel Carné, France, 1939
Last Tango in Paris, Bernardo Bertolucci, France, 1972
The Man with a Movie Camera, Dziga Vertov, USSR, 1929
Manhatta, Charles Sheeler and Paul Strand, USA, 1921
La Marche des machines, Eugène Deslaw, France, 1928
La Maternelle, Jean Benoît-Levy, France, 1933

Les Ministères de l'art, Philippe Garrel, France, 1988
Miquette et sa mère, Henri Diamant-Berger, France, 1933
Modern Times, Charlie Chaplin, USA, 1936
Mourir à Madrid, Frédéric Rossif, France, 1962
Nana, Jean Renoir, France, 1926
Nice, à propos de Vigo, Manoel de Oliveira, France, 1983
Nogent, Eldorado du dimanche, Marcel Carné, France, 1929
Nuit et brouillard, Alain Resnais and Jean Cayrol, France, 1955
On purge bébé, Jean Renoir, France, 1931
On the Waterfront, Elia Kazan, USA, 1954
Parlons cinéma: les anti-cours de Henri Langlois, H. Fischbach, Canada, 1976
People on Sunday, Robert Siodmak and Edgar Ulmer, Germany, 1929
Le Petit Chaperon Rouge, Alberto Cavalcanti, France, 1929
La Poison, Sacha Guitry, France, 1951
Psycho, Gus Van Sant, USA, 1998
Quai des brumes, Marcel Carné, France, 1938
Quatorze juillet, René Clair, France, 1932
Les Quatre cents coups, François Truffaut, France, 1959
Qui êtes-vous, Polly Magoo?, William Klein, France, 1965
Le Rapt, Dimitri Kirsanoff, France, 1934
Rien que les heures, Alberto Cavalcanti, France, 1926
La Roue, Abel Gance, France, 1923
Le Rouge et le noir, Claude Autant-Lara, France, 1954
La Seine ou la vie d'un fleuve, Jean Lods, France, 1931
La Souriante Madame Beudet, Germaine Dulac, France, 1922
Les Statues meurent aussi, Alain Resnais and Chris Marker, France, 1953
Such Is Life, Carl Junghans, Czechoslovakia, 1929
Three Songs of Lenin, Dziga Vertov, USSR, 1934
Tire-au-flanc, Jean Renoir, France, 1928
Travelling avant, Jean-Charles Tacchella, France, 1985
Un carnet de bal, Julien Duvivier, France, 1937
Un chien andalou, Luis Buñuel, France, 1929
Underground, Emir Kusturica, Federal Republic of Yugoslavia, 1995
Vénus, Louis Mercanton, France, 1929
La Vie d'un honnête homme, Sacha Guitry, France, 1953
Les Voyages de L'Atalante, Bernard Eisenschitz, France, 2001
When Father Was Away on Business, Emir Kusturica, Yugoslavia, 1985
The Wonderful Lies of Nina Petrovna, Hanns Schwartz, 1928
La Zone, Georges Lacombe, France, 1928

Select bibliography

Texts by Jean Vigo

Although neither a theoretician of cinema nor a film critic, Vigo produced a number of rich and suggestive texts, which he wrote for particular occasions, such as the presentation of a film. The article about Jean Painlevé was only rediscovered in 1990, so we can hope that more material will be discovered in future years.

'Présentation d'*À propos de Nice*', 14 June 1930
> Also known as 'Vers un cinéma social'. Vigo's presentation of *À propos de Nice*, at the Théâtre du Vieux-Colombier, Paris. Reproduced in Lherminier, P. (1985), *Jean Vigo: œuvre de cinéma*, Paris, Cinémathèque française/Pierre Lherminier, 65–7.

'Telle est la vie', 1931
> Vigo's presentation of Carl Junghans's film *Such is Life* (*Takový je zivot*, Czechoslovakia, 1929), at the Amis du Cinéma film club in Nice, 1931. Reproduced in Lherminier 1985: 54.

'Jean Painlevé à Nice', *Le Petit Niçois*, 6 November 1931
> Vigo's presentation of Jean Painlevé, and his particular brand of experimental scientific cinema, written for the Amis du Cinéma film club. Reproduced in *Positif*, 348, February 1990, 35.

'Sensibilité de pellicule', *Sésame*, Brussels, 1 December 1932
> This text about the relationship between technique, art and ethics, was written by Vigo in September 1932, at the request of the Belgian filmmaker, Henri Storck. Reproduced in Lherminier 1985: 51–3.

'Présentation de *Zéro de conduite*', 17 October 1933
> Also known as 'Responsabilité de l'auteur'. Vigo's presentation of *Zéro de conduite*, at the Club de l'Écran, Brussels. Reproduced in Lherminier 1985: 123–6.

In addition to the five short pieces listed here, a number of Vigo's private letters, as well as his schoolboy diary, have been published in various journals over the years. In particular, see *Positif*, 7, May 1953; Chardère, B. (1961), *Jean Vigo*, Lyons, Premier plan; *Centro-film*, Turin, 18–19, February–March 1961; *Jeune cinema*, 15, May 1966.

Further reading

Archives, Institut Jean Vigo, Perpignan, 90–1, March 2002. Special issue, including articles by F. de la Bretèque, 'L'histoire sans fin du "texte" filmique' (7–13), and F. Porcile, 'La musique de *L'Atalante*' (15–16). Also contains a selective bibliography by B. Bastide (20).

Bourgeois, N., Benoliel, B. and Loppinot, S. (eds), *L'Atalante, un film de Jean Vigo*, Paris, Cinémathèque française/Pôle Méditerranéen d'Éducation Cinématographique, 2000. Collection of numerous interpretative essays and historical articles, notably regarding the different versions of the film. Contributions by A. Bergala, 'Le plan aquarium' (153–61), N. Brenez, 'Vrille blanche du désir éperdu' (201–4), B. Eisenschitz, '*L'Atalante*, film russe ?' (141–51) and D. Païni, 'Au film de l'eau' (83–9).

Buache, F., *Jean Vigo*, Documents de cinéma, 4, Lausanne, Cinémathèque suisse, 1962. Collection of testimonies and critical articles.

Centro-film, Turin, 18–19, February–March 1961. Special issue devoted to Vigo, including correspondence with Henri Storck.

Chardère, B. (ed.), *Jean Vigo*, Lyons, Premier Plan, 1961. Contains many invaluable documents, including testimonies by people who knew Vigo, and criticism from a wide variety of sources.

Ciné-Club, 5, February 1949. The first special issue devoted to Vigo, including texts by the filmmaker, testimonies and other documents about his life and work.

Colaprete, P. (ed.), *Jean Vigo*, Florence, Controcampo, May 1952. Brochure including texts by Colaprete on 'The social cinema of Jean Vigo' and a 'Chronicle of the critical edition of *L'Atalante*' (in Italian).

Études cinématographiques, 51–2, Paris, Lettres Modernes, 1966. Special issue devoted to Vigo, including essays by A. Virmaux, '*L'Atalante* et l'univers surréaliste' (31–41), and B. Amengual, 'Monde et vision du monde dans l'œuvre de Vigo' (49–87).

Feldman, H. and J., and Weinberg, H. (eds), *Jean Vigo*, London, British Film Institute/New Index Series, 1951. Collection of essays and documents, including reviews of *Zéro de conduite* and *L'Atalante* by James Agee, plus G. Barbarow, 'The Work of Jean Vigo' (17–21) and S. Kracauer, 'Jean Vigo' (26–8).

Jeune cinéma, 15, May 1966. Contains a number of Vigo's previously unpublished letters (3–6).

Lherminier, P., *Jean Vigo*, Paris, Pierre Lherminier/Filméditions, 1984. Text substantially revised from first edition, Paris, Seghers, 1967. Contains many useful documents, including testimonies and critical articles. Excellent bibliography (185–91).

Lherminier, P., *Jean Vigo: œuvre de cinéma*, Paris, Cinémathèque française/ Pierre Lherminier, 1985. A remarkable collection of documents, including shot-by-shot accounts of the four films, and other written material by Vigo relating to these works. Also reproduces Vigo's theoretical writings (see above), as well as his notes for future projects. Finally, a number of synopses and scenarios written by potential collaborators, such as Claude Aveline and Blaise Cendrars, and extensive material related to the project *L'Évadé du bagne*.

Positif, 7, May 1953. Special issue devoted to Vigo. Contains texts by Vigo, notes for some of his future projects, letters and his schoolboy diary. Also, several testimonies by friends and acquaintances, many of which were later reproduced in Chardère 1961. Important articles by B. Amengual, 'Essai pour situer Jean Vigo' (48–58), B. Chardère, 'Jean Vigo parmi nous' (9–21), and P.E. Salles Gomes, 'L'œuvre de Vigo et la critique historique' (66–76).

Salles Gomes, P.E., *Jean Vigo*, Paris, Seuil/Ramsay, 1988 (first edition 1957). This exemplary biography remains the starting point for anyone interested in Vigo's life, and the historical and cultural context of his work. Published in English by Faber & Faber, 1998.

Simon, W., *The Films of Jean Vigo*, Ann Arbor, UMI Research Press, 1981. A thorough academic study of life and work.

Smith, J.M., *Jean Vigo*, Movie Magazine/November Books, 1972. Close linear analysis of all four films.

Temple, M., 'Dreaming of Vigo', *Sight and Sound*, 8:11, 1999, 14–16. Journalistic article about 'myth of Vigo'.

Terzi, C. (ed.), *Jean Vigo*, Bergamo, Italian Federation of Film Clubs/La Cittadella, April 1952. Brochure containing analysis of films and biographical information.

Vigo, L., *Jean Vigo: une vie engagée dans le cinéma*, Paris, Cahiers du cinéma, 2002. A brief and enlightening study of Vigo by his daughter, Luce. Contains some previously unavailable documents.

Warner, M., *L'Atalante*, London, British Film Institute, 1993. Interesting reading of film, undermined by numerous factual errors.

Index